# THE ASTROTWINS' LOVE ZODIAC

## The Essential Astrology Guide for Women

Tali & Ophira Edut

sourcebooks
casablanca

Published by Sourcebooks Casablanca, an imprint of Sourcebooks, Inc.
P.O. Box 4410, Naperville, Illinois 60567-4410
(630) 961-3900
FAX: (630) 961-2168
www.sourcebooks.com

**Library of Congress Cataloging-in-Publication Data**
Edut, Tali.
The astrotwins' love zodiac : the essential astrology guide for women / Tali &
Ophira Edut.
p. cm.
Includes bibliographical references and index.
1. Men—Psychology—Miscellanea. 2. Astrology. 3. Mate selection—
Miscellanea. 4. Interpersonal relations—Miscellanea. 5. Love—Miscellanea. I.
Edut, Ophira. II. Title. III. Title: Astro twins' love zodiac.
BF1729.M45E38 2008
133.5'864677—dc22
2008020018

Printed and bound in the United States of America
POD 10

# Dedication

To all our loved ones, whose lives served as "divine inspiration" for this book.

# Acknowledgments

We want to extend our most heartfelt thanks to the following people:

Our interview subjects (you know who you are): thank you for generously opening your hearts and being our case studies. Your wit and wisdom added so much dimension to the book, and made us deeply appreciate the beauty in every sign.

Our parents Doris and Shimon Edut and our little sister Leora, and our aunt Carolyn Mickelson—we're so grateful to have been born into a family that loves and supports us on every career path we've ever taken. Even astrology.

Our brilliant, trusting Aries editor Deb Werksman and our fierce Leo literary agent Donna Bagdasarian.

Our innovative Virgo coach Lois Barth and her program Luscious Living with Lois, which turned our writing process into a fabulous, rewarding adventure.

All our friends, family, clients, and colleagues who nurtured our astrology career and cheered us on. Call us anytime to find out what's in the stars.

Ophira sends special thanks and love to her Taurus husband Jeffrey and stepdaughter, Clementine, who helped inspire the book's first chapter and continues to support us every step of the way.

Tali sends a cosmic shout-out to the Playa!

# Contents

# Introduction

Here's a no-brainer: Raise your hand if you've ever felt heartbroken, let down, betrayed, or just plain frustrated by a man.

Sound like the makings of a bad country music song, doesn't it? But face it: We've all been there. For every man claiming that women are impossible to understand, you'll find at least five females crying themselves to sleep and wondering why the guys in their life think and act the way they do.

Women are relationship-oriented. Whether it's by nature or nurture doesn't really matter—at least not when you're pumped full of adrenaline, every abandonment fear triggered as you obsessively check your cell phone for a call, a text, any contact from Him. Women spend so much time on drama—analyzing why he slept in the fetal position instead of spooning us, or what he meant when he said whatever—we should all win emotional Emmys.

For years, we two found ourselves in a common predicament. Here we were, educated and ambitious women who felt totally lost when it came to men! We couldn't understand why our relationship track records didn't match our career success. If we were so smart and self-determined, why did we keep ending up with men who were clearly commitment-phobes? Or sabotaging things with the ones who weren't? Embarrassing as it is, we had to admit: We were total clichés.

We studied human psychology, learned the ways of Mars and Venus, and sat through 40-hour workshops on understanding men. In the course of our exploration, we also discovered astrology.

We began to study the astrological charts of every man we met. We were amazed to discover time-tested patterns. We analyzed current boyfriends, past boyfriends, friends' boyfriends—and the data was consistent. This knowledge began to heal years of heartache ("Ohhhh, that's why he did that!") and saved us from wasting energy on needless future struggle. Astrology transformed our love lives—and the relationships of thousands of our friends and clients.

This book is the "user's guide," the companion, the (ahem) *manu*al we wish we'd had. We're absolutely thrilled to offer it to you. In our 15-plus years as professional astrologers, love is always the first thing people want to know about. Is he the One for me? Should I stay in this relationship? Why does he do that? What can I do to make my relationship work? Does he love me, or should I move on? Will he ever come back?

Don't misunderstand us—we know that people are unique individuals, that your special relationship is unlike any other love, yada yada. For the record, we both have degrees from a Big Ten university, we're spiritual but sensible, and we've never owned a storefront psychic parlor, a muumuu or a crystal ball. We're modern women just like you who want to enjoy rewarding relationships now—without the pain, drama, or frustrating dead-end attempts. We know that the world can't be reduced to a cliché of 12 zodiac signs, and astrology runs much deeper than that, anyway.

Yet, time and again, we've seen the patterns. We've coached thousands of friends, readers, celebrities, and private clients. And once we explain the secrets of astrology, we hear the same basic response: "Holy s**t, that is so TRUE!"

But far more rewarding than the quick satisfaction of being right is seeing the light return to people's eyes... and their love lives. Astrology, when done right, provides clarity. When you're stuck at a crossroads, it helps get you unstuck. That frees you up to move, and there's nothing like momentum to bring freshness back into your love life.

## Rule #1: Trying to change him is a waste of time

If you want to hit the bar and cry into a flavored martini, you'll have to call someone else. We know that when you're bitching to your friends about how your boyfriend ignored you at a party, or what a jerk he is for not calling, you're secretly wondering: Was it something I did? You're frustrated as hell. And you'd give anything—anything—to know how to make it all better.

You could spend years doing all the stupid things we've done. Believing the cheating louse who claimed he had to "work all night." Dumping the loyal guy who swore he didn't stray. Identifying with every hopeless *Sex and the City* scenario—and staying home to watch the DVD boxed set instead of going out to meet a guy with real potential. You could repeat our mistakes—and you probably have. Or, you could take a shortcut.

In our opinion, trying to change a guy is a huge waste of time. We think it's better to know exactly what you're dealing with—then ask yourself if you can live with it. Yet, every woman on the planet has tried to reform her boyfriend at some point. And it never, ever works. He either turns you into his mommy (a job you don't want), resents you for "nagging" him, or leaves you for someone who accepts him as he is... smelly socks, public farting, and all.

The real problem? You keep trying to change him—or yourself—instead of changing your approach.

Chances are, you're reading this because you'd love some insight into what makes him tick, what ticks him off, what he cherishes most. You may be blind to the ways that you—yes, you—could already be the woman of his dreams. Simply put, if you don't understand your man, how can you accept him? Love begins with acceptance. It's what we women want, too! (Don't believe us? Ask your cellulite.)

In our opinion and "field research," men don't really change unless they have a damn good reason. It's much better to scope out what you're really getting into with him. If you choose this mission, grasshopper, you must embrace the good, the bad, and the infuriating. And so must he. You may have to face some difficult choices, to be brutally honest with yourself. Although it's hard at first, we do believe that the truth sets you free.

### Are you doing the wrong thing with the right guy?

Love and commitment mean something different to each specific sign. In practical terms, what turns on a Pisces ain't gonna rev up a Virgo's engine. But since your Pisces ex-boyfriend loved you in heels and black fishnets, you mistakenly assume your virginal Virgo will get all hot and bothered when you slip on the stockings. (Hopefully, you've at least bought a new pair. Virgos are clean freaks!) Instead, he runs for the hills.

Or, you read in *Cosmopolitan* that "stripper chic" is the latest seduction craze, so you take one of those pole-dancing classes that's all the rage at your gym. Your Gemini man loves it and enjoys a few encores before he disappears. But when, months later, you stage the routine for your new Taurus guy, the curtain falls faster than you can say "lap dance."

**Maybe you're doing the right thing... but with the wrong guy.**
Not sure? We are. We've been studying the secrets of every sign for years. And our advice has gotten actual results. We've helped friends get married, gently steered others to better matches, gotten the drama queens to actually communicate with their partners (for the record, yelling, sobbing, and making life-or-death demands do not count as communication).

See, once you learn the basics—what to expect and not expect from a particular sign—you're free to make choices in your own best interest. There's nothing more relieving than to discover that you're not defective ... you're just applying the wrong techniques to someone who could very well be the right person. Or that your nagging suspicion is true: You've been casting your pearls before swine, and it's time to move on to a better match.

**Is there a "right" sign for me?**
The answer is yes... and no.

Once you start learning astrology, you'll probably hear some misleading match-up advice. For example: If you're a Leo (a passionate Fire sign), you should date another Fire sign (Aries, Sagittarius). Weed out three-quarters of the population, and bada-bing, you'll find Prince Charming in no time. Or, if you're a moody, emotional Cancer, you should avoid cooler Air signs like Gemini and Aquarius, who squirm at sentiment. Eliminate your way to cosmic compatibility.

The truth? You can make it work with any zodiac sign. Sure, it might take more effort with some signs than others. Much more. But maybe not, as you'll discover reading this book—and possibly notice when your so-called perfect match still manages to break your heart.

Besides, who said easy was always good? Sometimes, we need a challenge to raise our frequency, to loosen the hardened earth around our hearts, to drag up an issue we've buried and allow it to be healed. Sometimes, similar is boring, and a challenge stimulates our growth.

At the time of writing this, Tali is enjoying the single life (so many zodiac signs, so little time). Ophira is five months into married life with her Taurus husband, Jeffrey. When people ask Ophira if Jeffrey's Taurus is a good match for her Sagittarius, she honestly answers no—at least, not according to conventional astrology advice. Taurus is a couch-loving, regimented Earth sign that likes red wine, luxury goods, and a steady paycheck. Sagittarius is a globe-trotting entrepreneur in rumpled jeans who refuses to follow a schedule or "settle down."

Without a full understanding of astrology, Ophira might not have given Jeffrey a fair chance. She would have seen his Wall Street-area apartment in a luxury high rise (never!), spotlessly cleaned and decorated in sophisticated browns, and said "hell no." She would have fled to her down-at-the-heels East Village pad, its walls painted apple green and fuchsia, the dog's failed attempts at paper training (well okay, her failed attempts at paper training the dog) on display.

Instead, she thought, "Hmmm. An Earth sign could be grounding for me. I'm all over the place, and he's stable. Let's see what happens." The two found common ground bonding over food, wine, and conversation. Independent-Sag Ophira discovered she really did enjoy having a steady guy who came through for her. She didn't feel suffocated; she felt supported.

When Jeffrey inevitably sank into the comfy couch most nights, a glass of red wine in one hand, remote in the other, Ophira knew this was heaven to a Taurus. Rather than vie for his attention, she let him be, and he was ever thankful. She curled up with a book and her dachshund (the Sagittarius version of heaven) beside him. A year later he found a tasteful but unique Art Deco engagement ring and the rest is astrological history.

Oh—by the way, Taurus men are very good dog trainers (Cesar Milan, the Dog Whisperer, shares a birthday with Jeffrey). It takes consistency and a commanding voice, both Taurus traits, to get a stubborn breed of dog to pee outside. Being a stubborn breed of man, Bull-boy Jeffrey knew how to tame a headstrong dachshund—and his wild Sagittarius owner—without breaking their spirits. Good thing Ophira gave her "astrologically incorrect" future husband a chance!

### Life is short, so take a shortcut.

Think about it: Couldn't we all use a shortcut, a decoder to this love thing? How many of us actually understand what it means to be in a relationship? With a skyrocketing divorce rate, it's obvious that our generation is lost, if not clueless, about relationships. Men and women simply don't understand each other. Turn on any daytime talk show if you don't believe us. And with children being affected by our love casualties, it's clear we need a whole new approach. Maybe it's time for a little magic… to learn what the ancients knew and see if they were onto something.

So maybe you're saying, "Oh, come on. You really expect me to take astrology this seriously?" To that we answer: Read it and decide for yourself. Even if your skepticism remains firmly intact, it never hurts to have an extra tool in your romantic arsenal.

The moral of the story? You could do this the hard way… or the easy way. It's always your choice. We know you're gonna date whomever you want, even if you earn an astrology PhD. We know that no matter how spot-on we are, you might just stay with that guy who calls you "fat," cheats on you, never calls, or tells lies that you accept because you're desperately clinging to his validation and would rather take crap than be alone. (No judgment; we speak from experience.)

We want you to know that regardless of your romantic path, you DO have other choices—of how to react, whom to date, what to tolerate, and how to deal with whatever baggage this particular man brings. Our wish for you? That you have everything you imagined love could bring, in an even better package than you thought possible. Knowledge is power, so go magnetize the perfect man for you. Who knows… he could already be there, just waiting for you to recognize what he's known all along.

# Astrology Basics:
# A Guide to the Zodiac's Men

## The 12 Zodiac Signs

| Sign | Dates | Ruling Planet |
|---|---|---|
| Aries | March 21-April 19 | Mars |
| Taurus | April 20-May 20 | Venus |
| Gemini | May 21-June 20 | Mercury |
| Cancer | June 21-July 22 | Moon |
| Leo | July 23-August 22 | Sun |
| Virgo | August 23-September 22 | Mercury |
| Libra | September 23-October 22 | Venus |
| Scorpio | October 23-November 21 | Pluto, with minor rule by Mars |
| Sagittarius | November 22-December 21 | Jupiter |
| Capricorn | December 22-January 19 | Saturn |
| Aquarius | January 20-February 18 | Uranus |
| Pisces | February 19-March 20 | Neptune, with minor rule by Jupiter |

# In His Element: Fire, Earth, Air, & Water

The twelve zodiac signs are grouped into four "elements"—fire, earth, air, and water. Each of these elementary groups has distinct traits, so the men of each element will share a common orientation to life, or have similar tastes and values. Of course, his actual Sun sign will add more dimension, but you'll find that your man's attitude is much like the element that represents him.

**Fire Signs:** Aries, Leo, Sagittarius

**Earth Signs:** Taurus, Virgo, Capricorn

**Air Signs:** Gemini, Libra, Aquarius

**Water Signs:** Cancer, Scorpio, Pisces

## The Masculine Signs: Fire & Air

We're not saying that these signs are more manly or macho than others. However, they tend to be external, forceful, and action-oriented. They are the "yang" (versus the "yin") signs, more prone to act or speak without thinking ahead. Independent and leadership-oriented, they answer to nobody.

### Fire Signs (Aries, Leo, Sagittarius)

Dynamic and passionate, Fire sign men are the gallant knights of the zodiac, forever in motion or fighting for a cause. Even when this guy sits around, he's learning, reading, dreaming, or talking about something. Fire can keep you warm, or it can cause great destruction. While fire burns out quickly without fuel to keep it going, it can also regenerate its power. A single spark can set off a forest fire. As a result, Fire sign men need to be managed carefully, lest they burn out of control.

**Best if you value:**
- Adventurous relationships
- Passionate affairs
- Ambitious types who want to take over the world together
- Lots of action
- A warm-blooded, warmhearted companion
- Sexual and emotional expressiveness
- Outspoken people who say what they think

- Traveling together
- Memorable fights, and even more memorable makeup sex
- Somebody who's always on the go, trying something new
- Constant change and evolution

## *Air Signs (Gemini, Libra, Aquarius)*

Like a cool wind (or an occasional tornado), Air signs are always in motion, sweeping you into a bluster of ideas, activities, and conversations. Intellectual and rational, Air signs are far more comfortable in the realm of thought than feeling. Don't expect too many emotional outpourings from these signs, although their tantrums can be memorable. Gifted at communication, these are the zodiac's messengers, carrying news, ideas, and gossip to the masses. Air sign men make excellent playmates. They're great if you're an "activity girl," open to new experiences and adventures. Traditional types could feel threatened, even abandoned, by the free-spirited Air sign man, who has many hobbies and interests outside of the relationship. If you're the type who needs "space," he'll give you plenty.

**Best if you value:**
- Intellectual and mental chemistry
- Creative inspiration
- Great conversation and exchanging ideas
- Unconventional relationships
- Retaining independence
- Your "space"—and a non-clingy partner who gives it to you
- Keeping things light, flirty, and fun
- Sexual experimentation
- Open relationships
- Talking in bed

# The Feminine Signs: Water & Earth

Receptive and internal, men of these signs tend to be more sensitive and intuitive. If you're looking to settle down, start a family, or buy a home, these signs are far more likely to go along with your nesting campaign. Chivalrous and old-fashioned, they can be more romantic than some of the women you know. Don't hurt their tender feelings by being too direct!

## Water Signs (Cancer, Scorpio, Pisces)

Hello, Mr. Sensitivity. Intuitive Water sign men can be as deep and mysterious as the ocean. Being in their presence can have a healing effect on your life, and they can be caring companions. They're often "one of the girls," and can be as catty as a junior high cheerleader. They notice everything! Water sign men's tendency to be oversensitive can set them adrift on a sea of self-absorption. At such times, you have to be careful not to drown in their depths, or be pulled into a needy undertow. Security is important to them—after all, water needs a container, or it dries up and disappears. These signs often have intense dreams and borderline-psychic intuition.

**Best if you value:**
- Emotional exploration
- People who work in the healing arts
- Security and comfort, but a little edge of mystery
- Being coddled and babied
- Sarcastic jokes
- Playing a nurturing role
- A man who's not afraid to cry
- Family and kids
- Dressing up and being appreciated for your beauty
- "Just the two of us" intimacy

- Working on your issues together
- Anything domestic: cooking, cleaning, decorating for the holidays
- A guy who might be willing to be a stay-at-home dad
- A man who can be "one of the girls"

### Earth Signs (Taurus, Virgo, Capricorn)

As grounded as the earth beneath your feet, stable Earth sign men can put your life on a solid foundation. Dutiful as military officers, they like to be there for friends in need. Slow and steady, these "builders" are loyal and stable, and stick by their people through hard times. On good days, they're practical; at worst, they can be materialistic or too focused on the surface of things to dig into the depths. Change is not their forte; they often need a more dynamic partner to keep them from getting stuck in a rut.

**Best if you value:**
- Stability and security
- A realist type, rather than a dreamer
- Having a long-term mate who fits in with your family and friends
- Building a future together
- Money and financial responsibility
- Substance and style
- A "daddy" type
- A more conservative disposition
- Traditions
- Fine dining, five-star hotels, luxury goods
- A touch of snobbery
- A "director" or "manager" type: someone who handles the decisions and manages practical matters you prefer to avoid (bills, taxes, mortgage payments, reservations)

# His Sign's "Quality": Cardinal, Mutable, or Fixed

Is he a starter, a doer, or a finisher? The quality of each sign shapes your man's temperament, and makes him better in certain situations than others. For example, a fixed sign might stand loyally by your side in a crisis, but his tenacity can also make him a stubborn son of a bitch. Call on him when you need a hero, but if you want adventure or a no-strings fling, a mutable sign might be best. Here's how to find his sweet spot:

## Cardinal Signs (Aries, Cancer, Libra, Capricorn)

Cardinal signs start every season—Aries kicks off spring, Cancer starts summer, Libra begins fall and Capricorn is the first winter sign. These men like to be first, to win, and to be admired. They're the leaders and "idea people" of the zodiac. Cardinal sign men can seem cocky and full of themselves, too driven by pride. These signs prize originality and like to be first in everything they do. If you want a dashing, gallant knight who will sweep you off your feet, call a Cardinal sign. He's sure to get the adrenaline coursing through your veins, jump-starting your motor after a long, lonely winter.

## Fixed Signs (Taurus, Leo, Scorpio, Aquarius)

These signs fall in the middle of every season. They're the stabilizers—the ones who set up a solid goal or foundation, then start building. Fixed signs can take the enthusiastic ideas that cardinal signs spark, and craft them into something real. They pick up the ball when the cardinal sign passes it, and run the distance to the goal. Fixed signs are the trustworthy types who like "to-do" lists and fancy titles. If a cardinal sign says, "Let's go on vacation!" the fixed sign will call the travel agency, book the tickets and hotel, and send everyone a list of what to pack. This is the guy you marry or lean on in a crisis. He's also the guy you want to kill because you can never, ever control him or change his mind. Exhausting!

### Mutable Signs (Gemini, Virgo, Sagittarius, Pisces)

These signs end every season—and have learned the hard lessons taught by spring, summer, fall, and winter. They know that all good things come to an end, and their role is to prepare everyone for the changing of seasons. Mutable signs are the adapters of the zodiac, a little bit older and wiser. More flexible and comfortable with change than other signs, they can "chameleon" themselves to fit into a variety of situations. Mutables are also the editors of the zodiac—the ones who complete the package with a winning touch. A plan can be sparked by a cardinal sign, built by a fixed sign, then perfected with the critical eye of a mutable sign. If you want to shake things up, or if you love conversation, flow, and adventure, mutable sign men bring excitement and variety back to your life. He's the guy you marry because he's also your best friend.

# Aspects: The Secret of Distance
## What the Distance Between Your Signs Says About Compatibility

In astrology, the distance between two signs on the horoscope wheel forms an angle called an "aspect." Aspects create a unique energy pattern that's either harmonious or challenging. The astrological signs of your past and current partners are part of that story.

As the cliché goes, people come along for a reason, a season, or a lifetime. Sometimes, a seemingly mismatched partner will inspire necessary growth. Perhaps you need to develop your generosity, learn to assert yourself, resolve an old drama with your parents.

It might be a short-term kick in the butt, a call to action. So when you dump him, don't shoot the messenger!

For example, Tali had a semi-torturous relationship with a musical, artistic Scorpio man who spent most nights composing amazing songs, then bingeing on Scotch. His extreme behavior was a wakeup call. Tali realized that she was repressing her own desire to sing and express her creativity. While she skipped the hard liquor and hangovers, she did pick up the microphone and let herself belt out some tunes. The relationship has faded into history, but Tali hits the karaoke bar several nights a week.

As long as you're taking the leap into love, you might as well get something out of it. Here's how astrology and aspects can help you turn your relationships into soul-elevating personal growth.

## Same Sign (Conjunct)

**Energy: Self-acceptance**

| | | |
|---|---|---|
| Aries-Aries | Taurus-Taurus | Gemini-Gemini |
| Cancer-Cancer | Leo-Leo | Virgo-Virgo |
| Libra-Libra | Scorpio-Scorpio | Sagittarius-Sagittarius |
| Capricorn-Capricorn | Aquarius-Aquarius | Pisces-Pisces |

As they say, how can you love somebody else unless you love yourself? If you date someone of the same sign, congratulations. You've probably embraced your quirks and accepted your humanity. Now, you can celebrate that with a kindred spirit! If you haven't learned to love yourself, warts and all, this relationship can inspire some crucial self-acceptance. Remember, though: being Bobbsey twins might be comfortable, but autonomy is important to stave off boredom. Keep some separation between your lives, even if it's easy to hang out together. Otherwise, passion may cool to a brother-sister vibe.

**Why You've Attracted Him & What There Is to Learn:**
- To experience what it's like for someone to be with you
- To see your best and worst qualities mirrored back
- Ease
- Self-acceptance
- Working through sibling rivalry

## *1 Sign Apart (Semisextile)*

**Energy: Friction**

| | | |
|---|---|---|
| Aries: Pisces, Taurus | Taurus: Aries, Gemini | Gemini: Taurus, Cancer |
| Cancer: Gemini, Leo | Leo: Cancer, Virgo | Virgo: Leo, Libra |
| Libra: Virgo, Scorpio | Scorpio: Libra, Sagittarius | Sagittarius: Scorpio, Capricorn |
| Aquarius: Capricorn, Pisces | Capricorn: Sagittarius, Aquarius | Pisces: Aquarius, Aries |

Like next-door neighbors with completely different styles of decorating, gardening, and living, the signs on either side of yours can stir up an instant love/hate vibe. Of course, all that friction can lead to explosive sexual chemistry, even an obsessive desire to figure each other out (you never will). Some astrologers believe that each sign is an evolved version of the one before it. The sign after yours is a teacher, although like a rebellious teen seeking emancipation from a parent, you may never admit it. This combination makes for painful breakups, and a seething sexual tension that lingers for a lifetime.

### Why You've Attracted Him & What There Is to Learn:

- To see how the other side lives
- To channel the love/hate tension into hot, round-the-clock sex
- To team up with a mate who has qualities you don't (and vice versa)
- Deep healing and transformation, often through painful growth
- To learn from each other's differences
- To force you out of your fear-based comfort zone or emotional paralysis
- Growth through challenge or contrast
- How to assert or express yourself with someone who doesn't instantly "get" you
- Making peace with "the enemy"

## 2 Signs Apart (Sextile)

### Energy: Friendship, communication

| | | |
|---|---|---|
| Aries: Sagittarius, Aquarius | Taurus: Pisces, Cancer | Gemini: Aries, Leo |
| Cancer: Taurus, Virgo | Leo: Gemini, Libra | Virgo: Cancer, Scorpio |
| Libra: Leo, Sagittarius | Scorpio: Virgo, Capricorn | Sagittarius: Libra, Aquarius |
| Capricorn: Scorpio, Pisces | Aquarius: Sagittarius, Aries | Pisces: Capricorn, Taurus |

It's easy and breezy to date a man who lives two zodiac signs away. Your signs are always of a compatible "element" (e.g., he's a Water sign and you're an Earth sign). You'll often have similar values and attitudes about politics, raising a family, which movies to rent. Friendship and communication are the hallmarks of this aspect. Being best friends is easy. Keeping the spark alive? A little challenging. You'll need to structure "date nights" or set up scenarios that get you out of buddy mode.

**Why You've Attracted Him & What There Is to Learn:**
- To be "best friends with benefits"
- The possibility of great communication with a mate
- How to speak up, listen, and be heard
- How to keep the spark going when it stops automatically lighting itself
- To enjoy romance that forms out of friendship
- A no-pressure gig with someone who doesn't demand more than you can give

## 3 Signs Apart (Square)

**Energy: Tension, power, tug of war**

| | | |
|---|---|---|
| Aries: Cancer, Capricorn | Taurus: Aquarius, Leo | Gemini: Pisces, Virgo |
| Cancer: Aries, Libra | Leo: Taurus, Scorpio | Virgo: Gemini, Sagittarius |
| Libra: Cancer, Capricorn | Scorpio: Leo, Aquarius | Sagittarius: Virgo, Pisces |
| Capricorn: Aries, Libra | Aquarius: Scorpio, Taurus | Pisces: Gemini, Sagittarius |

Mommy and daddy issues, anyone? The square aspect is a harsh, 90-degree angle between two signs that creates a push-pull dynamic. It's the relationship that helps you work through issues with a difficult parent, usually by reactivating old, painful wounds. There can be power struggles and clashing agendas. Don't expect to kick back and put your feet up in this match. The dynamic tension will keep you active and keyed up. Of course, that could be exactly what you want. The opportunity of the "square" aspect is to teach you how to compromise with an equally strong-willed partner. When you strike that delicate balance, you can make an undeniable "power couple"—a true force to be reckoned with.

**Why You've Attracted Him & What There Is to Learn:**

- Compromise
- Conflict resolution
- Balancing your dynamic, sometimes clashing, personalities
- Where you can be stubborn and unyielding
- Healing old wounds/baggage related to your parents

## 4 Signs Apart (Trine)

**Energy: Harmony, ease**

| | | |
|---|---|---|
| Aries: Leo, Sagittarius | Taurus: Virgo, Capricorn | Gemini: Libra, Aquarius |
| Cancer: Scorpio, Pisces | Leo: Aries, Sagittarius | Virgo: Taurus, Capricorn |
| Libra: Gemini, Aquarius | Scorpio: Cancer, Pisces | Sagittarius: Aries, Leo |
| Capricorn: Taurus, Virgo | Aquarius: Gemini, Libra | Pisces: Cancer, Scorpio |

Ah, home sweet home. The trine sign mate has the same "element" as yours (fire, earth, air, or water), creating an unspoken kinship and harmony. At last—you don't have to constantly explain yourself. You've never felt so comfortable, so understood on a core level. This is the guy you can burp and fart around, or pee with the door open when he's home. But don't invest in a wardrobe full of elastic waistbands just yet. In trine relationships, you'll need to preserve some mystery to keep things exciting. Make sure you stay active and on the go, and don't do everything together. A little autonomy goes a long way to keep the passion alive.

**Why You've Attracted Him & What There Is to Learn:**
- To feel at home with yourself and a mate
- How to let down your guard and be yourself
- To be understood without explaining yourself
- To rest and relax together
- To have a best friend and partner in one

## 5 Signs Apart (Quincunx)

**Energy: Karma, compromise, mutation**

| | | |
|---|---|---|
| Aries: Virgo, Scorpio | Taurus: Libra, Sagittarius | Gemini: Scorpio, Capricorn |
| Cancer: Sagittarius, Aquarius | Leo: Capricorn, Pisces | Virgo: Aquarius, Aries |
| Libra: Pisces, Taurus | Scorpio: Aries, Gemini | Sagittarius: Taurus, Cancer |
| Capricorn: Gemini, Leo | Aquarius: Cancer, Virgo | Pisces: Leo, Libra |

This is a fascinating, complex combination that defies explanation—the original odd couple. You'll either feel like you're with your soul mate or the devil incarnate. "How did those two end up together?" people will wonder. Your bond is intense, unspoken, almost secretive in a way. The person five signs away from your sign has nothing in common with you astrologically. You'll need to adapt to your differences, which could take a great deal of adjustment, even discarding a former lifestyle. For one of you, the relationship will be about sex and intimacy; for the other, duty and service.

**Why You've Attracted Him & What There Is to Learn:**

- Karmic repair; healing a "past life contract" with each other
- Exploring and expanding your sexuality
- Diving into deeper intimacy
- Developing your selfless side, learning to serve/give
- How to adjust to someone vastly different from you
- What it feels like to meet a soul mate

## 6 Signs Apart (Opposite)

**Energy: Perspective, contrast, responsibility, growing up**

| Aries-Libra | Taurus-Scorpio | Gemini-Sagittarius |
|---|---|---|
| Cancer-Capricorn | Leo-Aquarius | Virgo-Pisces |

Your opposite sign lives directly across the zodiac wheel from you. However, you've got more in common than the name suggests. This sign can be highly compatible, even a soul twin match. You each have a distinct role, but you're a tag team, too. With an opposite sign, you're challenged to grow as a person and take responsibility for your part of the relationship. It's like taking a big step back to get a clear perspective of your life. We tend to view things from a close-up, missing the whole picture by hyper-focusing on a detail or two. With an opposite sign, your life appears in full relief, like a finished painting. Suddenly, it all makes sense. This can be a little uncomfortable, but if you've manifested an opposite sign, it means you're ready to grow up.

**Why You've Attracted Him & What There Is to Learn:**

- To see yourself from an enlightening "bird's-eye view"
- To create a powerful tag team
- To join forces and create something bigger than the two of you
- To balance extremes in yourself, like selflessness or selfishness, too much independence or dependence
- He's a mate who complements your undeveloped side
- To discover a new, even inspiring perspective on life
- To develop the art of compromise

# Recommended Reading

Here are a few books that made a difference for us on our quest to understand relationships and find lasting love.

*He's Scared, She's Scared: Understanding the Hidden Fears That Sabotage Your Relationship*

Steven Carter and Julia Sokol

Why do you keep attracting unavailable men—or overly available ones that make you want to run? Essential insight into the ways a commitment-phobic person acts in a relationship. Bonus: discover and heal your own fear of commitment (surprise—you've got it, too).

*Calling in the One: 7 Weeks to Attract the Love of Your Life*

Katherine Woodward Thomas

Ophira read this and met her husband three weeks later. She passed it along to a friend, who's now engaged. An amazing workbook that leaves no stone unturned.

*Are You the One for Me? Knowing Who's Right and Avoiding Who's Wrong*

Barbara De Angelis

*Why Wait? Create Your Soul Mate Now!*

Frank Polancic

A tiny, power-packed book to help you clear your space and manifest a great match.

*The Commitment Dialogues*

Matthew McKay and Barbara Quick

Written by a couples therapist; especially helpful if you're dating a commitment-shy sign or struggling with myths around commitment yourself.

*Mars and Venus on a Date: A Guide for Navigating the 5 Stages of Dating to Create a Loving and Lasting Relationship*

John Gray

Who cares what anyone says, this guy has some great points. Finally, an explanation for "why didn't he call?"

*Making Sense of Men™: A Woman's Guide to a Lifetime of Love, Care and Attention from All Men*

Alison Armstrong

Armstrong studied thousands of men and designed a whole curriculum to help women understand why men do what they do. This book summarizes her workshop series, Celebrating

Men, Satisfying Women® (well worth taking!). Visit www.
understandmen.com

*What Shamu Taught Me About Life, Love, and Marriage: Lessons for
People from Animals and Their Trainers*

Amy Sutherland

*Mating in Captivity: Reconciling the Erotic and the Domestic*

Esther Perel

Fascinating treatise on how autonomy and healthy separation can
help long-term couples maintain intimacy and sexual attraction.

*Ask and It Is Given: Learning to Manifest Your Desires*

Esther and Jerry Hicks

Recommended when you want to take a more mystical approach
to love, this book explains the Law of Attraction, and how to
visualize and create what you truly want.

# The Aries Man

Dates: March 21–April 19
Symbol: The Ram
Ruling Planet: Mars, the planet
of action, energy, and war
Element: Fire—passionate, dynamic, active
Quality: Cardinal
Mission: Passionate Playmates

**Natural Habitat—Where You'll Find Him:** Reading a great American novel in paperback, surrounded by women on the dance floor, shouting at the TV at a sports bar, leading a youth group through a community service mission, playing or watching violent sports like pro football, hockey, wrestling; competing in an Ultimate Fighting Championship, playing chess or strategy games, expressing himself passionately through writing or speaking, debating politics, leading a military faction, potato-ing on the couch in a wifebeater and boxers, lost in obsessive thoughts, crafting a philosophy or argument to help himself win a long-standing debate

**What He Does for a Living:** Lawyer, politician, strategist, military officer, chef, writer, comedian, DJ, professional athlete, leader of a company or corporate division, entrepreneur, motivational speaker, salesperson, hairdresser, magazine editor, children's coach, advocate, activist, stuntman, fireman, professor

**Noteworthy & Notorious Aries Men:** Eddie Murphy, Vince Vaughn, Hugh Hefner, Zach Braff, Marc Jacobs, Jackie Chan, Al Gore, Thomas Jefferson, Kevin Federline, Martin Lawrence, Heath Ledger, Alec Baldwin, Spike Lee, Haley Joel Osment, Robert Kiyosaki, Hayden Christensen, Q-Tip, Ewan McGregor, Mark Consuelos, MC Hammer, Redman, Steven Tyler, Babyface, Eric McCormack, Steven Segal, Method Man, Christopher Walken,

Cesar Chavez, Conan O'Brien, David Letterman, Eric Clapton, Quentin Tarantino, Leonard Nimoy, William Shatner, Pharrell Williams, Marvin Gaye, Matthew Broderick, Warren Beatty, Michael Rapaport

# Aries: How to Spot Him

- Strong brow, often looks like he's frowning or angry
- May walk with his head forward, like a charging ram
- Assertive or dominant body posture that says "I own this place"
- Moves around quickly and energetically
- Powerful, straightforward gaze
- Oozes raw sexual energy
- Nearly naked (wifebeater, open shirt, flip-flops, baggy shorts drooping off his ass)
- Sarcastic and brusque
- Shouting, bellowing, whooping, or cheering
- Pacing around nervously, running his hand through his hair
- Wearing a hat, baseball or trucker cap, or bandanna (Aries rules the head)
- Sexy, powerful body and combat-ready stance

# Aries: How He Deals With...

### Money

Burns a hole in his pocket. Can become a multimillionaire as an entrepreneur, like Aries Robert Kiyosaki of *Rich Dad, Poor Dad* fame. May tank several businesses and lose the family fortune on his road to riches.

## Family

Strange dynamics—can be totally dependent, but also have babyish blowouts, giving relatives the silent treatment for months.

## Love

Has such an idealized vision of it, it's almost impossible to achieve. Refuses to settle for less.

## Sex

As necessary as oxygen.

## Children

Either wants no kids (doesn't want the responsibility or to share your attention), or a huge family. A strict father who can be a little too demanding, but also attentive.

## Pets

Too many germs, but enjoys their unconditional love and affection.

## Your Meltdowns

An amazing, helpful hero, as long as they're not about him.

## His Meltdowns

Explosive, mind-melding, intense arguments. Could send you to the psychological trauma ward.

## Breakups

If mutual, he'll be your friend for life. If you dump him out of left field, he's devastated. Once he's in, he wants to remain that way—it took him long enough to get there!

# Aries: What He's All About

Want to set the women's movement back to prehistoric times? Drop an Aries man into a room full of educated, self-aware women. Backs straighten suddenly, lashes flutter, hair is gamely twirled around fingers. The virile Knight/Caveman has arrived, victorious from the hunt, slain beast in tow. He's here to protect and defend the fair maidens of the land.

Surely there are some damsels in distress here? The Aries man has a way of "outing" you. His masculinity brings out a primal instinct you have the good sense to be embarrassed about. Thought you were too smart to go weak-kneed over some macho stud, right? After spending years earning college degrees, buying pepper spray, and learning to take care of yourself (thankyouverymuch), you're a modern-day version of Xena: Warrior Princess.

Until Hercules shows up, that is. Eons of feminist progress vanish like the dinosaurs. Blame it, perhaps, on your Darwinian DNA. Research suggests that women are still biologically hard-coded to seek out the hardiest mate, he who can guarantee our survival in case of flood, harsh winter, or famine. Whether it's with physical or intellectual might, the Aries man is an Alpha male whose presence, like a radio signal, beckons this archaic part of the female brain.

Of course, the Caveman must return to his hunt, so the "distressed" damsel must be a good provider herself. She needs to be independent enough to amuse herself while he's off on the hunt, sexy enough to satisfy his all-consuming libido, credentialed enough to support his under-earning bouts, and intelligent enough to compensate for his immaturity. Will he appreciate her? Not to the degree she deserves. In the Aries man's confident mind, there is no such thing as "out of his league." He's an Aries. He always gets the best.

Perhaps that's because he knows he's the best at what he does. It might take him years before he's ready to unleash his unique gifts on the world, but when he does—wow. This proud peacock arrives feathers out, ready to smoke his competition and impress you into a state of weak-kneed awe. If he doesn't do it with raw sex appeal, he uses his intellect, musicianship, jokes, political savvy, quick thinking—whatever he's got. Credentials and prior experience are irrelevant. He strives to assert his individuality, to be his own man. Skim through any industry and you'll find an Aries man who charged in out of nowhere and broke the mold. Democracy: Thomas Jefferson. Fashion: Marc Jacobs. Pop music production: Pharrell Williams. Comedy: Eddie Murphy. Environmental awareness: Al Gore. Stunts: Jackie Chan. Babymaking music: Marvin Gaye, Al Green. Late night TV: David Letterman. Acting: Marlon Brando. And the list goes on. He's number one. Get it? And like revolutionary Ram Thomas Jefferson, the Aries man holds that truth to be self-evident.

He can come across as a real arrogant prick, but underneath, he's terrified of being anything but numero uno. Aries Marlon Brando once said, "I put on an act sometimes, and people think I'm insensitive. Really, it's like a kind of armor because I'm too sensitive. If there are two hundred people in a room and one of them doesn't like me, I've got to get out." The Aries man is neurotic this way, constantly threatened and fearful of losing top billing. Because he covers this up desperately, he comes across as either breathtakingly egotistical or trying too hard. This can evoke your violent, immediate dislike of him—but wait. Stumble on a stiletto, and in a flash he's catching you, lifting you back on your feet. You feel weightless, feminine, cherished (dare we say it?) saved. Whoops. You've fallen in love with the guy you love to hate.

Of course, other men are glad to follow this natural leader. There's a raw, masculine quality that men admire in him; being around his testosterone wellspring makes them feel more manly. He's the ultimate frat boy, a man among men. He can whip ass in a political debate, annihilate a chessboard, hold court at the head of any dinner table with side-splitting jokes and stories. His friendships have a "bromosexual" quality, a backslapping, circle-jerking camaraderie that no woman will ever fully understand. Picture Aries Russell Crowe in *Gladiator*, Hayden Christensen swinging his light saber as a young Luke Skywalker. These films are probably in every Aries man's personal video collection, as he loves war movies about bands of brothers. Ophira dated an Aries for two years who watched either *Lord of the Rings* or *Gladiator*—sometimes both—every single night before bed. He also won a national jujitsu tournament without any training. Men adored him.

Still, underneath the Aries man's chest beating, there's also the most exquisitely vulnerable little boy you'll ever meet. He's a heartbreaking angel on a good day, an utter terror when he's off. As the zodiac's first sign, the Aries man is a bit of a paradox. Essentially, he's a "macho baby." While his ruler, warrior-planet Mars, makes him a fierce fighter, he's also the infant of the horoscope. And like a baby, his primal needs and abandonment fears are more immediate than any other sign's. The Aries man may cry for freedom, yet there's a side of him that's as dependent as a newborn. His version of "mother's milk" is to build an elaborate defense system that guarantees he'll never be left in the cold. For example, is octogenarian Hugh Hefner, with his Playboy mansion and three porn-star girlfriends, a sexual renegade? Or is he just making sure that he's never left alone without the reassurance, sexual attention, and devotion of a woman? Probably both.

The Aries man has a reputation for having anger issues. Indeed his temper and demeanor can be fierce and intimidating. But what's behind anger? Usually, pain and a sense of powerlessness.

Now let's go back to the image of the baby, the innocent. When he loves for the first time, the Aries man will hand you his entire heart, whole and beating wildly, with full trust. He has no idea that anything bad could possibly happen. He believes—he trusts the outcome purely, without a single, tarnishing thought. Like a child playing in traffic, he doesn't see the cars or imagine they could hit him.

There's a saying that fools rush in. The Fool is the first card of the Tarot deck. It depicts a merry, spirited young man on the edge of a cliff, carrying a small hobo sack. The Fool is so enraptured in his blissful adventure, he's unaware that his next step will send him plummeting right off the mountain. The Aries man begins each venture as this kind of "fool"—throwing himself headlong into the flames, with utter faith that he's fireproof.

Then—uh-oh. He gets burned. He sneaks downstairs to catch Santa Claus and sees his mother putting gifts under the tree. The woman he thought would be his wife has been cheating on him. Worst of all, EVERYONE KNEW BUT HIM. Now, he feels like a different sort of fool. The kind that's an idiot, a sucker. And this sucker punch knocks the wind right out of Aries. As the saying goes, the first cut is the deepest. He may never fully recover from this primal wound.

That's when the Aries man creates his "ego defense" to protect himself from reliving that pain. He might become a player, seducing and dumping women ruthlessly. He might swear himself to celibacy (so wrong for the sign with the highest libido), fall into drug abuse, even suffer a nervous breakdown. He can become tough, suspicious to the point of paranoia, obsessed with never getting "played" again. Aries Alec Baldwin was exposed to the media shouting into his pre-teen daughter's answering machine that she was a "rude, insensitive little pig." What really happened? She didn't return his calls and he was HURTING. Everything is pure and undistilled for the Aries man—his pain, anger, and outrage. He takes everything personally. He shouts, he pouts, he broods, he kicks over the Monopoly board because he's losing. Our Aries uncle Sami, visiting New York from Tel Aviv, stewed for a week because he paid (gasp) three dollars for two tomatoes. "In Israel, I get a BUSHEL for one shekel," he spat, invoking the open-air market where shoppers bargain for produce. "What does this guy think—I'm stupid?"

What really hurts the Aries man more than paying retail at a Korean deli, though, is denying his voracious, innocent spirit its lifeblood: adventure. Now, he's abandoned himself. He longs desperately to give his heart fully to life—to love and express his passion—every moment. So his heart continues to beat wildly, but rather than leaping through his chest, it now flings itself against an ironclad fortress, against the steely armor of a knight who once threw off his helmet and charged onto the battlefield naked.

So how does the zodiac's Superman regain his powers after a nasty clash with Kryptonite? As we write this on March 21—the first day of the Aries cycle and Spring—we're reminded that trees blossom even after the hardest winters. When the Aries man allows his heart to thaw, he can heal into a powerful force of nature. Often, it takes the unconditional love of someone he admires—a person who believes in him with the same purity that he lost—for the warrior's courage to return.

## What He Wants in a Woman

What do you get when you cross a kindergarten teacher, Superwoman, and a porn star? The perfect wife, according to Aries. He wants a lifelong personal lap dancer with natural sweetness, maternal instincts, passion, and star power. (Doesn't hurt if she's an amazing cook and domestic goddess either.) Being his woman is no easy task—in fact, it's a demanding gig that will keep you on your toes. He's the cream of the crop, and cream always rises to the top. In his mind, he's always entitled to the best. The rules and norms don't apply to him—and he'll go out of his way to prove it.

The spirited adventuress of his dreams can keep up with his tireless libido, advance his social status, and still coddle the fragile "baby" part of him. We said his dreams, right? Because let's face it, most of us have overdeveloped one of those qualities, usually at the expense of the others. We fall into a role: We're either the sexy temptress, or the smart chick, or the always-a-bridesmaid caretaker type. But deep down the bookish honor-roll girl yearns to be homecoming queen. The human Barbie doll wants to be taken seriously in spite of her double-Ds. Mommy wants those screaming brats to know she's a person with needs of her own.

So perhaps what looks like an arrogant, selfish demand is just Aries upping the ante for us. Haven't feminists fought to be seen as multidimensional creatures who can be wildly sexual and intellectual and nurturing? Don't working moms dream of calling the babysitter, leaving the job for an hour, and indulging in a steamy midafternoon tryst? Why can't the homecoming queen be a history professor, too? Aries has no problem with that.

Still, if he had to choose one dominant quality, the Aries man will go with the motherly type. He doesn't trust the porn star, because he's way too possessive and jealous. The bookworm might be too sexually inhibited for him. So… Mommy. She's a great fit for the part of him that needs constant attention and reassurance. As we said, he's the zodiac's baby, and the center of mama's universe is her little boy. She cooks, cleans, and cares for the family, leaving him free to play. She handles all the details he's too impatient to bother with, keeps money in the bank, and might even support him. Like a private therapist, she listens to his endless anxieties and neuroses. Even her body is available 24/7—it's a one-stop shop for all his most primal needs, from affection to sex.

Now, for the warning label. All that doting might keep your Aries fat and happy, but it will leave you completely miserable, with a spoiled brat to raise. Because his appetite and ego are huge, he doesn't really have limits. He'll heap his plate high with whatever you give him—your time, energy, body—then return to the buffet again and again. Do you really want to quit your job, greet him with pipe and slippers, listen while he rants about his "incompetent asshole" of a boss or our idiot of a U.S. president, serve him elaborate dinners followed by two-hour marathon sex, then tuck him in with a lullaby? He'll let you. But it will drain the life out of you. Suddenly, you'll understand why 1950s housewives devoured martinis and prescription painkillers, and why escort services charge $1,000 an hour. Attention is a valuable commodity.

The two most important qualities you'll need? Passion and patience. "I waited fourteen years for Peter to marry me," says one woman of her Aries husband. "He was unhappily married to someone else when we met. We worked together and had this ongoing flirtation for years. But his wife had been abused as a girl, so he felt like she needed him and he couldn't leave her. Finally, she moved out and they got divorced. I think his ego kept him from breaking it off—he imagined somehow she couldn't live without him. Even now, if she ever needs something, he'll help her out."

So why does this happen so often? The Aries man is extremely sensitive to stress—and he needs to vent this to the woman he trusts. He gets anxious and freaked out, down on himself and the world, and it's really hard to be around. He might even cry. It's a side so few people see of him. He has moments of such extreme vulnerability that you want to take him in your arms, rock him, tell him it will be okay. You might think, "I'm the only person in the world he can open up to. I'll be his rock. As long as he needs me, he'll never leave." It brings out the mother in you, but don't mistake his outpouring for weakness. It's actually a test.

In biblical lore, mighty Samson (surely an Aries) confided in beautiful Delilah that his long hair was his strength. She seduced him into cutting his hair and losing his powers. This is the Aries man's worst nightmare. What if you betray him and he's left completely impotent? He knows that he's easily swayed by sex. When Tammy Wynette sang "Stand By Your Man," she probably spoke right to the hearts of women who have valiantly stood by an Aries, while he subjected them to endless loyalty tests and delays. There could be a long waiting process before he feels "ready" for a real-deal adult relationship.

Don't rush his process by trying to make it "easier" for him to commit. This has the same effect as Kryptonite on Superman, or a buzz cut on Samson. He needs to fight for you, and without this, he loses his strength. Before you know it, he quits his job, and spends the day sitting around in sweatpants, stewing in a funk, or downloading videos instead of applying for a new job. You're now saddled with being the breadwinner and his personal servant. You might pay dearly for this in the end, too. Who can forget Sagittarius Britney Spears and her Aries ex-husband Kevin Federline? An unknown backup dancer of dubious talent, "K-Fed" landed a multimillionaire pop star who raved about his sexual talents and bore his children. After their divorce, he won child support, a mansion, and came out looking like Father of the Year while she had a bipolar breakdown.

So if you don't want this to happen to you, give Aries the best—and hardest—gift: boundaries. Know your limits and stick by them. It's hard to say no to this charmer, to deny a screaming infant the breast. But Samson needs to let his hair grow back naturally. He doesn't need you to sew him a toupee or enroll him in Hair Club for Men. He needs you to believe in him, encourage him and not interfere in his process. Practice the Japanese art of wu wei—doing by not doing (read up on it if you're with an Aries man).

Like the springtime that heralds the Aries cycle, there must always be a struggle, a fight for life to break through the frozen winter ground. Without this battle, there could be no crocuses, daffodils, or cherry blossoms. The "winter" of the Aries man is scary—everything looks dead and frozen, hopeless. Then… the tulips begin to peek out of the ground. Do you reach in and pull them out so they'll bloom faster? Only if you want to kill them. Leave the vulnerable buds alone and before you know it, you'll have a glorious outburst of magic, a garden filled with incredible colors, fragrances, and beauty.

## What He Wants from a Relationship

Let's start with a disclaimer: You might not like what you hear. Or, you might just shout "finally!" The Aries man has a very specific, grand, and demanding vision for his ultimate relationship. In life, he orders everything customized to his tastes, and those tastes are very particular. He may not subconsciously realize that human beings, imbued with things like personalities and free will, can't conform to his fantasies on demand. He'd rather just find that "needle in the haystack" relationship, the impossible dream come true. When he finds that, he gives it every ounce of his being. He turns off the selfish switch and pours on the giving. So why would he do that for just anyone?

The Aries man is great at either having lots of sex with lots of different people, or being completely devoted to one woman. Nothing in between. He's too impatient to master the finer points of courtship. It doesn't even occur to him. The Aries man is endearingly authentic to a fault. Even if he's dating multiple women when you meet, he'll just tell you outright. Although it may seem crude, his open-book policy can actually create a space of greater trust.

Take our friend Lois, a Virgo, and her Aries boyfriend Charlie. "He was exceptionally green when it came to courtship, since he had never been on a blind date before and was clearly the relationship or marrying kind versus a player," she recalls of their first date. "So he did all the wrong things, called at the last minute, talked endlessly about ex-girlfriends and wives, but there was this amazing sweetness about him. When I tried to end the first date early by saying I was tired, he offered to walk me home. 35 BLOCKS. On the way, I started to cough and said I needed to get cough drops and he insisted on paying for them—in addition to dinner. He blushed when he asked me out again, and looked at the ground. He was so shy and sweet, that it tugged at my heart. So there was a tremendous learning curve for him. But his courtship was largely based on acts of service. Cleaning out my storage closet in my apartment, buying tons of new plastic containers and organizing my tools. Buying me a new set of dishes because the old ones were pretty scary, fixing things. My kind of guy! All things I didn't even ask him to do, very thoughtful."

Besides, it's not like Aries thinks relationships are the be-all end-all of life. He gets restless, itchy for the next adventure. His eyes rove, his imagination wanders. Isn't there another damsel to save somewhere? Another sexual position he hasn't tried? He knows his desires may be more than one woman can supply—and he's not above shopping at a few different stores to complete his sexual grocery list. To this independent sign, bachelorhood is a cherished prize. It's his ticket to freedom, adventure, unlimited expression—his access to feeling truly alive. He'll never trade it in unless he truly believes a relationship will provide all those treasures and more.

What he needs is sort of contradictory: a relationship that gives him ultimate security and full freedom to roam. The Aries man is deeply driven by a fear of abandonment, so that should never be an issue between you. Once that's secured, he feels safe to spread his arms wide and pull life to him. He wants to live life like it's a huge playground—more like a carnival fairground—where he can wander, explore, win you stuffed animals, and enjoy a freak show or two. On Coney Island, reality is suspended. There's a different set of rules, or perhaps none at all, which is perfect because that means he gets to make them. We can't help but mention Aries Hugh Hefner again, who lives at the Playboy Mansion surrounded by half-naked centerfold models all day. Who cares if nobody else lives that way? That only makes it more appealing for Aries.

If you want to be with Aries for the long haul, you'll have to embrace his chosen lifestyle. Does that mean he wants everything on his terms? Well, everything that matters to him. We know tons of Aries men who are in long-term relationships, even married, but live in separate homes from their partners. Some even have open relationships, or some need that requires an "understanding" between you. If what's good for the goose ain't good for the Aries gander, he'd sooner fly away than change his migratory habits.

He eventually realizes that he's a high-maintenance diva, but he sees no need to apologize for that. He simply continues his search until he meets his match. A perfect Aries example is notorious ladies' man Warren Beatty, who supposedly inspired Carly Simon's hit "You're So Vain." Although he had a rep as a heartbreaking womanizer, what most people don't know is this: Beatty found and lost his ultimate woman years before he became a player. She was actress Julie Christie (also an Aries), whom he spotted in 1966 at a London screening of her film *Born Free*. Beatty and Christie were both attached, but realized they were soul mates who shared a rare level of passion. After a rocky start, they ditched their partners and dated for eight years. They kept separate homes throughout their affair. Beatty told the press that he considered her his wife, and would even pay her alimony if they broke up.

The only hitch? Julie Christie refused to marry Warren Beatty. The iconic lovers couldn't get past a sticking point: Beatty wanted children and Christie didn't. Of course, that wasn't enough to deter Beatty just yet. When he's truly in love, the Aries man won't go down without a fight. Beatty began setting up the chessboard to take his queen. In 1974, he bought his dream house and invited Christie over. She soon realized that he'd allocated several of the rooms as baby nurseries! He was determined to get his way. Unfortunately, he was dealing with another stubborn Ram, so Christie broke up with him by phone. And he left a trail of broken Hollywood hearts until 1992, when he got Annette Bening pregnant, then married her (in that order, of course). They now have four children, so he got his way in the end. Aries always does.

The Aries man is a natural leader, so if he does want kids, he takes great pride in being "head of the household." There's a tinge of chest-beating chauvinism to this, a sense that you could be cast into the roles of traditional, *Leave It to Beaver*-era husband and wife. Of course, you'll never sleep in separate twin beds like the Cleavers. Mostly it will all be for show, another part of the peacock you'll have to deal with. Even if you don't have kids, there will always be a very important third "member" of your household: his penis, that is. The Aries man is incredibly proud and fascinated by everything his can do. And you'd better be, too. There's usually plenty to appreciate there, anyhow. It will be obvious when you meet him that he knows that.

When the Aries man loves, he holds on tight. This can make him a tyrant who runs his home like a four-star general. He wants his kids to be successful and will hold them to high standards—

though he spoils them ridiculously, too. This won't always be an easy relationship. There could be episodes of screaming, tears, hurled objects, and slammed doors with your warrior prince. He can take you to the edge of a mental breakdown. But as our Aries uncle Sami once said, "If you can't fight with someone, you can't love them." For every shattered wineglass or hyperventilating meltdown, there will be passionate sex, unparalleled intimacy, and devotion so powerful it takes your breath away. Together, you'll write this unforgettable love story with blood, sweat, and tears—every drop that's in you.

# Sex with an Aries

If there's one thing the Aries man is known for, it's his libido. He's incredibly physical, and he'll take any opportunity to shed his clothes. This guy could screw all day long, and if he's not having sex, he'll think or talk about it nonstop.

As with everything, Aries is always chasing the ultimate high: an idealized moment of bliss where pure love and ecstasy conjoin, where his noisy mind finally shuts up and he surrenders to his senses. He can't stand restrictions—and that means anything from sexual inhibitions to condoms to time limits. Aries loves the rapture of feeling completely free. One Aries man says he had the best orgasms while trying to get his wife pregnant.

Since Aries rules the mind, his imagination is boundless when it comes to sex. His roguish nature can give his fantasies a teenage-boy twist. The *Playboy* centerfolds, swelling implants, cheesy garters, and money shots might just do it for him. "For me, dirty talk, when done right, is irresistible," says Dirk, an Aries writer. "And this might be cliché, but there's something about fishnets that I can't shake." Then, his mind wanders into "taboo" territory, which usually freaks him out and entices him all at once. Most Aries men dream of open relationships and threesomes, but they're too loyal to do it in reality—unless there's a willing partner. He needs a woman with a high sex drive who's willing to act out his fantasies and let him be dominant—his and only his. "One time, a girl I was seeing came over wearing nothing but a trench coat, knocked on my door, and we ended up screwing for hours," recalls one Aries. He's hungry, impatient, eager (the "Ram" can be an apt symbol for his technique). You might have to pace him, or he'll finish before you've even warmed up.

There's an experimental side to Aries that often includes homosexual play. Like a daring knight, he needs to try everything once—if only to disprove his paranoid fear that he's gay. Even notoriously well-endowed sex symbol Marlon Brando, an Aries, admitted in his biography, "Like a large number of men, I, too, have had homosexual experiences, and I am not ashamed." Who didn't get hot and bothered watching Aries Heath Ledger as a gay cowboy in *Brokeback Mountain*? Somehow, this only makes the Aries man seem like an even bigger stud. It's as though he needs to commune with his own raw, uninhibited, masculinity in its basest form—to skip the tenderness and get down to unvarnished, aggressive sex. "Gay" is too limiting a label for Aries. He's just sexual in an energetic way, and energy seeks whatever it wants without judgment.

In spite of being a sex god, he can suffer from paralyzing performance anxiety. After being unable to "get it up" one time, an Aries man we know couldn't have sex for over a year. He was terrified that it would happen again. This sign is incredibly paranoid, in completely irrational ways. A patient, noncritical, receptive mate will restore his confidence and get him back to being the sexual Casanova he was born to be.

# Aries: Turn-Ons & Turn-Offs

## Turn Him On

- Respect yourself—have an inner grace and self-assuredness
- Be a little bit of a tomboy—he doesn't like divas or overly delicate types
- Tease and flirt, but let him pursue you
- Be direct, bold, and outspoken
- Talk dirty in bed
- Let him be dominant in some areas
- See the glass as half-full: share a sincere sense of wonder and awe, without being overly naïve
- Share his sense of adventure
- Be passionate about your life and what you do
- Have credentials he admires, especially educational ones
- Make him feel like nothing short of a god
- Be an amazing cook (and appreciate his cooking)
- Think outside the box
- Have a strong sense of social justice
- Have "a sweet face and killer curves," as one Aries puts it
- Laugh at his jokes

## Turn Him Off

- Have sexual hang-ups or a prudish nature
- Try to control his sexual appetite, forbid porn, cancel his *Hustler* subscription
- Prevent him from going out at night or hanging with the fellas

- Be jealous of his fantasies or when he admires other women
- Embarrass him in public
- Boss him around
- Pursue him too heavily
- Tell him to "grow up"
- Have bad breath, body odor, or poor hygiene
- Challenge him too much
- Deny him the attention or affection he craves
- Flirt with other men in his presence
- Pressure him to have kids, move in together, or live a traditional life

# His Moves

## First Moves: How He Courts You

The Aries man has two styles of courtship: the preening peacock or the direct attack. When he's in peacock mode, he simply turns up the volume on his masculine mojo and lets the invisible rays of his testosterone do the work. He manages to grab your attention while seemingly doing nothing.

He can also charge after women like the Ram that symbolizes him, making his intentions clear as day. An Aries once walked up to Ophira on the beach in Israel and, without even introducing himself, said, "Want to go out tonight?" Of course, he was charming enough to plop down in the sand and engage her in a three-hour conversation about life, relationships, and the senselessness of monogamy. And he was so earnest about that, she went out with him anyhow. That night, he brought her an exquisite box of Max Brenner chocolates—"chocolates by the bald man"—because he, too, was bald. When the Aries man courts you, he always leaves you with something to remember him by. And indeed you will.

In the unlikely event that it's not obvious, here are some signs an Aries man likes you:

- He approaches you and starts a conversation
- He asks you all about yourself, or tells you all about himself
- He walks right up to you and tells you he thinks you're hot
- He directly asks you out
- He hits on you shamelessly (if he's feeling superconfident)

- He "hovers" and studies you to see if you're available
- He observes you from a distance
- He begins protecting you
- He says something sweet, boyishly sincere, and flattering

- He turns up the charm around you
- He plays peacock—showing off his "feathers" and letting you notice him

- He gets loud, funny, and cocky
- He baits the trap—talks about sex, other women, his fantasies—knowing you'll get all hot and bothered

- He calls you to talk for hours and hours

## He's In: How You Know He's Committed

Although the Aries knight may not leave bachelorhood behind without raising major hell, once he does, he can be fiercely devoted. It's not happening without a fight or a testing period, and possibly a few "do-overs" should he freak out and second-guess everything. Still, Aries is pretty much a direct kind of guy. So here's how he shows you his devotion:

**He tells you.** The Aries man isn't big on subtlety. He speaks from the heart and says what he means, especially if he's professing his love.

**He tells everyone.** Shouts it from the rooftops, even. Hey everybody! Look at my woman! She's MINE, all mine! (Translation: Look at me! I'm number-one and I've got the hot, sexy superstar babe to prove it!) It's endearing. Our friend Lois tells us that her Aries boyfriend, Charlie, writes "I love Precious" (her cutesy nickname) in the snow.

**He becomes your champion and one-man fan club.** When the Aries man is truly in love, he worships the woman he's with. Of course, being on a pedestal has its own set of problems, but he needs to idealize you. One woman who won an award from her women's professional group brought her Aries boyfriend to a dinner in her honor. The lone male among a hundred women, he was like a stud in the dairy barn, but he didn't care. After her acceptance speech, he leapt to his feet for a loud standing ovation and to bellow "Wooo hooo!" The women all looked at each other, at once shocked and touched by his obvious adoration.

**You're his confidante.** He rarely goes to bed without calling you, and you might talk for hours. He needs your opinion, your feedback, your listening ear. One friend confessed that she drifted off to sleep while her Aries was mid-monologue. But if he trusts you enough to be his sounding board, he won't want to lose you.

**He goes from "me" to "we."** That's a big step for a guy who occasionally forgets that the Sun is the center of the solar system, not him. Now, he's all about being a unit, taking vacations together, being the head of the household and whatever other perks come with trading his cherished independence for this.

**He cries on your shoulder—literally.** The little boy in Aries with all that pent-up stress and frustration secretly longs to sob in your arms and let it all go. If he trusts you with his tears, he trusts you with his life.

## Unfaithful Aries: Why He Cheats

When it comes to cheating, the Aries man has his own set of rules. If he truly loves you, it's almost impossible for him to stray. He's motivated by a very masculine honor code that's all about loyalty, nobility, and dignity… or whatever they talk about in those epic Mel Gibson war movies. But if every single fiber of his being doesn't shout "she's the One!" about you, he'll always sleep with one eye open, scanning for his true love. And if he happens to spot her while you're still together, so be it. He's not cheating—he's just leaving you for someone better. Don't you see the difference?

We don't either. But it doesn't matter, because he makes the rules. Here are a few reasons why the Aries man could stray:

**Revenge.** He's hurt immeasurably and seeing red. Most people don't understand how immediate pain is for Aries; he feels it in every part of his body. It just overtakes him, like any passionate emotion. He wants you to hurt as badly as he does, to experience his agony so you'll never dare to hurt him this way again.

**You're not his soul mate.** Or he suspects you're not, anyhow. His intuition is usually right. Couldn't he have told you sooner?

**You've eclipsed him and he feels like a chump.** Sure, he's proud to be dating a superstar. In fact, nothing less would do. But if people start whispering, "What's she doing with him?" his ego may not be strong enough to take it. He could bolster himself in that most cliché, knee-jerk way, by charming and seducing a sweet, worshipful young thing.

**He's still "experimenting" and not ready to settle down.** The Aries man is a late bloomer in the monogamy game. Sometimes, he forces himself into a relationship when he knows deep down he hasn't sown his oats. If he did, he might start having sexual adventures on the side.

**Hormones.** When his testosterone is rocking, don't come a-knocking. This is particularly potent in his younger years. But his youth can stretch well into his thirties, forties, and beyond, and his curiosity never dies. "It would be pure opportunism," speculates one Aries man, "being caught in the moment of a 'dream' woman of my sexual ideal type, who at that point would probably be much younger than me."

## Dig the Grave: It's Over

It takes a lot for the Aries man to end a relationship, because it takes him so long to actually commit to one. He likes to keep one foot in one foot out until he's really sure, a process that can take either five minutes or fifteen years. So before he jumps in all the way, here's what might make him run in the other direction:

**You have different sexual preferences.** Sex is the single most important factor in an Aries man's relationships. He can only accommodate your sexual differences so much before this becomes an absolute deal-breaker.

**There's not enough chemistry.** Beyond the physical, he needs mental compatibility, passion, and everything else on his lengthy demand list to really feel turned on. If that's not there, buh-bye.

**He ices you out with the silent treatment—and you don't beg for his forgiveness.** Aries is famous for that four-year-old pouting tactic: I'm taking my ball and going home! Of course, this really just means that he's seething mad, wounded to the core, and punishing you. He expects you to apologize, take full responsibility for the fight he probably started, kiss his ass for a month, and endure his torturous stonewalling. If you're up for this bullying, good luck.

**He hasn't established himself as the leader in his field yet.** The Aries man needs to be the Alpha in his circles. When he doesn't have a platoon to lead, he feels like a castrated schmuck around you. Let him go get his life together. Don't fight him on this one.

**He's a traditionalist and you're a feminist.** He wants to be head of the household and you're all about equality. He needs a certain degree of dominance, sorry to report. Better find yourself a Sagittarius or an Aquarius to play 50/50 with instead.

**You fight constantly, with no makeup sex.** He's no stranger to circular arguments and four-hour screaming matches. But if you're not ripping each other's clothes off after tearing the door off its hinges and hurling it at him, what's the point?

**You're moving away.** The Aries man can't live without his RDA of affection, sex, and physical contact—it's like his Flintstones vitamin that he needs every day. If you decide to take a yearlong teach-abroad gig in Beijing while he stays in Cincinnati, or you spend the summer in Europe, he'd rather just say bon voyage.

# Interpreting His Signals:
## *What does he mean by that?*

| When he | It means... | So you should... |
|---|---|---|
| Gets quiet | He's watching your every move.<br>He's pouting, brooding, or giving you the silent treatment. | Do your version of a "mating dance" and signal him toward you with body language.<br>Ask him if he wants to talk about it. If he won't, give him some time to cool off by himself. |
| Doesn't call | He's either intimidated or not interested. | Call him. You've got nothing to lose. If he doesn't like you, he won't call you back. If he's intimidated, your call will reassure him you're not a player. |
| Calls a lot | He really enjoys talking to you and he wants to know you better. | Only answer when you have time to talk. He's persistent; if he likes you, he'll call again! |
| Doesn't make a move after a couple of dates | He's scared of rejection. He wouldn't bother going on the date if he didn't like you. | Check your body language and attitude to make sure you're not giving off the signals of being "unsafe" or unavailable. |

| When he | It means... | So you should... |
|---|---|---|
| Doesn't make a move after a few weeks | You're his new best friend. | Stop spending all your time with him. He's zapping your "boyfriend energy" and you're getting zero ROI. |
| Moves fast | He's confident in your chemistry. When he knows it's right, he goes for it. | Enjoy some hot, steamy bumping and grinding. |
| | He's dating other women. He usually has a backup plan to hedge against rejection. | Have a conversation about monogamy and STDs to see where he stands. |
| Picks up the tab, gives flowers and gifts | He just got his paycheck and is already impulsively blowing the whole thing. | Prepare to pay for the next date because all of his money will be gone. |
| Introduces you to his family and/ or closest friends | He sees you as someone who will make a good impression, and will make him look good. Score! | Make them fall in love with you. |

# Your Moves: Tips for Flirting and Everlasting Love

## Flirting with an Aries

The way to an Aries' heart is through the mind. Even if he acts like a beer-soaked frat boy, he's no dummy. He notices everything. Chances are, by the time you approach him, he's already been scoping you out half the night. He might seem a little intimidating, because his guard is usually up to a degree. If you want to melt off the Aries mask and get him all hot and bothered, here's what to do:

**Engage in passionate conversation.** Your relationship will be largely centered around bonding through great talks. Open up and share from the heart. Don't interrupt him when he starts on a diatribe—he wants to know that you're fascinated by his opinions and observations.

**Tell him you think he's hot.** He loves a bold come-on that's delivered in his own straightforward style. The male peacock wants to be admired. It's survival of the fittest in the henhouse, so you might as well strut up and grab his feathers.

**Say something clever and edgy.** Make him laugh and show him that you've got sharp wit. He thinks he's smarter than everyone else, so if you start to establish an "us-against-the-world" camaraderie, you could soon be his favorite confidante.

**Do your own version of a mating call.** Show off your star quality, laugh loudly, be the sexiest one on the dance floor. Like an animal in heat, he'll hone in on your seductive signals.

**Remind him of himself.** There's a bit of a narcissist in every Aries. Did you take the words right out of his mouth? Do something exactly the way he would? It must be love! Our friend Lisa met her Aries husband Rob on the first day of grad school. The students went around and introduced themselves, saying why they enrolled in the master's program. "Rob told me that

I said exactly what he was going to say, almost word for word," Lisa says. He was in love from that moment on.

## Everlasting Love with an Aries

Getting to this point is a rocky road, one that might tempt you to turn back or take an easier path instead. The Aries man knows that, and he wants a woman who will stick by him when he's on his best and worst behaviors. Want to show him you're the woman of his dreams? Try this:

**Clean his apartment.** We swear to God, this has worked for several women we know. After walking into the disaster zone that passes for an Aries man's home, they rolled up their sleeves and spent the day organizing, decluttering, and cleaning. The relationship began immediately.

**Share his vision.** Want the same overall lifestyle he wants, and allow him to fully explore the parts you don't share. One couple we know loves Barcelona, philosophy, and also shares a passion for scuba diving. So they take courses and trips together all the time.

**Have a passionate sense of social justice.** Selfish as the Aries man can be, he can give back generously, too. He's often involved in civil rights, social justice, or community groups where he can make his mark on the world. He has a strong aversion to unfairness and human suffering. Working with children and youth groups like Big Brothers/Big Sisters is especially rewarding for Aries, since he loves to be looked up to as a mentor. If you're passionate about making a difference in the world and fighting for a cause, he'll deeply admire you.

**Put up with his quirks.** Beneath those rippling biceps, Aries can also be a needy, neurotic, OCD worrywart. He's usually developed an elaborate arsenal of coping mechanisms to deal. For example, he might be really paranoid about the E. coli virus, so he has to quadruple-rinse his spinach with that special vegetable wash from the organic market. Or he's always been terrified of dying in a plane crash, even had nightmares about it, so he refuses to fly. If you're willing to work around these limitations, he'll love you for it.

Be really, really patient. Aries wants to be a self-made man. He needs to grow at his own pace, to do things his own way, especially when it comes to his career. Stephanie, a graphic designer, offered to teach her Aries boyfriend how to build websites when he was out of a job for months. He refused her help. Years later, he secretly took out student loans to pay for an online web design course. Once he landed a job at an ad agency, he told her what he'd done. The Aries man has too much pride to let you interfere in his process. Let him become a man on his own terms.

# Prep Yourself For...

## Your First Date

Even though Aries is the sign of "firsts," he doesn't pull out all the stops on your initial date. It's a feeling-out process, his chance to observe what you're all about and whether you'd be a good companion for his adventures. Besides, he's probably kind of nervous, even though he tries to hide it. If the conversation and chemistry flow naturally, he'll start to relax. To him, passion is the key ingredient. If that's there, it doesn't really matter what you do or where you go, as long as there's a sexy charge between you. You might end up wandering all over town, guided by whims and the moment.

Besides, he hates doing things the typical way, and he usually has some reservations about opening himself up for possible rejection. "I honestly don't date much, and part of it is because I'm not at all interested in all the canned bulls**t that comes with dating," says Dirk. "There are too many rules, too many expectations. If I meet the right person, then of course I'm going to make an effort, but I don't want to conduct my relations via some sort of textbook or parameters that have been laid out for me by some editorial staff at a glossy mag or the producers of a cable show."

**The Basic Vibe:** If you want to be wined and dined, date a Taurus or a Cancer. The Aries man doesn't want to make a huge, high-maintenance fuss. He just wants to have fun, talk, and connect. "I'll go to a nice low-key restaurant, nothing trendy," says Dan, an art historian, "Then a drink after, very chaste, just to get to know the person. I'll plan something sexier for the second date." Prepare for intense conversation and spontaneity; be ready to go with the flow. Rest well and pamper yourself beforehand—not to get dolled up, but because you'll need to be focused and attentive. Make sure you're not drained or overworked when you go out with Aries.

**What to Wear:** No heels required! The Aries man likes a sexy tomboy who's more cute than sophisticated. He doesn't like being confined in too many clothes, so keep your formal wear in mothballs. Slip into something nonrestrictive that shows off your shape, skin, and cleavage—like a sexy backless halter paired with jeans and low-heeled shoes. Cliché as it is, he gets off seeing a thong peeking out of low-rise jeans, or a lacy bra strap under your tank. Bright colors catch his attention, so don't be afraid to wear bold shades like hot pink and red, or if your skin is dark, white. Since the night could be active, don't limit your physical movement in any way. Make sure your outfits allow you to freely walk, dance, and grind hips in an alley on the way home.

**What Not to Wear:** If it ain't sexy, forget it. Err on the side of youthful and playfully sexy with Aries. Anything too grown-up, sophisticated, stuffy will turn him off—there's no sense of play or flirtiness for him to enjoy. The Empire-waisted prairie-girl schmattes might look good in the window at Anthropologie, but he'll think "grandma." Ditto for the pearls, knit sweaters, and flowy skirts. On the flip side, don't sacrifice comfort for sexiness. Stilettos, corsets, and elaborate lace-ups might look hot, but if they're too hard to rip off in the throes of passion, or reminds him of a dominatrix (never!), scale it down.

**To Pay, or Not to Pay?** Aries is selectively chivalrous, and unfortunately, his old-fashioned values don't always include paying the tab. He tends to burn through cash quickly, rarely leaving enough left over to treat you. It's also a self-protection strategy, since he's hypersensitive to being "played." Bring enough cash to split the bill. Once he senses you're not using him, he may start footing the bill whenever he can. Aries becomes more generous with time and trust.

**Saying Good-night:** He's always in the mood for sex, but the Aries man is never up for rejection. If the night doesn't end with his tongue in your throat and his hand on your ass, it's only because he's afraid you'll shoot him down. He'll hover around to read your vibe, and if he doesn't get a clear signal, he'll sweetly say good-night. If your chemistry is obvious, you could be making out within the first hour of your date, and it might not end until the next day. Hot!

## His First Home Visit

Sound the trumpets and prepare for his royal welcome! Aries is coming over and you'd better get ready. Now, his own home may look like post-nuclear wreckage, with a mattress buried somewhere far under papers, clothes, and God knows what else. Do you think that means you can skip dusting the corners or leave scum on the shower tiles? Not a chance. Listen, a knight gets called off to battle on a moment's notice. You think he shouldn't defend his country because there are dirty dishes in the sink? Well, fair maiden, if you want him parking his white horse at your estate, you'd better prepare his throne. Here's how:

**Have a well-stocked kitchen.** The Aries man loves snack food. He could eat nonstop, really—it's one of his favorite activities. He eats because he's nervous, bored, horny, happy, hungry, tired, whatever. You'll need a Costco membership to keep up. So make sure he can amble in and out of your pantry without depleting the stash.

**Order delivery from his favorite restaurant.** The Aries man is a particular eater, and he likes his food prepared and arranged exactly to his specifications. He rarely orders anything the way it appears on the menu ("Can I have the seafood lo mein with only scallops, the carrots julienned at a 49-degree angle, and the bok choy on the side?"). He's happiest after having the perfect meal… and of course, he'll want you for dessert.

**Talk politics.** Or sports, philosophy, music, literature—whatever topic he knows a lot about. He loves to show off his mental prowess, spout and tout his opinions, and enjoy a spirited conversation on a hot topic.

**Don't invite him to the Barbie Dream House.** This is the über-masculine frat boy who'd rather be at a hunting lodge, a sports bar, or shooting pool in a dank basement. He can't stand fussy furniture and precious objects. Take the plastic off the couch and the canopy off your bed. Anything too princessy will make him gag.

**Hide the remote.** The Aries man goes into couch potato mode too quickly if you let him. Turn on the TV and he'll zone out like a high school boy after football practice. Before you know it, his clothes are on the floor and he's in his boxer-briefs watching CNN and eating Cheetos. What happened to the romance?

**Scrub and sterilize.** Aries is a hypochondriac and a germ freak, for starters, and he gets easily grossed out by a dirty house. One Aries we know walked into his now-girlfriend's house, sniffed and remarked, "It smells like cat pee in here." She was mortified.

**Save him a drawer.** He might be moving in soon, unofficially anyhow. Still, even if he loves being at your place seven nights a week, he might maintain his own scummy little bachelor pad, furnished with fruit crates and plastic storage tubs.

## Meeting His Family

Because he takes so long to figure out what to do with his life, the Aries man might still live with his family when you meet him. Until he decides to "settle down," home is little more than a crash pad for Aries, somewhere to shower between one-night stands, or have his socks and underwear washed. This can be convenient if you decide to live together, since there will be no tearful negotiations over whose place to move into.

Even if he's shacked up with mommy and daddy rent-free, his relationship with them can still be fraught with tension. Usually this stems from an early childhood trauma he can't seem to shake—divorce, not enough attention, some other failure on their part to live up to his incredibly high expectations. He might refuse to grow up just to punish them!

The Aries man always has mother issues. He either idealizes his mom or demonizes her. If she's on a pedestal, then don't dare to make a single critical remark to tarnish her sacred, saintly image. She probably treated him like a crown prince in his childhood, never criticizing or disciplining him, creating a monster along the way.

If the relationship is bad, it's usually because he feels "smothered"—too guilty to cut the cord, and perhaps secretly reluctant to give up the perks that go along with it to keep it intact. He longs to break away and be his own man, but knows he's also dependent, which can fuel some deep-seated hostility and anger issues. The family unit must be supportive, not restrictive, for him to be close to his relatives.

Still, don't think you can go criticizing them. He's like a mobster about other people bashing his relatives. Just because he made you think you're inheriting a monster-in-law or a henpecked future father-in-law, don't believe the hype. He may still hand over his paychecks, bail them out of prison, and dutifully serve them, even while complaining how terrible they are.

Deep down, he desperately wants his family's approval so if they like you, score for you and him. Your single job is to be as likeable as possible to his relatives. As they warm to you, his own broken ties with them may mend, which will be healthier for everyone in the long run.

# Saying Good-bye
## Breaking Up with an Aries

Breaking up with Aries isn't the hard part. Forcing yourselves to stay together, though? Brutal. There comes a time with Aries, after one too many screaming, crying fights, when you have to wave the white flag. Let it go. You've both taken this as far as you could, and nobody's willing to budge. No amount of couples therapy, sedatives, and Imago dialogue workshopping can save this *Titanic*. The barge has hit the 'berg and it's going down.

Once you mutually agree that it's best to part ways, conversations become downright civilized between you—even loving. You're setting him free to seek true bliss, returning him to his treasured bachelor roots. Aries wants to think of himself as a good guy, not that asshole who accused you of flirting with the bag boy at Stop 'n Shop. God, he can't believe he did that. He wants to remain friends forever, and listen—if you ever need someone to carry your groceries, just call him, okay? Not that chump from the supermarket. He'll knock that sorry sucker out.

Now, if you decide to pull the rug out from Aries or disappear, forget it. He has way too many abandonment issues to handle that well. He'll be devastated, and furious that you didn't just talk to him. One woman we know moved across the country from her Aries instead of directly breaking up with him. He never really forgave her.

## Getting over Him: When an Aries Dumps You

We hate to be the bearer of bad tidings, but if any Aries leaves you, either a) he was never really in love with you, b) you did him wrong in a completely unforgivable way, or c) it was just a manipulation tactic to see if you'd come around. This is the guy who storms off when he doesn't get his way, raises hell until you give in and do things on his terms.

If he's truly dependent on you, the zodiac's infant will never break the bond. Babies don't ask mommy to stop breast-feeding them, do they? Harsh, we know, but he really feels connected by some kind of spiritual umbilical cord to the woman he loves. Why would he cut off his life supply?

The only exception is if one of you moves away for an unforeseeable time period. Even then, if he's really in, he believes that love will conquer all. He might wait around for a while, but he does need regular sex, affection, and contact. Keep extending your travels or start putting down roots in a faraway location—in other words, make it clear that you're building the next chapter of your life without him—and he'll call things off. In that case, he'll want to tell you directly and remain friends for life.

**Have yourself one good last cry over...**
- How goddamn sexy he made you feel
- That roguish, cocky, bad-boy energy
- His h-h-h-hotness

- The way he could grab your hips and take you
- His edgy, sarcastic humor
- The way he just dug into life with both hands
- His moments of heartbreaking naïveté and innocence
- How sweetly loyal he could be underneath the agro armor
- Being appreciated in all your raw, tomboyish glory

**Praise the universe that you never have to deal with...**
- Paying his bills, washing his clothes, being "mommy"
- His immaturity and late blooming
- Waiting forever for him to make up his mind about you
- His uninterruptible tirades and rants
- His roving eye and musing about sexual fantasies that don't include you
- Buh-bye, Caveboy: Does he think "white-collar" means wearing a Hanes T-shirt instead of a wifebeater?
- How insecure he really can be
- How selfish he really can be

# Love Matcher:

## Can you find a common language?

| You are a(n)... | He thinks you're... | You think he's... | Common Language |
|---|---|---|---|
| Aries | Admirably ambitious, but a bit of a diva. A lot like him in some sexy, challenging ways. | A volcanic, brooding, complicated soul—the type nobody understands but you. | Arguing, competition, winning, high drives (sex and other), being a star, doing things on your own terms, freedom |
| Taurus | A beautiful, graceful, grounding force: the earth beneath his always-moving feet. | A sexy scamp who needs your patience and tender touch. | Intense sex, doting, food, massage |
| Gemini | His ideal playmate, with smokin' brains and body. | Someone to party with and talk to all night, but overthinks everything. Why can't he lighten up? | Books, ideas, music, politics, intellect, mind games, adventure, conversation, giving each other advice |

| You are a(n)... | He thinks you're... | You think he's... | Common Language |
|---|---|---|---|
| Cancer | The mommy type he loves (especially those boobs!), but also a tad too clingy. Breathing room, please! | So seductive, yet soooo immature. Willingly accepts your nurturing, but may take it for granted, too. | Catering to his needs, processing your emotions, taking everything personally |
| Leo | A fiery kindred spirit who's far too demanding and naively optimistic. | Passionate and intense, but also draining—too much of a downer. You wish he'd be a little more financially and emotionally stable, too. | Battling for world domination, love of attention and the sound of your own voices |
| Virgo | Insufferably uptight, but somehow you keep ending up together. | A complete disturbance of your inner peace. | OCD habits, neurotic oversensitivity to smells and sounds |
| Libra | Sweet and charming, but a bit too delicate for your straightforward style. | Too rough around the edges for your refined tastes. | Social causes, issues, parties, music, art |

| You are a(n)... | He thinks you're... | You think he's... | Common Language |
|---|---|---|---|
| Scorpio | The equally intense sex goddess of his fantasies. | A total porn star, but too hard to control for the long term. | Sex, intensity |
| Sagittarius | An inspiring go-getter, but a little too ambitious to make him the center of your universe. | Sexy but needs too much attention. | Travel, your love of freedom and independence |
| Capricorn | Parental in all the right ways, kinky in others. | The naughty little boy you can't want to punish. | The kind of sex found in special magazines on high-up shelves |
| Aquarius | An adorable best friend to have beers with, but lacking the passionate temperament he likes. | Hot and hilarious, but reminds you of your brother. | Sports, conversation, fitness, offensive jokes, hanging out, movies |
| Pisces | Just the damsel in distress he's been looking for. | A gallant knight in shining armor. Save me! | Romance, art, film, procreation, defying convention and rebelling against "the man" |

# The Taurus Man

Dates: April 20–May 20
Symbol: The Bull
Ruling Planet: Venus, the planet of beauty, art, and romance
Element: Earth—grounded, realistic, wants material security
Quality: Fixed
Mission: A Wife for Life

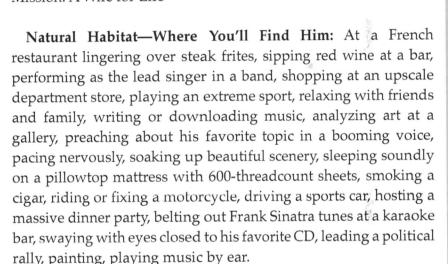

**Natural Habitat—Where You'll Find Him:** At a French restaurant lingering over steak frites, sipping red wine at a bar, performing as the lead singer in a band, shopping at an upscale department store, playing an extreme sport, relaxing with friends and family, writing or downloading music, analyzing art at a gallery, preaching about his favorite topic in a booming voice, pacing nervously, soaking up beautiful scenery, sleeping soundly on a pillowtop mattress with 600-threadcount sheets, smoking a cigar, riding or fixing a motorcycle, driving a sports car, hosting a massive dinner party, belting out Frank Sinatra tunes at a karaoke bar, swaying with eyes closed to his favorite CD, leading a political rally, painting, playing music by ear.

**What He Does for a Living:** Music, banking, real estate, sales, fashion designer, model, actor, fine artist, high school principal, public speaker, decorator, mechanic, political leader, dancer, film director, athlete, construction.

**Noteworthy & Notorious Taurus Men:** George Clooney, David Beckham, Jack Nicholson, Enrique Iglesias, Tim McGraw, Busta Rhymes, Jay Leno, Jerry Seinfeld, The Rock, Jason Biggs, Darius Rucker, Tony Hawk, Craig David, Lance Bass, Joey Lawrence, Al Pacino, Trent Reznor, Jason Lee, Ving Rhames, Jacob Underwood, Bono, John Corbett, Pierce Brosnan, Fred Astaire, Sigmund

Freud, Salvador Dali, Malcolm X, Karl Marx, Stevie Wonder, Billy Joel, Saddam Hussein, Adolf Hitler, General Ulysses Grant, Willie Nelson, Chow-Yun Fat, John Woo, George Lucas, Pope John Paul II, Dennis Rodman, Andre Agassi.

# Taurus: How to Spot Him

- Stylish dresser, either a debonair metrosexual or a total rock star
- Metrosexual Taurus favors suit jackets and button-downs with jeans
- Rock star Taurus may dress in all black, with motorcycle boots and hardware
- Defined chin and strong jaw
- Thick or long neck, broad shoulders
- Soulful eyes, intense gaze
- Deep, booming, or throaty voice
- Full head of hair, often styled distinctively
- Leather shoes, accessories—even leather pants
- Stocky or solid build, often short (but acts like he's seven feet tall)
- Thick or stubby fingers
- Walks with his chest puffed out
- Strong, forceful gestures and an air of authority

# Taurus: How He Deals With...

## *Money*

Loves it, needs it, wants to buy the best of everything. He's the sign of the provider and is usually a good money manager. His weakness for food, music, and designer clothes can empty his wallet in an afternoon. So can you.

### Family

He's a big-time family guy and can't wait to start his own. However, his rigid or explosive behavior can alienate his clan. He's either not on speaking terms with his parents or has them on speed dial.

### Love

He's a romantic in theory, a realist in practice. While he wines and dines many, his love is reserved for the wife he's certain he'll meet—and stay with forever.

### Sex

Loves it, needs it, but he'll go without it for months if the right woman hasn't come along. A monogamist in Casanova's clothing.

### Children

Can't wait to have his own—once he's got the money to provide for them. The ultimate daddy when that time comes.

### Pets

Not so much, unless they make you or his kids happy. Amazing dog trainer.

### Your Meltdowns

Barely tolerates them, but if he gets over it, gives great hugs.

### His Meltdowns

Red face, earsplitting yells, flying objects. Run for your life!

### Breakups

Hates change, and becomes bitter when it's imposed on him. Years can pass before he moves on. Too much pride to let you know he's pining.

# Taurus: What He's All About

So you're looking for a guy who's loyal and stable. Trouble is, you're afraid that spells B-O-R-I-N-G. With a Taurus, it can go either way. The Taurus man is who he is, and you should either love him or leave him alone. He's a creature of habit who loyally sticks to his deep-rooted opinions, favorite restaurants, and creature comforts. He loves his family and craves a conventional lifestyle, complete with kids and a thirty-year mortgage.

So where's the excitement? You have to be ultra-present to find it. Taurus men can appreciate life's simple pleasures like no other sign. They live in the now and soak up every delicious moment. Are you grounded enough to join him? If you're like most multitasking women, being in the moment can be a challenge. Date a workaholic Capricorn if your career eats up all your free time—he'll understand. Or, if you need to "process" your day instead of leaving it behind at the job, a Virgo will listen to you kvetch. Taurus wants to spend quality time as a couple.

The Taurus man loves art and culture. His sign is ruled by Venus, the planet of beauty and creativity. But he's an Earth sign, which makes him a realist. He may burst your bubble when you share your heartfelt dreams, but take a deep breath and listen. Taurus can provide a necessary dose of reality and structure. He'll champion your creative ambitions, as long as you're willing to be practical. Count him out if you plan on standing in a 10-mile line for *American Idol* auditions, or hitchhiking to Hollywood to be "discovered." He doesn't believe in overnight success. Taurus makes small, concrete steps toward a goal, and he'll help you map out yours.

A note to women who like to change your boyfriends: don't bother. Many women find power in leaving our mark on a man, being the one who helps him "see the light." Your shrink calls it codependence, but that hasn't stopped most of us from turning our relationships into Boyfriend Boot Camp. Setting up reform school for a Taurus guy is a total time-waster. The Taurus man doesn't believe in change, and it makes him queasy. He told you exactly who he was from the start. Therefore, changing would be a lie—and he can't stand liars.

With his stubborn personality, Taurus will only change if there's a damn good reason—like his family or loved ones will be threatened if he doesn't. Saving your relationship? Only worth it when kids, property, or joint investments are involved; in other words, when his life as he knows it is at risk. Taurus values the security of a stable life over a fleeting romance. Although he may charge in and out of affairs, he won't make a real move without asking himself, *Is it worth it?*

Do you believe that people can change? *Bah!* scoffs Taurus. He believes that what you see is what you get. "You can grow and learn from your mistakes," says Taurus Jeffrey. "But you're still the same person you were when you were a kid, and you always will be. You can get wiser, but you are who you are. End of discussion." If optimism, spirituality, and faith in the human spirit are among your core values, try a Sagittarius or a Gemini. The Taurus man will only snort and roll his eyes at your "childishness," infuriating the crap out of you.

Taurus is a provider. His sign rules material comfort and daily income, and that's his focus. If you're the kind of woman who brings home wounded birds, go thee and mother an Aries or a Scorpio. Taurus is fine with you bringing home a paycheck. But make no mistake: He brings home the bacon. You may realize it's the 21st century, but that means squat to his traditional sign. He'd rather you buy yourself something pretty with your earnings than spend them on the rent.

Love being spoiled? Taurus is your soul mate. Shameless gold-digger? Grab a shovel. If you're a 50/50 girl who wants to pay her own way, though, forget about dating this sign. You'll feel like you're setting the women's movement back 200 years every time the check arrives. And he'll feel like a castrated schmuck if he lets you pay it. Go split the bill with a budget-conscious Virgo or an equality-minded Aquarius. One woman we know tried to impress her Taurus love interest by treating him to dinner at a chic, upscale French restaurant for his birthday—a "see and be seen" kind of hot spot. Though it sent his account into overdraft, he still grabbed the check out of her hands and paid it. You can't buy the Taurus man's love!

If your conscience bothers you, give him gifts. Cashmere scarves, leather wallets, Godiva chocolate, a CD boxed set—he'll take 'em. Taurus men want the best of everything. Rip off the price tag and pay for gift wrapping. Pick up groceries or gourmet treats, and he'll happily indulge, too. As long as he doesn't see the receipts, he shouldn't mind.

Taurus is a fixed sign, which is exactly what it sounds like—a guy who's "fixed" in one place and doesn't budge. It's the frustrating side of his loyal nature. Sometimes, you need a partner who keeps you guessing, or whose nomadic spirit gets your own life out of a rut. If you find constant surprises and change exciting, try one of the four ever-evolving "mutable" signs: Gemini, Virgo, Sagittarius, and Pisces.

If you long for more excitement from your Taurus, be careful what you wish for, though. The Taurus man is stable 95 percent of the time, but when he's hotheaded, watch out. He's the sign of the Bull, and as you know, a threatened Bull charges. The angry Taurus morphs from Zen-boy into a hyped-up rage machine, hell-bent on destroying whatever's in his path. During these rare but frightening spells, he will repeat himself endlessly, refer to himself in the third person, punch walls, or shout at the top of his lungs. (We'll get into this more later. But if you sense the volcano's about to explode, run.)

Your Bull can also be a bulldozer. When the Taurus man pushes, you'll need the strength to push back. That means knowing and accepting yourself enough to stand for your beliefs. Otherwise, you'll feel like you're dating a dictator (Saddam Hussein and Adolf Hitler are both on the Taurus roster). Know thyself and thy boundaries. A woman who asserts her limits without attacking or putting him down will win the Taurus man's heart and his respect.

## What He Wants in a Woman

Taurus is the sign of self-esteem, and you'll need plenty to be with him. He loves a self-possessed woman who's beautiful, brilliant, and strong. A lot to ask for? Not in his mind. He's the kind of guy whose Match.com profile demands, "I'm looking for a woman who's equally comfortable in a ball gown as she is in sweatpants." Cheesy and conventional? Sure. Taurus wants the total package, and he'll hold out for it.

Although looks are important to him, the Taurus man needs a resilient mate who won't crumble when faced with life's challenges—or his own overwhelming personality. His ideal woman has a reserve of inner strength, the grace of a goddess and the wisdom to choose her battles. She won't push him to commit before he's ready, but when he does, she'll be totally receptive and available. Offended? Skip to the chapter on Gemini or Libra.

The Taurus man's head may turn at the sight of a supermodel (he's ruled by beauty-loving Venus), but he craves substance. What are you really about? A woman with the confidence to speak her truth will impress him far more than one who agrees with everything he says. In his world, a wishy-washy woman can't be trusted. He needs to know what team you're on. Don't get jealous if he admires another woman's beauty. If he's with you, he's with you.

Although he can play the "daddy" in relationships and may even financially support you, Taurus expects you to be an adult.

He'll hang back to gauge how in touch with reality you are. Some of his clues: you pay your bills, work a steady job, keep a full refrigerator (food is a top Taurus priority), and decorate with grown-up furniture. Cooking and cleaning aren't required (he thinks that's what restaurants and maids are for). Nonetheless, you should know how to do both. A primal part of his brain always wonders: If the stock market crashed tomorrow, would she be able to keep us afloat? His survival instincts won't let him marry you unless the answer is yes. On a more shallow note, he also can't stand filth and bad smells. There's a huge prima donna in every Bull.

Aggressive types will send a Taurus guy scurrying for shelter, so if you want to run the show, try a Pisces, the martyr sign, or a Scorpio, who loves a good power struggle. (Hey, there's a lid for every pot, right? We never said you should change yourself for a guy.) Passive or coy types don't reel in a Taurus either. A little mystique only goes a long way at first. Ultimately, Taurus will want to get to know you. Women who know the art of keeping it real are the Ones with whom Taurus men will form genuine and lasting connections. The Bull can smell bulls**t from a mile away. Say what you mean and mean what you say. A foundation of honesty is the key to winning a Taurus man forever.

# What He Wants from a Relationship

Simply put, the Taurus man is looking for a wife. He's all about putting down roots: the family, the perfect mate to grow old with, and a beautiful home to share. He'd rather follow the same routine for sixty years with one person than constantly swap partners. Sure, he's got a lusty appetite, but most Taurus men think variety means taking you to a new restaurant. Change is too much work, and he's not one to waste his time like that. He just wants to settle into a steady track with someone to adore. Your job is to show up and be that person. Not a bad gig, if you think about it.

The single Taurus man is constantly in "interview" mode. He carries a mental checklist and screens every woman he meets to see if she fits. Although he might accept a temporary substitute, he's not afraid to drop her if the perfect match appears. Generally, he'll hold out for the real thing, breaking many hopeful hearts along the way.

The Taurus man wants to pursue you, even against all odds. Why? Because if he's moved his sluggish ass enough to chase you, he intends to make it worth the trip. Taurus David Beckham, who's married to former Spice Girl Victoria "Posh Spice" Beckham (an Aries), is a perfect example. In 1996, superhottie Beckham saw the Spice Girls' video "Say You'll Be There" while traveling abroad. He pointed to Posh and informed his soccer teammates that she was the woman he wanted, and that if she wanted him, they would be together forever. Within months, they were an item. They now have three children and a relationship that's spanned a decade.

Such entitlement is typical Bull-boy behavior. The Taurus man fancies himself a prince. Naturally, he chooses his bride, and can't imagine being denied. He usually gets his way. If a Taurus wants to make you his princess, take the crown or else. He stubbornly persists, charging after his target until he reaches it. This guy is not easily scared off, so if you're not interested, forget about subtle hints—he won't get them. You'll have to make it crystal clear that you're not interested—and it's best to do it early, before he's set his mind on you being the One.

It's not uncommon for Taurus men to marry young. This nostalgic guy may even wed someone from his hometown, like Bono, who married his childhood sweetheart, Ali Hewson. A formidable activist, Hewson declined an offer to run for the Irish presidency because (in true Taurus style), Bono "would not move to a smaller house." Taurus men need their comforts.

Life with a Taurus man is comfortable and safe, save the occasional bullfight. Yes, he's demanding as hell, but he repays you with unparalleled loyalty. If you're tired of complaining to friends that "men don't commit," or you're ready to start a family, set your sights on a Taurus. You see, the real adventure with Taurus begins after the commitment. That's when he begins building a life filled with vacations, anniversary gifts, children to spoil, and lots of general coziness. If you dig this vision, sign up, and plan to stay for the long haul.

# Sex with a Taurus

When it comes to sex, the Taurus man swaggers around like he has a varsity letter in it. This guy knows he can deliver, and he oozes sexual confidence. He's always ready for an earthy roll in the hay with you. A slave to his senses, he loves to taste, see, touch, and smell. Your natural scent is the biggest turn-on. He loves to inhale your musk, before and after sex. (If he doesn't like your smell, consider it a deal-breaker.) He's in no rush to finish, either. When he takes you in, you'll feel like the main dish in a lavish, seven-course meal. Patience is his sexual virtue.

Atmosphere is important to Taurus, and he loves to create a lush setting for you to tryst the night away. He'll do rose petals, candles, pillows, hell—he might even break out a bearskin rug. A comfortable bed and clean, non-scratchy sheets are the absolute minimum requirement. An Earth sign, he'll go for an outdoor romp in the woods, too. He's a mountain man *and* a mountin' man.

Taurus rules the neck and throat, so you can expect a few grunts and growls of passion. He'll often rev your motor by kissing your neck, lightly at first, then with increasing pressure. Keep a few turtlenecks in your wardrobe if you date a Taurus man. Hickeys aren't just for high school anymore. In the throes of passion, Taurus doesn't realize his own strength.

When it comes to positions, the Taurus man is more consistent than experimental. You get one of two styles: slow and sensual (he'll start with a massage and go all night) or a charging Bull ramming into his target (ouch!). What he lacks in variety, he makes up for in endurance. You can expect to be saddle sore after riding this mechanical Bull!

That's not to say that he won't get kinky. He'll branch out if you initiate it. Being a Bull, he's familiar with a little cowhide, so feel free to break out the leather costumes and cuffs. Just don't expect to lay a lashing on this Alpha male's backside. Tease him with a pair of sexy stilettos or a corset; he loves when you put in a little effort to impress him. Still, he'd really rather just have you naked than play too many games. With this guy, your femininity and curves are the main event. He just wants to grab and go!

# Taurus: Turn-Ons & Turn-Offs

## Turn Him On

- Be consistent. Taurus loves the familiar and hates sudden change
- Be on time—this sign is punctual to a T!
- Love music, art, and be culturally literate all around
- Genuinely admire him—make him feel brilliant and successful

- Ask his advice and opinion and listen raptly
- Express your truth passionately—he thinks wishy-washy people are weak

- Be sensual, strong, and classy
- Love food and wine—and be willing to indulge in both with him
- Be fashionable, choosing elegant clothes with original flair

- Massage his neck, head, and shoulders

- Run your life like a well-oiled machine, balancing family, work, and fun
- Make time to share life's simple pleasures, like a sunset, or a stroll
- Want children and a family
- Be available when he needs comfort, affection, or attention
- Be warm, real, and down-to-earth
- Call it like you see it (in a supportive, noncritical way)
- Buy him expensive grooming products or other metrosexual accoutrements

## Turn Him Off

- Interrupt him when he's talking
- Talk too loud or make a scene
- Have an empty refrigerator or a messy house
- Try to change him or tell him what to do
- Compliment him too often—he'll think you have an agenda (do you?)
- Be scared to disagree with him
- Fight just for fighting's sake—Taurus needs peace!
- Be tacky or cheap
- Don't shower, or wear a scent he hates—his sense of smell is unparalleled
- Be cold or mysterious
- Play games or make him jealous—he'll just leave
- Come between him and his family or friends
- Show him up, embarrass him publicly, or make him look foolish in any way
- Insist on having the last word in an argument
- Rush him when he's fussing with his appearance, which could take hours

- Flirt with anyone else in front of him
- Stay out all night or be nomadic in any way

# His Moves

## First Moves: How He Courts You

So you think he likes you, but a nagging voice wonders if you're reading into things. With Taurus, that's a good thing to ask yourself. Taurus men are famous for acting committed when they're not (more on that later). This commitment-cautious sign definitely takes a "try before you buy" approach.

While a Taurus wines and dines you, he's observing how you fit into his world, how you carry yourself, and whether you'll embarrass him in public. Taurus is a status-conscious sign. He holds the old-fashioned view that as his wife, your public demeanor reflects on him. No matter how much he likes you, he needs to know that you'll make him look good in any situation. If you like him, put your best foot forward!

**Here are a few signs that he's checking you out as a prospect:**

- He pursues you relentlessly, immune to your resistance
- He invites you to an elegant restaurant and orders a bottle of wine
- He takes you to a concert, political rally, or play
- He shares his favorite music or book with you
- He gives you flowers or a thoughtful gift
- He tells you straight-up that he wants you

## He's In: How You Know He's Committed

Once you make it past a Taurus man's extensive screening process, he's decided that you're a keeper. Now, he begins setting up a life too good for you to leave. Here's how you'll know:

**He acts like you're married.** When a Taurus is committed, he starts to act like your husband. He may straight-up tell you that he's planning to propose. He calls you his girlfriend in public, becomes possessive at times, and generally acts like he's claimed you. He wants you to move in immediately.

**He stops pursuing, but the relationship is physically intimate.** Taurus men have two speeds: either full-on pursuit or totally chill. He's won his prize, and now he's downshifted to relax mode, where he can savor your company. While he wooed you with four-star restaurants and opera tickets, it's now Pad Thai delivery and Movies on Demand. What, is a comfy couch and surround sound so bad?

**He takes you shopping.** Once a Taurus claims you, your presentation reflects on him. You are now the pepper mill to his salt shaker, and must be outfitted in a complementary style. Those tutus and fairy wings he found cute as your friend are now his reputation's death knell. Buh-bye vintage, hello Bergdorf. Also, as a natural provider, he feels all manly putting warm clothes on his loved ones.

**He wants you to sleep over every night.** Sleep is sacred to Taurus, and if he needs you for a good night's rest, you're indispensable.

**You met his family (or closest friends) and they loved you.** Congratulations—you passed their litmus test! If his most important posse stamps you with their approval, don't be surprised if he brings you home for the holidays.

## Unfaithful Taurus: Why He Cheats

Taurus is a loyal sign by nature. It takes a lot for this guy to cheat. In general, he'll give you a ton of warning signs before taking such drastic measures. He's too practical to ruin his life with the drama of a broken home or family, and he cares too much about his reputation to mar it with a scandal. Chances are, he's hurting or lonely and you haven't noticed. Affairs can be easily prevented with this sign, so tune in to your Taurus on a regular basis.

**He doesn't feel like "the man."** Although he carries himself with pride, even cockiness, the Taurus man has a fragile ego. He needs to feel special and admired by you. Are you criticizing him or cutting him down? Do you interrupt him when he's sharing important news? Find a way to be wowed by him. Otherwise, he'll look for new fans elsewhere.

**He feels neglected, lonely, or forgotten.** Taurus men crave physical contact and affection. If your busy schedule has no room for him, he may find comfort in another's arms. Wanna keep your Taurus? Don't make him feel like he's second place to anything.

**His lusty appetite got the best of him.** Taurus rules the five senses, and occasionally, he gets intoxicated by a heady hit of feminine beauty. Only in rare cases does he act, and it's usually due to immaturity or one of the two reasons above. Make sure he's sown his oats before you commit to him.

**He decided you're not "the One" and it's over in his mind.** Although he may not have communicated the breakup to you, if he's made up his mind, he considers himself free to move on. Integrity is still important to him, so expect a "Dear Jane" phone call soon.

## Dig the Grave: It's Over

Taurus hates change, and it takes a lot for him to end a relationship. Once he makes this difficult decision, he commits to it with the same strength that he once committed to your romance. If he's dumping you, chances are you've f***ed up big-time—or he has—and he's deemed the wreckage beyond repair. How do you know there's no more hope?

**He stops pursuing.** When a Taurus thinks you could be "the One," he chases you. He's now quite likely chasing someone else.

**He wears a ratty T-shirt or sweatpants in front of you, and it isn't bedtime.** Translation: you're no longer worth dressing up for, and you're off the A-list. He doesn't care what you think of him, because you're no longer part of his life. He's got no intention of taking you out on the town tonight, or ever again.

**He doesn't pick up the tab.** Taurus loves to treat his ladyfriend. If he's not slapping down cash for dinner, he's either broke (see next item) or he hates your guts.

**He doesn't have the money to provide for you, or a family.** Taurus is the provider sign, and he's always thinking long-term. If he knows he can't offer food, clothing, and shelter to you (no matter how irrational this seems), he won't commit. To him, being in a relationship when he's unable to provide feels like the ultimate failure. Don't bother trying to change his view on this one.

**He tells you he doesn't see you as a couple.** Believe him. Trying to change his mind could take decades. A friend of ours spent almost two years convincing her Taurus boyfriend to date her! We don't recommend this exhausting path.

**Your fighting escalates to a scary level.** Taurus rules the throat, and this guy can yell at the top of his lungs, or intimidate you in a few other scary ways. When this happens, Taurus has been pushed past the breaking point. If a restraining order sounds like a good idea, get yourself out of this charging Bull's path—fast.

**You still want to change him.** Taurus men put it all out there and show who they are. Don't like it? He ain't changing. If you need a guy who's constantly evolving, try a Sagittarius or a Gemini. With Taurus, you get what you get.

# Interpreting His Signals:

## What does he mean by that?

| When he | It means... | So you should... |
|---|---|---|
| Gets quiet | He's digesting food, savoring the moment, or just relaxing. He's observing you to see if you're wife material. | Let the man digest, or vibe along with him. Express yourself! If you don't know what to say, ask his opinion on a topic he knows a lot about. |
| Doesn't call | He's decided you're not the One.<br><br>You insulted him and he's waiting for an apology. | If you think he's wrong, invite him out and show him otherwise. If he doesn't respond, move on.<br><br>Call and ask if you offended him. If you did, graciously apologize. Then, never repeat the offense! |
| Calls a lot | He thinks you might be the One and is eager to find out. | Only answer when you have time to talk. He's persistent; if he likes you, he'll call again! |
| Doesn't make a move after a couple of dates | He's interested, but still unsure. The Taurus man is looking for a wife, and doesn't want to start something he can't finish. | Be patient and take a cold shower. Never push or initiate physical contact with a Taurus, unless you want to chase him away. |

| When he | It means... | So you should... |
| --- | --- | --- |
| Doesn't make a move after a few weeks | He loves your company but doesn't see you as the One—wife material. | If you like his vision of the One—wife material, start being it and see if he responds. If not, forget it! |
| Moves fast | He's either 100% sure you're the One or 100% sure you're not. | Hold him off and see if he keeps pursuing. If he's after a fling, he'll stop calling. If he thinks you're wife material, he'll chase until he wins you over—no matter how long it takes. |
| Picks up the tab, gives flowers and gifts | Nothing. Tauruses treat and spoil people they like, whether it's romantic or not. | Enjoy, but don't interpret it as a love connection. If he wants more, he'll tell you. |
| Introduces you to his family and/or closest friends | He's seeing how you fit in. Taurus is a loyal person, so bad chemistry with his clan is a deal-breaker. | Family is personal, and when a Taurus man reveals something intimate, he cares about you. Be kind, interested, and make a good impression. Listen more than you talk. |
| | He trusts you. | Tell him you're honored. Be accepting, loving, and keep your opinions to yourself. |

# Your Moves: Tips for Flirting and Everlasting Love
## Flirting with a Taurus

Taurus men are flirty by nature. This sign is ruled by Venus, the planet of beauty and romance. Taurus men love to admire you, and it's not hard to engage them in a little playful banter. Leveraging a flirtatious interaction into a date takes a few key moves, though. How do you seduce this sign and get him to ask you out?

**Remind him of a black-and-white film star.** Taurus men love sophisticated women. Avoid coy or cutesy behavior or he'll see you as a little sister, not a potential date. To catch the Taurus man's eye, borrow the old-world glamour of film stars like Greta Garbo or Audrey Hepburn (a Taurus). He's a sucker for a class act. Skip the denim and minis and wear a sexy, business-casual silk shirt with a sleek pencil skirt and heels. Lift up your hair and twist it into an elegant chignon while he's watching. (No cheerleader-style hair twirling, though!) Move gracefully and articulate your words. He adores that long-forgotten art of classic femininity. Work it like a self-possessed, silver-screen heroine.

**Offer a bite of your dinner or a sip of your drink.** Taurus men love to eat, so food is a tried-and-true seduction. Order a bottle of wine and pour him a glass. He'll be yours until the cork dries up.

**Touch him lightly.** Sensual Tauruses respond to touch, so graze his arm or elbow when you talk. It will convey intimacy without too much forwardness, and makes him feel connected to you. Don't grab him, slap his back, or make crude gestures. Save that for a macho Aries or Aquarius man.

**Ask his advice.** Nothing flatters a Taurus more than being asked his opinion. He loves to nurture and protect, and welcomes an opportunity to provide that. Ask him to recommend a wine, or listen raptly as he shares his theories on art, politics, and family. Tell him about a crossroads in your life (as long as it's not too dramatic), and you won't have to make small talk for another second.

**Go shopping.** This is particularly useful if you want to transform a Taurus man from a friend into a lover. Head to a high-end store and let him help you pick out a perfume or an outfit. He'll feel like you're his girlfriend already.

**Be an *artiste* or a rock star.** Taurus may be a simple guy, but he loves a strong personality and a good performance. Seeing you "in the zone" turns him on. Invite him to hear your band perform, or to a lecture you're delivering. Let him hang around while you direct a photo shoot, or do anything that makes you look like you rule the world. If you're a star, he'll want to be part of your orbit. He's a fame whore, so be the name he wants to drop.

**Make him feel comfortable.** A simple smile may be all it takes to win this guy's attention. The Taurus man wants to be around a person who won't judge him. Your smile is the green light that says, "It's safe here."

## Everlasting Love with a Taurus

So you think he's the One. How romantic. Now, how do you kindle the flames of desire into your forever-after fantasy? The way you start is how you finish with Taurus, so your first moves are the most important. If you've struck up a connection, try these techniques to seal the deal.

**Have a stable life.** Other signs love a damsel in distress (hello, Virgo) or a drama queen (Mr. Aries). Not Taurus. He wants to lock you in and start building a future. Have you worked through your baggage? Are you earning a steady paycheck and handling your biz? If you've got more issues than a magazine warehouse, don't count on a proposal from him.

**Have a great work-life balance.** Taurus is a family guy. He needs to see that you make time for other things besides your career. He respects an ambitious woman, as long as she still has time for family and romance (read: him).

**Already *be* his wife.** Allison Armstrong, creator of PAX Programs, researched thousands of men and found that most men marry women who are already being, or acting like, their wives. For Taurus, this means fitting his vision of an ideal mate (detailed earlier in this chapter).

**Be a woman, not a little girl.** Have adult furniture, pay your bills, handle your psychological issues, and know what you're passionate about in life. He'll nurture you, but he won't coddle you. Yes, he wants to raise children, but that doesn't include you. He wants to see that you'll be an equally strong partner. He'll gladly support you if he knows you can support yourself.

**Let him be your knight in shining armor.** That doesn't mean you should pretend to be helpless or ditzy. Never! Just let a Taurus provide for you, open doors, help you even if you don't need the help. He's dying to make a difference and make you happy. Let him!

**Don't be too available.** When a Taurus likes you, he'll chase after you like a charging bull. If you want a long-term relationship, make him wait a few days for the first date. We hate to sound like *The Rules* here, but the Taurus man only commits to women who have full lives of their own. If your calendar seems empty, he'll lose interest fast. Also, Taurus can be possessive as a boyfriend. Being overly available opens the gates for him to steamroll you. Set firm boundaries early on, and you'll enjoy a relationship with balance and equality.

# Prep Yourself For...

## Your First Date

So you're going out with a Taurus. What to expect? Here's how to make your first date a success, and have a good time no matter what.

**The Basic Vibe:** Taurus men love to eat, and they adore music. Chances are, he's taking you to dinner, a concert, or both. If you're a healthy eater, don't even think about ordering salad as an entree, or splitting anything besides dessert. Taurus is a steak and potatoes kind of guy. Plan on appetizers, a decadent French or international dinner in a romantic setting, a bottle of wine, and a rich dessert.

Got a hectic week? Don't pencil a Taurus into your calendar. He will expect to linger over a multicourse meal and savor a long, delicious conversation. Afterward, he'll want to hit a lounge, see a movie, or take a stroll. Excusing yourself early makes him think you're rude, or not interested. Block out at least four to six hours for the date. Come on, you work hard enough—let yourself enjoy a night out!

**What to Wear:** Taurus men love sophisticated elegance, so choose tasteful but sexy cuts in a classy fabric. Get your nails done, or at least file the suckers, because he'll definitely notice your hands. Go upscale-funky with heels, designer jeans, and a silk top, or a cashmere tank under a blazer. Bright colors are a plus, as long as they're cheerful but not blinding. Wear elegant, natural makeup; even have it done professionally at a makeup counter. This date is a good excuse to indulge in some girly pampering. Easy on the perfume. This sign has a super-strong sense of smell.

**What Not to Wear:** Just say no to anything low-cut, ultra-short, or made of cheap or synthetic fabric. Taurus rules the five senses, and he'd rather not run his hands over 100 percent polyester tonight. On the flip side, don't wear anything more expensive than what's in his closet, either. Heels are sexy, but don't wear stilettos so high you'll break your ankle hailing a cab. Be comfortable in your goddess gear tonight. You'll probably cruise around town on your date, so dress for a long evening out.

**To Pay, or Not to Pay?** Although some signs are thrilled to go Dutch, Taurus wouldn't dream of letting you finance a date. Just say thank you, but keep it in your pants (your wallet, that is). Enjoy being treated tonight.

**Saying Good night:** Unless you want this connection to tank fast, don't plan on a slumber party after your first date. Taurus men like to set the pace, so be responsive if you like him, but don't initiate physical contact. A small good night kiss is enough to reassure him you're interested, while holding him off a little. If he pushes for more, hold your ground. Thank him for the evening and set another date. We're not telling you this because we believe in retro gender roles (we don't). We're just letting you know what works with this sign if you want a second go-round.

## His First Home Visit

So he's coming over. Should you leave that pile of papers on the coffee table, or your bra casually draped over the doorknob? Nuh-uh. Forget those myths about filthy bachelor pads, because they don't apply to Taurus. He's a consummate metrosexual, sensitive to his environment, with definite opinions on decorating. Unfair but true, he will evaluate your home to gauge what kind of nest you could feather for him (and your kids) one day. Unless you have a live-in maid and a full refrigerator, never invite him over for a spontaneous first visit.

**Clean like your name was Molly Maid.** Taurus is a clean freak, and will definitely want to know that you are, too. Get rid of the dust and grime, especially in the bathroom. This is a good time to call that cleaning service you've been thinking about.

**Add sensual touches.** Fresh-cut flowers, scented sprays (light ones only; he's got a strong sense of smell), framed pictures of friends and family, and ambient music will all set the mood he loves.

**Don't assume he'll spend the night.** And don't be offended if he doesn't. The Taurus guy can move slowly, and it doesn't mean he's not interested. Besides, he probably really loves his own bed and is worried he won't get a good night's sleep in yours.

**Display cultural collections.** Books, music, art—he wants to know who you are and what you're passionate about. This is an opportunity to get more intimate with him, so put your interests on display. If he doesn't get it, better to find out now!

**Stock your refrigerator.** Sorry to say, he's no cheap guest. The night before his visit, grab $60 from the cash machine. Swing by the gourmet deli for olives, crackers, and a few rich treats, like specialty potato chips and Godiva ice cream. Add some imported beer and a nice bottle of wine to your cart (research the vineyard; he could be a wine snob). Anything you could feed each other, like grapes, is a plus. If you think he's sleeping over, buy some fresh-ground gourmet coffee and half-and-half (no skim milk for the Bull—ever!)

**Put anything overtly sexual, kinky, or suggestive of an "alternative lifestyle" in your bedroom drawer.** Should you hide your true self from this man? Hell no. But Taurus is traditional, and needs to get to know those sides of you slowly. At the very least, keep your toys in the bedroom.

**Make sure it looks like a grown-up lives there.** Are you still eating off TV trays, sleeping on a futon and stashing books in milk crates? If you haven't upgraded from the college life, at least make it comfortable. Throw out melted-down candles, take the batik blanket off the wall, and add a few womanly touches, like fresh flowers, books, scented candles, and throw pillows.

**Have massage oil handy.** Sensual Taurus loves touching, and it's a great way to warm up to each other. Have a small bottle of lightly scented oil handy. Make sure it's brand-new. We think that's obvious, but nothing turns this possessive sign off more than imagining you rubbing down another guy from the same bottle.

**Remove anything work-related from your field of vision.** Shut down your computer, pack up your files, and put away any work distractions. He will demand your full attention!

## Meeting His Family

If a Taurus is on good terms with his family, they mean the world to him. He now takes you seriously enough to introduce you to them. Is this a test? Better believe it!

Meeting the parents is a high-pressure scenario even without astrology involved. But while some signs don't think it's a big deal for you to mix with their relatives, Taurus does. How to avoid a nervous breakdown? The advice is basic and straight from a 1950s charm school handbook. Dress appropriately, bring his mom flowers, don't talk politics or religion, and be a warm, grateful guest. Send a thank-you note, and if his mother asks you to drive to the store with her, go. While a Scorpio or an Aries might freak if you get along TOO well with his clan, Taurus is judging how well you fit in.

What if you don't get along with his family? It's entirely possible, after all. We suggest seriously thinking about how much (or if) you love this guy. Loving a Taurus means accepting his family—or the baggage he has around them. Can you put aside your distaste long enough for a few family outings and holidays? Are you willing to complain to your therapist about his irritating sister, instead of to him? If you think he's worth the trouble, stick around. But if you know they'll be an eternal sore spot, it might be better to part ways.

# Saying Good-bye
## Breaking Up with a Taurus

The Taurus man hates change, and that goes for breakups. Once he fully settles into a cozy coupling, he's lazy and doggedly committed. He'll only do something major like ending a relationship if he decides it's "worth the trouble," as one Taurus man puts it. When your love hits the rocks, he'll first run a mental cost-benefit analysis of leaving you. If the discomfort of leaving outweighs the pain of sticking it out (e.g., the kids will be devastated, you have a shared mortgage, he can't live without your veal scaloppini), he'll stay put. At least he doesn't have to peel his ass off his favorite leather club chair and find a new address for it.

Still, just because he's in denial, doesn't mean you have to be. Just remember that the Taurus man sees everything as a possession, including you. In his mind, once he chooses you as his mate, you're his. If the relationship has gotten to the point of no return, you'll have to be the one to end it. He'll make it difficult for you to go, possibly even staging a temporary "honeymoon" to change your mind.

Should you be immune to his charms, watch out. Hell hath no fury like a Taurus scorned. He'll be doubly pissed off by inconvenience to his comfortable routine. The bigger the surprise, the worse his reaction. Expect him to bellow, break things, slam doors, and generally blow his top. Scary! Getting him out of your life could involve a restraining order or a cross-country move.

## Getting over Him: When a Taurus Dumps You

Bitter and volatile as he can be when you leave him, the Taurus man doesn't hesitate to serve you walking papers. Can you say double standard? If he thinks your relationship is a waste of his time and resources, don't expect him to stick around. There's not much convincing the stubborn Bull to change his mind. Chances are, he's done a thorough evaluation and has determined your relationship doomed. Once he's set his compass in a new direction, you might as well follow suit with yours.

In this case, make as clean a break as possible. Even if it means relocating or traveling for a few weeks, alter your reality fast. Taurus is a habitual creature, so you've probably established a preset lifestyle or routine together (rise at 7 A.M., meet at the wine bar after work, Wednesday dinner at your favorite Italian spot…). Mix it up as dramatically as you can to avoid feeling lonely and hopeless about your romantic future without him.

**Have yourself one good last cry over…**
- Having to pay your own way again
- Losing your shopping buddy—he had such good taste
- The feeling of security he gave you
- The amazing dinners and nights on the town
- Marathon sex
- The way he would drink you in with his eyes
- Feeling safe and protected, like a little girl
- Having to make your own decisions again
- Having a well-dressed, sexy companion who could go anywhere with you

**Praise the universe that you never have to deal with…**
- Being bossed around and treated like a child
- Having to argue—and lose—all the time
- The way he'd never admit that he was wrong
- Going to the same six places all the time
- Dragging his lazy ass out of bed or off the couch
- Listening to him rant, rave, and repeat himself
- His snobbery and label whoring

- The embarrassing scenes and public blowups when he lost his cool
- His 45-minute showers and vain primping—you get your mirror back!
- Pandering to his playboy streak (where was he until 4 A.M., anyway?)

# Love Matcher:

## *Can you find a common language?*

| You are a(n)... | He thinks you're... | You think he's... | Common Language |
|---|---|---|---|
| Aries | A fascinating fireball. | A solid provider and a Sugar Daddy. | Getting dolled up for each other and the world, sex for means of procreation (you'll have multiple kids) |
| Taurus | B-ooooooring. | Hotheaded and infuriatingly set in his ways. | Music, fashion, fighting to be right about everything |
| Gemini | Interesting, eclectic, but ultimately insane. | Blunt, unimaginative, and not playful enough. | Pushing each other's buttons |
| Cancer | Classically feminine, a trophy wife. | A romantic choice, though at times insensitive. | Home, family, and a love of the arts |
| Leo | Beautiful, passionate, a breath of fresh air. | The perfect sounding board for your ideas. | Being each other's creative muse |
| Virgo | Interesting, but you make everything too complicated for this "keep it simple" guy. | Romantic and sweet, but also overly simplistic and insensitive to life's subtle nuances. | Financial security, long-term planning, a love of nature |

| You are a(n)... | He thinks you're... | You think he's... | Common Language |
|---|---|---|---|
| Libra | Charming, beautiful but lacking common sense and punctuality. | Overly strict and demanding. | High-rolling nights on the town, designer clothes, snobbish tastes |
| Scorpio | Intense. | Intense. | Passion and strong feelings and opinions about nearly everything |
| Sagittarius | A fun playmate; a little rough around the edges. | A good activity partner; a little too hung up on appearances. | Being know-it-alls, bossing people around, calling it like you see it, forcing things to go your way |
| Capricorn | Elegant, polished, but a tad too stiff. | A bit of a loose cannon. | Money, status, investing, long-term goals and planning, building a family |
| Aquarius | Nuts. | An asshole. | Sex |
| Pisces | Creative, imaginative, his fantasy girl. | Too good to be true. | Music, arts, cooking, hosting elegant parties, namedropping |

# The Gemini Man

Dates: May 21–June 20
Symbol: The Twins
Ruling Planet: Mercury, the "messenger" planet of communication and the mind
Element: Air—intellectual, changeable, social
Quality: Mutable
Mission: Meeting of the Minds

**Natural Habitat—Where You'll Find Him:** Writing a screenplay or novel, closing a deal, talking smack, behind a camera, in a DJ booth or a recording studio, arguing both sides on a debate team, buying and "flipping" properties, engaged in intense conversation, at a comedy club, reading yet another book, watching crime shows or cartoons, annoying people by reciting movie lines, pushing someone's buttons, attending a gallery opening or book-signing, browsing shelves at a bookstore or library, stirring up a political debate, downloading or writing music, working with his hands, channel-surfing at home, hopping on his bike or in a roadster and taking off on a day trip, IMing or chatting online for hours, refilling his antidepressant prescription, dancing at a club while people watch in awe.

**What He Does for a Living:** Choreographer, dancer, writer, graphic designer, radio broadcaster, day trader, entrepreneur, hair colorist, promoter, publicist, recording artist, poet, actor, voice-over artist, stage technician, biologist, elementary school teacher, web designer, seminar leader, motivational speaker, singer, journalist, screenwriter, interpreter, mechanic (especially motorcycles or rare automobiles), collector, stockbroker, network marketing shareholder.

**Noteworthy & Notorious Gemini Men:** Johnny Depp, Tupac Shakur, Ice Cube, Dave Navarro, Morrissey, George Michael,

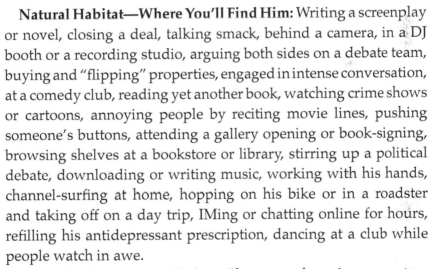

Andre 3000, Donald Trump, Mark Wahlberg, Boy George, Andy Warhol, Mike Myers, Biggie Smalls, Kanye West, Paul McCartney, Lenny Kravitz, John F. Kennedy, Drew Carey, Morgan Freeman, Allen Ginsberg, Tim Allen, Newt Gingrich, Michael J. Fox, Clint Eastwood, Tom Jones, Liam Neeson, Rudy Giuliani.

# Gemini: How to Spot Him

- Eyes that twinkle and dart around, taking everything in
- Looks like he just told a lie, heard a private joke, or knows some privileged information that he's dying to share
- Nervous gestures and speech, contrasting with a laid-back, come-to-daddy posture
- Dimples and a boyish, pretty face
- Long, well-shaped fingers and nice hands
- Strong forearms with pronounced tendons and muscles
- Long, lean torso

- Gender-bending outfits that somehow make him look even more manly
- May dress in a stuffy, overly formal way: sweater vests, watches, button-down shirts, shiny leather shoes
- Carries around a notebook or messenger bag holding his laptop, script, half-finished novel, etc.
- Evades personal questions and keeps conversation in realm of ideas and theories

# Gemini: How He Deals With...

### Money

In extremes: either holds on tight or blows it all on an impulse buy, risky venture, or get-rich-quick scheme. May go from bankrupt to billionaire several times over. Keep separate bank accounts. Never, ever cosign a loan for him.

## Family

A love/hate relationship, checkered with sibling rivalry, a few secrets, and a sense of duty. Craves his family's approval but hates that he wants it. Tends to either idealize or demonize his father.

## Love

Views it with cool, rational skepticism. He doesn't trust most feelings to last. What is love, anyway? At the same time, has an adolescent-level notion of true love.

## Sex

Imaginative, touch-oriented, great with his hands. Dirty talk—any talk—is always welcome. Potential porn addict.

## Children

His true soul mates. Although he may shy away from fatherhood, he makes an excellent father who's inspired by his kids' curiosity and wonder.

## Pets

An animal lover through and through, but may be too nomadic or undisciplined to take on the responsibility. Will gladly have a menagerie if you pick up the poop.

## Your Meltdowns

Will hold, comfort, and talk to you—for a little while. Too much emotion wigs him out. Might make it worse by arguing with you, trying to have a rational conversation about emotions, playing devil's advocate, or just shutting down. Keep your therapist on speed dial instead.

### His Meltdowns

Implosion and internalized angst that manifests as depression.

### Breakups

Completely obsesses if you leave him. Pretty good at getting over it otherwise. Tries to think his way out of emotions.

# Gemini: What He's All About

He's two, he's three, he's four boyfriends in one!

Gemini is the sign of the Twins, as you know. With his multiple personalities, he makes monogamy feel like a gang bang. You never know who he'll be at any given moment—but then, neither does he. Gemini is ruled by impish, quick-thinking Mercury, the planet of communication. Like a Pentium processor, his mind and mouth move at warp speed. Mercury is the "messenger," and the Gemini man is a lightning rod for new ideas, trivia, and information. He's like the interplanetary newsboy, getting the first crack at the morning headlines and shouting "Extra! Extra!" as he trumpets them to the world.

With his observant nature, the Gemini man can mirror and mimic like no other. Mike Myers channeled his Gemini "shape-shifting" abilities into his Austin Powers series, playing both Powers and his rival, Dr. Evil. It was like a big-screen tableau of the Gemini man—embattled with his own inner demons, saving the world while at the same time plotting its demise.

"I'm at least four different types of people—and those identities can be hard to juggle," admits Bryan, a Gemini publicist who's married with a four-year-old son. "I could be the obnoxious potty-mouth with Group A, then in Group B, I'd be the studious bookworm. I used to go out of my way to make sure those groups never intersected. I was afraid I'd shock people."

Among his magnificent panoply of personas, we've seen a frequent recurrence of Old Man Gemini and Gender Blender Gemini. Your Gemini can morph from tattooed club kid into a stuffy, vest-and-pocket watch-wearing curmudgeon who just wants to read a novel or go fishing. Other Gemini men make an art out of melding the genders in their style and expression. (Witness: Prince, Dave Navarro, Lenny Kravitz, Andre 3000, and Fall Out Boy's Pete Wentz who inspired the term "guyliner" by lining his eyes with a kohl pencil.) This is the guy who can look smokin' hot wearing lace and heels. Even former New York City mayor Rudy Giuliani hits the town dressed in drag every Halloween, leaving people wondering—just what the Gemini man loves! As long as you're left guessing, he's still free to flit among characters and identities.

He never wants to be tied down to anything, least of all an identity. The Gemini man often speaks in "you" rather than "I" or refers to himself in the third person—almost like he's talking about somebody else. He makes an excellent entertainer, and a memorable politician, like Geminis John F. Kennedy and Clint Eastwood.

Gemini has an active, restless mind that must be managed. Trapped by his own turbulent thoughts, "analysis paralysis" can cripple him. Too much of this fragmenting can take a toll on his mental health. Depression, even bipolar disorder, can afflict this sign, and a good therapist can be essential. Many Gemini men turn to antidepressants, alcohol, or other addictive escapes from their inner woes. He'd do well to avoid Happy Hour and plant his ass in the self-help, neuropsychology, or metaphysical section of his local bookstore. Consciousness work does the Gemini man wonders. Once the Gemini man becomes a master of his mind—demystifying his knee-jerk reactions and learning to track his impulses—he can use his intellectual force for great things. Meditation or martial arts can also be useful; anything that decelerates his impatience and helps him "be with" his thoughts instead of running away from them.

He's an excellent student, luckily. Mercury makes his brain a sponge for facts. The Gemini man's nimble fingers fly through a search engine, and he'll find you the most obscure data in half the time of a trained librarian. Don't ever challenge him to a crossword puzzle competition, unless you plan to lose.

Gemini rules communication, and this silver-tongued chap can turn quite a phrase. His gift for stringing together words can land him a career in writing, speaking, or media. Three of the most celebrated rappers—Tupac, Biggie Smalls, and Kanye West—are all Geminis admired for their creative wordplays, not to mention their extravagant egos and fearless trash-talking. Who can forget Gemini Donald Trump's curt dismissal on *The Apprentice*: "You're fired!"

The Gemini man may earn a reputation as a liar, which is not always true—although in some cases, it certainly fits. It's more like double talk. Words are his toys, and he tends to use them too lightly. His penchant for playing the devil's advocate gets him in hot water, and he loves debate. Conversations with him can feel like the ultimate mind-f**k. Believe it or not, he doesn't always realize he's doing it. The Gemini man means what he says… when he's saying it. He just forgets a few minutes later, or changes his mind, and that's where all the trouble starts. George H.W. Bush, a Gemini, famously promised "Read my lips: no new taxes," then proceeded to hike taxes two years later.

Mischief has a way of finding him, and the trademark twinkle in his eye suggests he may court it, too. In his youth, Gemini can be quite the troublemaker, dabbling in shoplifting, sports betting, petty theft, and drugs. His curious mind is quicker than most, and he thrills at discovering just how much he can get away with. Mark Wahlberg, now a serious actor, reinvented himself from his earlier incarnation as Marky Mark, the trou'-dropping Calvin

Klein underwear model and cheesy rapper with a long criminal rap sheet.

The mature Gemini man learns to honor his personality shifts, whose onset can be swift and sudden. Pity the Gemini man who grew up in a home that either had too many rules, or lacked discipline. He needs permission to be his own person (or people, as it were), but he also needs healthy boundaries (if only to experiment with testing them). He thrives with tolerant, mellow parents who repeatedly answers Gemini's favorite question—"Why?"

In the end, the Gemini man's abundant sense of wonder is still his best trait. While he can be maddeningly immature or indecisive, his eternal youth also makes him a fascinating seeker. Sure, he may watch Cartoon Network and eat sugared cereal well into old age. But he can also chase a morning of Lucky Charms and Sponge Bob with a well-chosen Cabernet and tickets to an off-off-Broadway opening that he found on an obscure culture website. If variety is the spice of life, Gemini is one of the zodiac's most well-seasoned men.

## What He Wants in a Woman

Picky, picky. With the Gemini man, it's easier to talk about what he doesn't want in a mate than to pinpoint what makes this astrological Peter Pan grow up and commit. He's a natural editor, pickier even than Virgo and far less tolerant of your "flaws." Quick to dismiss, he gathers his prospects' initial data, runs it through his microprocessors, then swiftly votes them off the island.

Topping his list of undesirable traits: wide-eyed innocence, saccharine sweetness, and wholesomeness. A lack of curiosity, cultural literacy, or imagination. Too much "take home to mama": traditional values, doting, and dependence. Anyone easier to figure out than a Rubik's Cube (he might solve his in an hour).

Nope, the Gemini man needs variety and range, and an alter ego or two. If you're the girl next door, then "next door" had better be a burlesque club. On top of that, your peep-show profits should be financing a biochemistry PhD. He needs smart and smut in equal measure. Never, ever should you fit neatly into a checkbox if you want to capture Gemini's fleeting attention.

The Gemini man needs a sophisticated, multifaceted woman who's always a few steps ahead of him. She must keep him on his toes, but still spare his dignity and be duly impressed by his mind. Mutuality is important to him. He loves a worldly woman who enriches his life with new ideas, conversations, and experiences—a female Marco Polo who, like him, is also an adept chameleon.

For Gemini, an intellectual Air sign, attraction happens in the mind. Whether you're curvy or scrawny, zaftig or runway-thin, he doesn't always care. Far more important is that you're intelligent and sharp. Boredom sets in quickly for Gemini. Remember, this is the sign that can solve the *New York Times* Sunday crossword without a dictionary. His ruler, Mercury, makes him highly discriminating and opinionated. This guy is a serial dater who may prefer his romanticized idea of a relationship to the reality of one. Because his mind and tastes change so quickly, he'll log years of bachelorhood rather than take the boring, conventional road. Then, just as abruptly, he'll be at the altar saying "I do"—possibly for the fifth or seventh time.

The Gemini man's standards can be schizophrenic, and might change hourly. Tali had a brief Internet dating exchange with a Gemini man (by "brief" we mean two hours, which can qualify as a long-term relationship for some Geminis). Said Gemini advertised that he wanted an open-minded, free-spirited woman who was off the beaten path. Check. After a few flirty emails, they set up a phone date. When Tali revealed that she was an astrologer, he rudely barked, "I'm sorry, this isn't going to work. That hippie, granola, 'om-shanti' crap just kills it for me. Good-bye, Tali." With that, he hung up the phone. Huh?

This sign plays the eternal bachelor well, like Gemini Colin Farrell. Dimpled and boyish, the twinkle in his eye beckons you to be bad together. Nonetheless, he's the sign of the Twins, and he needs his complement, his mirror image, to be complete. When he's bad, he needs you to be good. When he tucks away his cloven hooves and forked tail, that's when he needs you to stab his ass with a pitchfork.

So if you're one of those people that's constantly growing, evolving, and searching—great. Where does he sign up? Bring all your messy, complex layers. Go ahead and contradict yourself a little. Be passionate and live out loud with him. Be a saint with a dark side. As the old song aptly goes, you've got to be cruel to be kind… in the right measure. How else will you recognize heaven, reasons Gemini, unless you occasionally visit hell? Let him keep his *pied-à-terre* in Hades and in return he'll create paradise on Earth with you.

# What He Wants in a Relationship

First, the disclaimer: Commitment is not a natural state for the Gemini man. He's a mutable Air sign, which keeps him in constant flux, happiest in the cooler climate of ideas and intellect, rather than the emotional frying pan. The idea of "forever," if it doesn't freak him out, is laughable to Gemini. The only fairy tales he believes in are the ones he writes himself. He watches enough movies to know that just when you think you've found happily ever after, the sequel comes out a year later.

Gemini lives in his imagination, and real-world relationships can be a bit too grounding for his sign. Until then, the Gemini man avoids committing by being a little bit committed to everyone and everything. Like Sagittarius, he's a dilettante who craves variety, and prefers breadth over depth. He might even marry a very practical or maternal type, just so she'll handle the everyday reality while he retains his boyish freedom.

That's not to say that Gemini men don't commit for the long haul, because they do. In fact, this man is capable of becoming the most boring, bathrobe-wearing, remote control clutching cliché of a husband ever. He may marry just to "get it over with." Once he's comfortable, he can stay put. The last thing he wants to do is climb the rickety roller-coaster rails of a new relationship all over again. The emotional blowups, the misunderstandings, the soul baring—ugh! He'd rather just put on his favorite sweater and go to the multiplex for the latest action movie, or burrow into a book while you entertain yourself. Sure it's a snoozefest. But it's better than being with a needy, attention-hungry Daddy's girl who distracts him from his dreaming and downloading.

Still, turning into Al Bundy is far from the Gemini man's dream. He just needs relationships with a single key ingredient: space. He must have distance in order to come closer. His inner Twin needs this contrast, to switch the intimacy button on and off. "I need variety; I don't want to talk to you all the time," says John, a Gemini IT specialist. As much as he may seek fame or a public career, the Gemini man needs to slip into the shadows at will, retreating into his own anonymous world to recharge. When he's not making films, Gemini Johnny Depp lives a private, idyllic life in Southern France with his Capricorn partner and children. These polar extremes are essential to his sanity (a term we use loosely with Geminis).

The Gemini man thrives in a long-distance relationship for that reason. Our Aquarius friend Neda is married to a Gemini who lives almost 6,000 miles away in Iran, while she lives in New York. She met him while producing a documentary film in Tehran called *Nobody's Enemy*, about Iran's first public elections. Yas, her husband, is Iran's first recorded hip-hop artist. Neda filmed him in the studio reciting his fiery political verses. (Only a Gemini could get away with recording conscious rap under a totalitarian government.) Both passionate about change in their native country, their intellectual chemistry sparked a romantic connection.

Oh, did we mention that Yas is also twelve years younger than Neda? Fairy-tale romances with Gemini, should they happen, always have an interesting plot twist—the more unpredictable the better. And feeling like he's getting away with something could inspire the Gemini man's adoration. He loves a challenge! "He knew he would get me—he just waited for me to realize it," Neda recalls of her courtship. "He introduced me to his mom and family without me knowing what he was up to (because I was filming and in work mode). When he confessed to me his feelings and I responded positively, he said, 'Well then, my last question to you is, shall I wait for you?' I said yes and the next day, it was as if we were a married couple—that comfortable! No guesses, no games."

Truthfully, Neda may have the better end of the deal. The Gemini man is not always easy to live with. Phone relationships suit him well, since Gemini rules the voice and communication. Before he's gonna reach out and touch someone, or let his fingers do the walking, he needs to know he can talk to you for hours without getting bored. "Back in college, I knew I was in trouble," says Gemini Bryan. "I had a great friendship going with a woman I met in class, and I realized I'd rather talk to her on the phone than to my girlfriend." When he noticed he was putting his hometown honey on hold, he decided to mute the relationship and put his new friend on speed dial. They eventually married, and have been together over fourteen years now.

The older he gets, the more the Gemini man needs space—especially once he's married. Take our friend Amanda's Gemini dad. Every day after work, he retreats to the bedroom where,

Amanda says, "He watches crime shows, reads at least eight books, and drinks a six-pack of Diet Coke. He then eats an entire package of ham, which he wraps around hot dogs and shares with the dog." Another Gemini man built his personal playroom in the attic, where he surfs the Internet, watches TV shows, and downloads video games. The Gemini man absorbs so much information that he gets easily overwhelmed. "A giant Whole Foods makes me anxious," admits one Gemini. "I like defined spaces. I need to know where I am so I can make an informed decision. Besides, I don't like to waste time."

To stay interested for the long haul, the Gemini man needs a mate who's interested—in all kinds of stuff—and interesting by default. When (and if) things get routine, you need only ask him a smart question or solicit his opinion about something happening in the news. The Gemini man always has an opinion. If he doesn't, he's lying or being polite. It just means he thinks your question was inane and not worth dignifying with a thoughtful answer.

As Gemini Clint Eastwood once said, "They say marriages are made in Heaven. But so is thunder and lightning." Well, he has a point. Doesn't the Gemini man always? And as long as he sees a point to being with you, he's not likely to go elsewhere—at least, not unless he sees an equally valid point in that. Oh, brother.

# Sex with a Gemini

Gemini rules the hands, and his long, nimble, well-shaped fingers know exactly what to do with whatever ends up in them. He also responds well to your touch, so be sure to return the favor with a massage or lots of caressing. Kiss or nibble on his fingers if you want to give him an extra thrill.

Gemini is mutuality-minded, and he likes sex to be a give-and-take. He's also a talker. Since Gemini rules communication, talk dirty and vocalize your pleasure. Tell him where to touch you and get him talking back. Your voice will be a major turn-on. You can also seduce him with racy emails or IMs during the day. Just get his imagination going. He'll be home from work early!

The Gemini man's curiosity can take many forms. He may keep your sex in semi-vanilla territory, while he saves his most outrageous fantasies for himself. As we said, Gemini rules the hands—so he can always find a willing "partner," if you will. With his love of the Internet, he may prefer to download before he can unload. Take our word: just let him. Many women get jealous of their man's fantasy material, but as long as he's not subscribing to *Barely Legal* or *Inches,* don't freak out. He's got room in his vast sexual universe for your A-cups and the triple-Ds he gapes at on Bustybroads.com.

If you think it won't freak him out, you could learn a few burlesque or striptease moves, then surprise him. But just because he goes wild over it, that doesn't mean you should install a pole and an adult swingset in the bedroom. "I am a big fan of dirty talk, and when there's a trust there, I love acting like porn stars together," says Tyler, a Gemini actor. "High heels or boots in bed works for me."

The key with his sign is variety. Even Gemini rocker Dave Navarro grew bored with his Pussycat Doll ex-wife Carmen Electra (a Taurus), and she pioneered the pole-dancing craze. Keep him guessing, waiting, wondering a little. Throw in a costume or two, and remember that spontaneous, unpredictable sex is always his favorite kind.

The thrill of almost getting caught will drive his inner daredevil wild, too. A semipublic tryst will always be memorable. "My favorite sexual experience was hiking six miles to the top of a waterfall in Yosemite national park," recalls Sam, a Gemini writer. "We reached the top with a bunch of random strangers who all rested at one peak, then climbed a little bit higher to a pool of ice cold water, where we got naked and had sex on a roasting hot slab of rock that was up against the ice cold pool... dipping in and out of the pool with everyone just out of earshot below us. HOT!"

# Gemini: Turn-Ons & Turn-Offs
## Turn Him On

- Be up on current events, the latest books and music
- Have a big, ambitious project that gives your life purpose and passion
- Look like a total girlie-girl, but be a whip-smart tomboy on the inside
- Have a beautiful voice and hands

- Be intelligent and observant
- Call him on his s**t, but do so in a playful way
- Appreciate and compliment his ideas and intellect
- Give him constructive criticism and support his creativity

- Listen to his demo, read his screenplay, attend his spoken word performances
- Understand his need for variety
- Give him lots of time to himself
- Be his best friend and perfect complement

## Turn Him Off

- Have a shrill, piercing, or annoying voice
- Lack edginess, and be too wholesome, sweet or naïve
- Let him get away with murder—he wants you to be onto his game (mostly, anyhow)

- Mother him, nag, or boss him around too much
- Be insecure or needy

- Lose your autonomy: want to do everything together, or be two halves of a whole rather than two whole, separate people
- Suggest he "grow up" and get a traditional 9-to-5 job
- Eat an unhealthy diet, neglect your fitness or appearance
- Make him dress up or play along with family politics
- Show no interest in the trivia and hobbies he enjoys
- Need him to financially support you
- Expect to be spoiled, coddled, and paid for 100% of the time—he needs a give and take
- Demand consistency or try to put him in a neat little checkbox

# His Moves

## First Moves: How He Courts You

Talk may be cheap, but to the Gemini man, it's worth a lot. As the sign that rules communication, he needs to connect through conversation and intellect. With his curious nature, he loves to ask questions. He loves it even more when you question him, as long as you keep it in "safe" terrain that's not too personal.

While he may charm you into spilling your secrets, if you're too forthcoming, he'll grow bored. So even if he peers right into your soul, or reads you like one of his many books, the more you intrigue him, the more excited he'll get.

**Here's how a Gemini signals his interest:**
- He can't shut up—he babbles nervously around you, even blushes
- He asks about your favorite books, music, film, TV shows
- He engages you in a deep, mind-melding conversation
- He bases a song, poem, or character in his novel on you

- He reads you a favorite book passage, or buys you a book
- He IMs you all day, sending you little snippets of information, web links, and flirty messages
- Titillation and teasing: He tells you that he's imagining doing something really provocative to you
- He actually gives you his full attention

## He's In: How You Know He's Committed

Getting here may be the hardest part, but the Gemini man can be faithful as a hound dog once he's met his soul mate. Since he's a verbal sign, he'll usually tell you straight-up. Here are some other signs that he's there to stay:

**He doesn't want to end your conversations.** If you're the first and last person he talks to each day, and he loves to discuss everything under the sun with you, you've got a leg up on the competition.

**Eye contact.** You know how it can feel like Gemini is always trying to hide something from you? Well, whatever poet said the eyes are "windows to the soul" had a point. If he pulls up the shades and lets you peer deep into his, he trusts you. And that, girlfriend, makes you one of a privileged few.

**He accepts your ultimatum.** With this sign, you might have to force a deadline on him. He's in no rush to be pinned down, but he respects you for having the guts to be firm with him.

**He stops taking his antidepressants.** The Gemini man is an anxious creature, and he may dip into the pharmaceutical buffet to calm his neurotic nature. Did he stop refilling his prescriptions, but still seems happy? Congratulations—you've become his personal Paxil. (Warning: may cause side effects such as headache, dizziness, and nausea.)

**You become his muse.** The Gemini man is artistic, and he adores a woman who inspires his creativity. He'll be very vocal about it, too. When he's truly in love, the Gemini man will gladly tell the world. He might name a pet after your favorite movie character, or do something boyishly sweet and charming like that.

**Your intellect is greater than or equal to his.** If you've got a beautiful mind, there's far less need for him to seek outside stimulation.

## Unfaithful Gemini: Why He Cheats

The Gemini man can suffer from a terminal case of "grass-is-greener syndrome." In his early years, he may eternally try to "trade up." Plagued by indecisiveness and still seeking his own path, he finds it difficult to commit to another human being. Until he makes his mark, or defines himself through some kind of achievement, the Gemini man struggles to be satisfied with what he has. Of course, if he could stick with anything for longer than a month, he might find that fulfillment. But never mind; he'll have to figure that out the hard way.

Because his sign has a sneaky side, the immature Gemini man might be caught creeping around. Still, the lies will take their toll on him, eventually forcing him to grow up. As one Gemini man eloquently put it, "I realized it was easier to make one hard decision than to cover up 20 bad ones." Until then, here's what might lead him astray:

**Pure impulse.** When asked why he'd cheat, one Gemini man responded immediately, "Because she was there." (Of course, that was the same reason he gave when we asked why he'd commit to someone.)

**Boredom.** A lack of variety or spontaneity is a buzzkill for Gemini. You don't need a full costume wardrobe or a dungeon, but an overly predictable sex life could find him seeking thrills elsewhere.

**You're gullible or "too nice."** As much as he loves sweetness, too much can send your Gemini into a sexual diabetic coma. One Gemini man got turned off by his "bleeding-heart girlfriend" who naively loaned money to her family, and offered up her apartment to every out-of-town guest. "I feel like she has the word 'sucker' written on her forehead," he confesses. "It made me worry about her, and that's not sexy. It took some of the hotness away."

**To prove something or see what he can get away with.** The Gemini man loves the thrill of tempting fate, achieving the impossible, and winning. Generations later, we still see iconic footage of Gemini president John F. Kennedy being serenaded by his rumored mistress Marilyn Monroe (also a Gemini), as she cooed "Happy birthday, Mr. President"—seducing him shamelessly on camera.

**Curiosity.** Hello, midlife crisis. The repressed Gemini man who had a strict upbringing is especially susceptible to wanderlust. If he grew up believing his natural curiosity was "bad," he probably repressed his experimental nature. Years later, after marrying and starting a family, he'll quietly sow his oats.

## Dig the Grave: It's Over

No stranger to snap decisions, impulsive Gemini is quick to move on if he stops feeling the love. The Gemini man can be slow to commit, and fast to exit. His roster often has a trail of two-week "relationships." In long-term affairs, he may tough it out past the expiration date, torturing himself with guilt or inventing reasons to stay. "But she's so nice, and my family loves her." Or, "What kind of fool leaves an Estonian lingerie model with a Yale PhD?" Mentally, though, he's already checked out of the relationship—and you'll know it. When he's done, there's no turning back.

**He describes you as a "doll" or a "total sweetheart."** Sound like a compliment? With Gemini, it's actually the kiss of death. Nice girls finish last with this edgy dude. If you're too wide-eyed and accommodating, he'll steamroll you in seconds, then move on to his next plaything. He needs a bitch with some bite!

**You're not sharp enough for him.** The Gemini man can be a snob, and he loves to show off his avant-garde tastes. He needs a companion who can hang at his level. One Gemini man complained that his girlfriend doesn't read enough. "If I buy her a book, she'll read it," he gripes, "but she doesn't initiate that or buy books on her own." With Gemini, you've got to love ideas, culture, and media—the more obscure, the better.

**He has to take care of you.** Do you love a man who spoils you, dotes on you, and calls you cute nicknames? Call a Taurus or a Cancer. Gemini has no interest in being your codependent life coach or in playing daddy. The Gemini man is an eternal boy, which means he'd rather be out playing pirates than babysitting your inner child. If you can't grab a sword and swashbuckle with him—or entertain yourself until he gets back—your relationship will sink.

**No spark.** Whatever that playful burst of initial chemistry is, it needs to be prolonged for the entire lifespan of your relationship. Like two tigers circling each other, it's a dance that's at once dangerous and enticing. Once the dance is over, so too is his attraction.

# Interpreting His Signals:

## *What does he mean by that?*

| When he | It means... | So you should... |
|---------|-------------|------------------|
| Gets quiet | He's in his own world, and probably happy to be there. | Take a time-out. He's had enough together time, so now he needs to be alone with his thoughts. He'll miss you soon enough. |
| Doesn't call | He doesn't think you have enough in common. | Gemini connects through conversation. If he's not eager to talk to you, he may have written you off already. |
|  | It's your turn to call him. | Has he done an inordinate share of the calling? Send him an email or pick up the phone. He likes 50/50 relationships. He might feel he's putting in more effort than you are. |
| Calls a lot | He's really interested. He may also IM, email or SMS you. | Answer, but don't be constantly available. Tease him back with bits of witty banter, then return to your day job (somebody's gotta have one) so he doesn't think you're too easy to catch. |

| When he | It means... | So you should... |
|---|---|---|
| Doesn't make a move after a couple of dates | He might be shy, nervous, or still unsure about your chemistry. | See if he keeps asking you out. If he does, that means you're still in the running. Don't give him exclusive access just yet, though. |
| Doesn't make a move after a few weeks | He's either on a celibacy kick or intimidated by you. | Throw caution to the wind and kiss HIM! At least you'll find out what's up. |
| Moves fast | He's impulse shopping and feels like taking a chance. He's not thinking about consequences, but he's not ruling out a love connection, either. | Some of Gemini's great true love moments happen spontaneously. Forget the old-fashioned crap and let his imagination take you to exciting places. |
| Picks up the tab, gives flowers and gifts | He's in courtship mode. | Be gracious and grateful, but don't expect this to go on for much longer. He's not into buying your love. |
| Introduces you to his family and/ or closest friends | He's seeing how you fit in. Gemini is a loyal person, so bad chemistry with his clan is a deal-breaker. | Family is personal, and when a Gemini man reveals something intimate, he cares about you. Be kind, interested, and make a good impression. Listen more than you talk. |

# Your Moves: Tips for Flirting and Everlasting Love
## Flirting with a Gemini

Like the proverbial cat who eats the canary, the Gemini man's flirting style is both playful and premeditated. He teases with carefully chosen words, provocative comments, and a minefield of mind games. He likes to test your limits, and he bores easily. To amuse himself, he'll smugly rile you up or piss you off intentionally.

You'll either burst into tears (as Ophira once did after a quick-thinking Gem took a debate too far), or rise to the challenge. Study the game of tennis and you've got a perfect formula for flirting with Gemini. Read Sun Tzu's *The Art of War* as if it was a dating manual. Whatever he serves you, serve it back twice as hard. The challenge will excite him. Since life is a game to him anyhow, he doesn't mind if you're a little bit of a player. Here's how to win the match point and score love with this short-attention span sign:

**Spark an intellectual or political debate.** Isn't it hot? All that tension from sparring, the adrenaline of fighting over facts and figures… you can really work up a sexual appetite. One Gemini man recalls a memorable first date where he "argued psychology for three hours."

**Let your fingers do the talking.** Verbal stimulation works wonders for Gemini, who can get insanely turned on by the written word. Instant Message banter can heat up quickly with him. Or, pick up your cell phone and text for sex.

**Invite him for a spontaneous adventure.** Out of the blue, casually call him and invite him to a reading, a bar with live music, a swingers club, whatever night on the town you dream up. He loves surprises, and he's not one of those old-fashioned guys who balks at being asked out by a woman.

**Transport his imagination to another reality.** To the Gemini man, it's a thin line between fantasy and everyday life. He likes to keep at least a gentle blur between the two. Take Dan, a Gemini computer programmer, who had his best "true love" moment with a woman he never officially met! "It happened in the airport in Rome," Dan recalls. "There was a woman sitting behind a counter, about 20 feet away. We couldn't take our eyes off each other. It lasted about two minutes. We never spoke. She got called away, and I got on a plane." Talk about a quickie!

## Everlasting Love with a Gemini

Getting a Gemini to settle down is like trying to catch a butterfly in a net. You might do it, but the poor creature will beat its beautiful wings relentlessly in protest. Soon, you'll feel like a monster holding it captive. If you want to keep Gemini fluttering in your garden, drop the net and sprout some wings yourself. Then fly around with him—or without him. With this Air sign, the magic really happens when you're aloft, above it all, marveling at the world below together. Here's how to sail on the breezes with Gemini forever by your side:

**Be emotionally intelligent.** If you've got a firm grip on your issues (rather than dwelling on old baggage), he'll see you as a stable long-term bet. He may keep his own therapist on speed dial, and he won't mind if you do, too. Better that than you dump your crap on him. The Gemini man is fascinated by human nature, at least from a scientific perspective. Bonus points if you know about neuroscience and brain chemistry (hint: "hypothalamus" and "amygdala" are not dirty words).

**Be culturally literate.** Information-magnet Gemini is always up on the latest books, politics, movies, TV shows, and music. Even if he turns his nose up at pop culture, he needs you to be a doyenne of ideas, words, and information.

**Love his mind.** The Gemini man will come up with the most out-there ideas. But you know what? He might just make them happen. He needs your eyes to light up at his treasure trove of inventive thoughts and get-rich-quick schemes. Those are his best offerings, after all. If you ignore his visions or roll your eyes, he'll think he's casting pearls before swine. Cherish his bountiful brain, even if you secretly wonder whether he's a genius or totally nuts. (Likely he's both.)

**Inspire his sense of childlike wonder.** Our Gemini friend Douglas nostalgically describes kissing a woman he met in Brazil. "It was like a first high school kiss," he recalls. "I didn't know I could still feel like that." The boyish side of your Gemini is here to stay, so the more you bring it out, the better.

**Evolve continuously and defy classification.** You must never fit neatly into a checkbox, and if you do, you shouldn't stay there for long.

# Prep Yourself For...
## Your First Date

So you've been asked out by a Gemini. Join the club. The Gemini man looks at nearly every woman as a prospective mate. Just as he tears through books, websites, and information at warp speed, he takes the same quick-sorting approach to dating: Yes/no, yes/no, yes/no. His time is a precious asset to him, so he wants to spend it well. Here's how to make it to the next round:

**The Basic Vibe:** Try not to judge him by the first date, which could be a bit schizophrenic. In his usual bipolar style, your Gemini will be trying to connect with you and not connect with you—all at the same time! Hey, he loves a challenge. More than that, he hates to feel vulnerable too soon. Gazing dreamily into each other's eyes? It's not gonna happen until he loosens up. You may have to endure a lot of nervous chatter, awkward pauses, and surface talk at first. *If he's not gonna open up, I'm not going to either,* you might think. However, the more you show bits of vulnerability, the more this anxious guy will drop his guard.

Still, there are safer relaxation techniques than baring your soul. Keep it friendly and fun. The Gemini man does well on activity dates. Never have we met a sign so into comedy clubs; don't be surprised if he shows up with tickets to a local improv theater. If he's a more highbrow Gemini, he might have museum passes, concert tickets, or an invitation to a reading by his favorite new author.

"I like to do something where you can just be together, talk, and learn about each other," says Gemini Tyler. "It's going to sound corny, but the best first date I ever had was at Color Me Mine. We just sat and painted these queer little pieces of pottery, but it kept the focus off of each other directly and still let us talk quite a bit."

**What to Wear:** Honestly? While he'll notice your style (since he likes personality), your best accessory will be your brain. And hey, the brain is the largest sexual organ after all. So flash your intellect and a hint of cleavage to spark his curiosity. Let him notice your wits and your tits. As for the outfit, follow the 80/20 rule. Make it 80 percent basic, then add a few cool, feminine details: pretty shoes with an unusual accent, a flirty ruffle on a short leather jacket, dangly earrings. Go for simple, well-made clothes with unique tailoring and feminine accents, like a pintucked ballerina-style corset under a denim jacket, or a structured dress with a floaty handkerchief hemline.

**What Not to Wear:** The Gemini man loves a confident woman. If your outfit screams "high-maintenance," he'll assume that you are, too. And in his world, that means you'll need far too much attention, money, and time from him. He wants a woman who supports his many hobbies, not a needy distraction. Don't wear anything too outrageous, bright, or flashy just yet. You can trot those clothes out later when his other side emerges. Err on the side of understated or everyday feminine glamour. Think of Giselle

Bundchen when she's off the runway, hanging out in downtown New York City. She always looks cute and chic, but clearly not trying too hard.

**To Pay, or Not to Pay?** Gemini is the sign of the Twins, and he appreciates mutuality. While he may pay for the first date or two, it might not go on forever. He's a 50/50 guy, and he likes to trade off. He may also be an artist or an entrepreneur, so be sensitive to his budgetary constraints and skip the market price Maine lobster.

**Saying Good night:** If a Gemini man likes you, he'll often play the proper gentleman, leaving you at your doorstep with a gentle kiss. "What did he mean by 'thanks for the lovely evening?'" you'll wonder. Lord only knows. Especially since it's just as likely that his hands will be all over you, trying to score a cheap feel. There are no rules with this impulsive, unpredictable dude. You just never know! If he calls you for a second date, that will be far more telling.

## His First Home Visit

Opinionated Gemini is always looking for clues to your real personality, and he gathers them visually from your environment. His own place is probably a cluttered mess, filled with newspaper clippings, books, albums, DJ equipment, and a million accessories from his gazillion hobbies (which change every 4-6 months). When he visits your place, it's often a sign of trust: he's no longer afraid of giving you the "wrong idea." Here's how to make for a great time hosting him:

**Keep a little clutter out.** Fire your Feng Shui master! Cancel your *Martha Stewart Living* subscription! Piled-up projects, manuscripts in the works, even a few dust bunnies convey one important truth: you've got a life. The Gemini man would rather you prioritize that than hone the art of ancient Chinese space clearing or play domestic goddess.

**Serve wine.** The Gemini man, if he drinks, can be really into wine. Our theory is that since he rules communication, his talkative tongue is also sensitive to flavors, notes, and subtleties of the grape. Bring out the fruit of the vine—or better, ask him to bring one of his favorite bottles and you provide the dinner.

**Make it a Blockbuster night.** Gemini rules media, so a great movie or a rented season of a great TV show will give you lots to discuss.

**Host "game night" for two.** Playful Gemini loves games of any kind: board games, video games, mind games. Start with a tame one like Scrabble so he can impress you with his wordsmithing. Work your way into Trivial Pursuit (another coup for his amazing memory), then suggest a challenge round where the loser takes off a piece of clothing. Or, plug in the karaoke machine and loosen up with a little cheesy songfest.

**Let him go home if he needs to.** The Gemini man needs to slip between alone time and together time, and is very sensitive to reaching an overload of either. If he calls it an early night, don't take it personally. He's probably just obsessing over one of his own issues—or maybe he was struck by an "aha!" moment of how to finish his novel and needs to go write it now.

## Meeting His Family

If a Gemini man reveals anything personal to his family, it's usually serious. Don't expect to meet them immediately. Privacy is important to him, and he doesn't want everyone up in his biz. If anyone knows how changeable he is, it's his family, and they'd rather not get attached to someone who will be traded in two weeks later.

Gemini is the sign that rules siblings, and he can have a strange rivalry with his older brothers and sisters. On the One hand, he can be awestruck and worshipful. At the same time, the Gemini man needs to be praised for his own achievements, and will compete to win the "golden boy" title. As an older sibling, the Gemini man is a doting and protective brother. You'd best get along with his little brothers and sisters, because you'll be seeing a lot of them.

The Gemini man may idealize, even worship his mom. That means mommy had better love you like you emerged from her own womb. It won't seal the deal, but it will certainly break it if she doesn't approve. He may even describe her as his best friend, or be a bit of a mama's boy. (Gemini rappers Kanye West and Tupac Shakur both penned hits titled "Dear Mama.")

His father also occupies a pedestal, but the Gemini man usually tries to prove his manhood to daddy, rather than being best friends. Since his sign's dual nature makes him both masculine and feminine, the Gemini man will suffer with a macho, militaristic or unexpressive dad. If daddy's a drill sergeant, hope that your Gemini has a good therapist. Otherwise, he may spend years trying to prove his manhood, earning endless degrees and obsessing over his career.

Your job is to remain respectful and sweet, and to make him look good. Bonus points if you become best friends with his sister and mom (as long as he doesn't think you're talking behind his back). He needs to keep his family off his case and win their admiration. Keep your own wild side under wraps around them—he certainly will.

# Saying Good-bye
## Breaking Up with a Gemini

The Gemini man can be so passive about commitment, that you might just ditch him in sheer exasperation. His wishy-washy drama is enough to drive any woman insane after a while. If your ultimatum fell on deaf ears, it may be all you can do to scrape your dignity off the floor and move on. Because he rarely wears his heart on his sleeve, you probably won't see it break when you leave him. Often, he'll sink into a quiet depression, nursing his wounds with prescription drugs or sleepless nights on the Internet.

Since he's such a thinker, the Gemini man is good at reasoning himself out of feeling any deep emotional pain. This, of course, can cheat him out of the essential healing and grieving processes. He may drag around years of unresolved baggage, which can express itself as pathological behavior. He may obsess over the facts, but never delve into the necessary introspection. Unfortunately, dealing with relationship issues like a forensic scientist never gets the girl back. Sometimes, a person has to hit emotional rock bottom before he can truly heal. The Gemini man often needs one important, excruciating breakup that brings him to his knees and ultimately connects him with his feelings.

Then, there are cases where Gemini deserves to be dumped cold—when it's time to play the zodiac's player. He slept with your roommate, committed bank fraud in your name, or told his friends he only married you for a green card. If his "other side" turns out to be a total psycho, don't stick around for an encore.

## Getting over Him: When a Gemini Dumps You

Considering that Gemini relationships can have a very short shelf life, getting over him may be as simple as re-posting your Internet dating profile (which is probably still completely current). However, if he ended something long-term with you, it probably involved a lot of back and forth and hashing things out. You saw it coming—no surprises. You may have heard a painfully vivid litany about all the reasons he loves you, and all the reasons he's not sure you're meant for each other. This is where the Gemini gift of dialogue becomes a curse. Did you really need to hear that he's not sure you're smart enough for him, or that you're a little bit boring in bed? Or he may have just drifted away, let go of the wheel, and let the relationship fade to black.

If you're not a shell of the woman you once were, you're probably exhausted! First things first, you'll need to sleep for 96 hours. Maybe take a trip to visit a friend, a spa, or both. You're probably all talked out, so you might even want to escape alone. Read some self-help books on the beach (not the ones he bought for you as part of his campaign to change or improve you). Better yet, read books that are completely unrelated to him—maybe those chick lit classics he scoffed at so disdainfully ("I can't believe you're reading that," one Gemini we know sniffed).

Once you get over him, you might become friends again. He'll certainly keep you in his address book. Gemini men do like to stay in touch, if only to say an occasional hello, meet for coffee now and then, and make sure you're well. In some ways, he might be a better friend than boyfriend—and there will be a lot less crap to deal with.

**Have yourself one good last cry over...**
- The hilarious, incisive, insightful observations
- Dating a walking encyclopedia and cultural connoisseur
- His intelligence and fascinating ideas
- The great conversations
- The things... oh, the things... he could do with his hands (adios, Mr. Magic Fingers)
- The romantic promises he made in the beginning and never delivered
- His sweet, shy, heartbreaking, tender little boy side that needed you so

**Praise the universe that you never have to deal with...**
- Begging for his fleeting attention
- The verbal diarrhea and insensitive criticism

- Being embarrassed at parties when he starts sharing his renegade political beliefs and arguing with your best friend
- His absolute refusal to be told what to do or compromise
- His insistence upon doing things the hard way just to prove a point
- Waiting… and waiting… for him to "figure out" what he wants
- His annoying insecurities and refusal to be satisfied with what he has
- His bouts of dark depression that left you feeling completely iced out
- Constantly worrying about him

# Love Matcher:

## Can you find a common language?

| You are a(n)... | He thinks you're... | You think he's... | Common Language |
|---|---|---|---|
| Aries | Smart, sophisticated, and respectful of his space, but a little bit of a diva. | A little neurotic and needy. | Intellect, books, poetry |
| Taurus | Way too conventional. | Way too out there. | Affection, touch, food, and wine |
| Gemini | As wild and crazy as he is—a potential wife. | Eccentric, intelligent, and wild—just the way you like them. | Everything |
| Cancer | Someone who will take care of all the bulls**t he doesn't want to deal with. | Exciting but irritatingly irresponsible. | TV shows, cultural activities, music, books |
| Leo | Bossy, dominating, and emotionally over the top. | Cold, callous, and emotionally clueless. | Winning arguments, debating, politics |
| Virgo | Intelligent, savvy, a great conversationalist. | Smart, interesting, but a little scattered. | Words, writing, politics, ideas |

| You are a(n)... | He thinks you're... | You think he's... | Common Language |
|---|---|---|---|
| Libra | A little too girlie and high-maintenance. | Cheap and self-involved. | Parties, socializing, wine, restaurants |
| Scorpio | An electric connection and sexy challenge. | The perfect slave for your dominatrix fantasies. | Kinky sex, music, debauchery, exploring the underworld |
| Sagittarius | His competition: annoying, undermining, brash, and unsophisticated. | A flaky, neurotic, uptight snob. | Fighting and writing, stringing words together into the perfectly crafted insult |
| Capricorn | Composed in a way he wishes he could be. | Quirky in a way you wish you could be. | Acting out each other's repressed alter ego |
| Aquarius | His eccentric kindred spirit and playmate. | An independent thinker you admire. | Revolutionary thought |
| Pisces | An adorable mess. | Your poetic, tortured soul fantasy boy. | Neuroses, music, art, the underground scene |

# The Cancer Man

Dates: June 21–July 22
Symbol: The Crab
Ruling Planet: The (ever-changing) Moon
Element: Water
Quality: Cardinal
Mission: Domestic Bliss

**Natural Habitat—Where You'll Find Him:** Running the family business, cooking a gourmet dinner, sampling Cabernets at a vineyard, helping friends decorate their homes, hosting an elegant party, cheering on "his team" at a sports bar, sightseeing at historical ruins with an out-of-print guidebook tucked under his arm, hand-engineering an elaborate art project in the basement or garage, rocking out at an indie concert, huddled with friends at his favorite dive bar, camping out (with his two dogs) at a lakeside cabin, leading a troop of Boy Scouts on a wilderness adventure, coaching a youth soccer team, the lone straight guy at a bachelorette party or Girl's Night Out event, attending a charity dinner for the Leukemia and Lymphoma Society, training for a triathlon, traveling to remote corners of the Earth with a backpack and a smile, sailing around the harbor on his boat

**What He Does for a Living:** Real estate agent, interior or set designer, architect, fashion designer, comedian, actor, art collector, electrical engineer, chef, bartender, TV writer, financial planner, videographer, digital designer, special effects coordinator, journalist, restaurateur, critic, therapist, songwriter/composer, local politician, human rights activist, soldier, poet, novelist, English teacher, defense attorney, Olympic swimmer/diver, head of human resources, construction manager, pediatrician, Ob/Gyn

**Noteworthy & Notorious Cancer Men:** Robin Williams, 50 Cent, Tom Cruise, Beck, Derek Jeter, Tobey Maguire, Will Ferrell, Tom

Hanks, Harrison Ford, O.J. Simpson, Sylvester Stallone, Prince William, Carlos Santana, Bill Blass, Geraldo Rivera, Josh Hartnett, Adrian Grenier, Chace Crawford, George Orwell, Ringo Starr, the Dalai Lama, John Glenn, Ernest Hemingway, John Cusack, Neil Simon, Giorgio Armani, Bill Cosby, David Hasselhoff, Forest Whitaker, Nelson Mandela, George W. Bush, George M. Cohan, Pierre Cardin, Richard Simmons, Arthur Ashe, Milton Berle, Andrew Wyeth, Thurgood Marshall, Kevin Bacon, P.T. Barnum, Mel Brooks, Larry David, Chris Cornell, Randy Jackson, Hunter S. Thompson, Alex Trebek, Mr. Rogers

# Cancer: How to Spot Him

- The Crab's most sensitive spot is his chest, and the Cancer man often walks with his puffed out—at once offering you his heart and shielding it
- Buying everybody shots at the bar—he wants you out of your shell before he'll come out of his
- Preppy-conservative: button-down shirt, sweater, vest, or blazer (Mr. Rogers meets captain of the varsity lacrosse team)
- Metrosexual clothes like slightly tight shirts, revealing his (often well-defined) pecs
- Round "moonlike" face or rounded body
- Baseball cap and ratty college T-shirt, flip-flops—the sentimental value wardrobe he won't let go of
- Holding court among a gaggle of girls
- Soft, nurturing gaze… if he likes you; a cold, distant one if he doesn't
- Standing in a huddle with a group of guys, usually his frat brothers or childhood friends
- Actively involved with a pool table, video game, or pinball machine—Crabs love to play games

- Listening quietly and intensely to a friend over dinner, with a sympathetic, "there, there now…" look on his face
- At a cafe with his laptop, a well-worn notebook, or dog-eared novel
- Browsing for hours at a used bookstore or indie video shop
- Dumpster diving for goods to sell on eBay; dragging a curbside furniture find up five flights of stairs
- Rushing to the DJ booth to fix a power outage during a party
- Milk-fed features: creamy skin and rosy cheeks

# Cancer: How He Deals With…

### Money

Financial bulimic. Pinches it tightly in his crab claws (one Cancer man we know hid over $100,000 in his mattress!), then splurges without sense on food, travel, or equipment. Repeats famine cycle until he's re-earned his fortune.

### Family

Intensely emotional, complex, and codependent connection with his family. Forms a clique with his favorite relatives (usually female) and ostracizes the ones he hates. Cancer is the sign associated with the mother—watch out for Crabs who clash with their mamas or you could be the brunt of his issues for life.

### Love

Seeking domestic bliss with a willing dependent.

### Sex

Connected to his emotions, even when just a fling. It's all about "taking care of the ladies," so save your pole dancing moves for a

Gemini and just let him know he's pleasing you. Cares enough to call in the morning, even if it was a one-night stand.

### Children
Wants at least five. Total Soccer Mom.

### Pets
Nurtures all creatures without prejudice. Loves a good shelter dog and will spend hours in the park playing Frisbee with Fido.

### Your Meltdowns
Lives for them—this is his time to shine, provided you're not pissed at him. Will spend hours soothing you at his bosom. If you freak out on him, he'll freak out right back. Don't wound the crab's soft underbelly. He'll lash out blindly in an emotional outburst that can even get violent (Mike Tyson and O.J. Simpson are Cancers).

### His Meltdowns
Pure emotional rage. He'll either completely withdraw into his shell (leave him alone and lock up the liquor!) or take off to rage and beat the crap out of the nearest door, wall, or other (hopefully inanimate) object. May head to a bar and start a brawl.

### Breakups
More complicated than your average divorce trial—good luck dividing up the assets. Will keep your favorite possessions for sentimental value… or spite.

# Cancer: What He's All About

Paging the guy in aisle seven of Williams-Sonoma! There's a sale on chafing dishes and copper-clad sauté pans. What's that? You already have a full set? Ohhhh, you're looking for an espresso machine to surprise your girlfriend. She doesn't have a tricked-out kitchen like you do. I see. You must be a… Cancer?

Okay, ladies, let's talk straight here. We're officially in the post-post-feminist era, or something like that. We can't keep track. The point is, there's a good chance that right now you're a successful, working woman, and that whole Betty Crocker thing is actually just a crock of s**t. You don't have time to cook and clean and wipe up baby drool—at least not on your own. You don't need a husband. You need a wife.

Enter the Crab. Dinner's on the table (or reservations have been made), the kids are nodding off to his classical music collection, and he's already painting your picket fence white. A trip to Pier One or Pottery Barn is like foreplay to your little Crabcake. He'll do the dishes, the laundry and you. Does it get any better than that?

Cancer is the sign that rules women and femininity. Domestic bliss is his number-one mission. His idea of nirvana is a cozy, well-appointed home filled with art, music, and an ever-expanding brood. (Bonus points if you cook together, since this emotional eater loves food almost as much as he loves you.) Home, family, and security are his top priorities—along with Taurus and Capricorn, he's a major "family man."

So where's the downside? Well, he can be sensitive, even whiny. Oh, who are we kidding? On bad days, he's a total bitch. His sign is ruled by the Moon, which causes his moods to fluctuate with the tides. That's right—just like yours. You'll have as many Kotex moments as you will Kodak moments with him. Were someone to conduct a study, the Cancer man could prove that "male PMS" is no myth.

Although he loves to be around women, sometimes the Cancer man is the "woman." Want to find out? Just push his buttons. He reacts in all the stereotypically feminine ways, taking every slight personally, wondering "what she meant by that," and stewing in a funk. He gets easily attached to his possessions, too. One Cancer friend loved a certain style of Adidas flip-flops so much, he wore them for years. After scouring eBay (they finally fell apart), he bought five pairs, which he estimates will last him for the next twenty to thirty years.

Girlie as he can be, the Cancer man will defend you like a gallant knight. He's fiercely protective of his loved ones. In the animal kingdom, the mothers are often the most ferocious, and like a mama bear, he'll tear a limb off anyone who messes with his clan. In rare cases, the Cancer man's pent-up frustrations can erupt in a fearsome or violent rage. As a kid, he might even have been the neighborhood punk. It's not easy being as sensitive as Cancers are, and like an angry crab, he may pinch anyone who gets too close. This guy definitely needs lots of emotional outlets: martial arts, sports, the stock market, or beating up a pinball machine—something he can "conquer" when he feels out of control.

Loyal to his crew, he's a band of brothers kind of guy. In college, the Cancer man is often a frat boy—though we suspect it's because he just wants to secure housing for himself. As the sign that rules family, he needs to belong to one. Until he can start his own, he'll fashion a pseudo-clan by going Greek, joining a sports team or arts club, visiting the same bar every night, or getting jumped into a gang. There's a doggedly patriotic quality to the Cancer man. Gone too far, he can be xenophobic, like George W. Bush. Is it any surprise that a Cancer president would be preoccupied with "homeland security"?

Fortunately, he's also concerned with yours. If you want the kind of guy that understands women, cares how you feel, and will stay by your side in exchange for being your macho-yet-motherly hero, the Cancer man has a cozy spot waiting in his shell.

# What He Wants in a Woman

The Cancer man wants an intelligent, powerful woman who will never leave him. He's looking for his dream wife, the mother of his children. Simple enough, right? You can do that. You're smart, you own your s**t, and you've hit "snooze" on your biological clock too many times. Bring it!

Well, sister, there's a catch: The Cancer man doesn't like his women prêt-à-porter. To win his heart, you need to be a little rough around the edges. He's a bit of a Svengali, and he loves to use his magic touch to transform a willing Pygmalion into a goddess.

Although he adores feminine sophistication and grace, he'll gladly teach you those skills. The Cancer man prefers a scrappy lady in the making—someone whom he can civilize and bring over to the right side of the tracks.

The Cancer man is a "horse whisperer" when it comes to women. He knows how to lull you into feeling so safe and trusting, you'll remain willingly under his command. Before you know it, you're all saddled up, happily leaving the reins in his control. Although you may miss your wild days, it feels good to be led around, too, letting somebody else make all the decisions.

That's why Cancer men are often found with a younger woman on their arm. Plainly stated, they need a colt to break. This right here could explain the mysterious bond between Tom Cruise, a Cancer, and Katie Holmes. Katie is a Sagittarius, one of the most rough and tumble, independent signs of the zodiac. Much like wild colts, Sags are a challenge to tame. The experienced Cancer man knows how to give women the illusion of freedom and adventure (read: Armani wardrobe, private jets, and Colorado ranches belonging to the once-hottest man on the planet). Soon, free-spirited women like Katie will barely even notice they're wearing a harness and saddle, and being led around by the nose.

Stockholm Syndrome is the Cancer man's specialty. If you don't know what that is, it's a phenomenon where a prisoner identifies with her captor, even develops a bond that resembles love. We're not saying that being with a Cancer is akin to being abducted by a psychopath (our Cancer guy friends would never forgive us if we did). But when the Crab lets you into his shell, or grasps you in his claw, don't expect to get out easily. You might as well fall in love with the guy, because he won't let you go without a fight.

Now, let's talk about the mom thing. Unlike Scorpio, he doesn't have an Oedipus complex, thank God. But as the zodiac's "mother sign," the Cancer man has a significant relationship with his mama. Often, she's his best friend and confidante. (Tom Cruise's mother and sister live with him.) In some cases, he sees her as a patron saint who can do no wrong. At the very least, he respects her powerful role. Woe betide the Cancer man whose mother abandoned or abused him. He may punish every woman he meets for her transgressions.

Will he expect you to win his mom's approval or live up to her legacy? To a point, yes. At the very least, never knock her off her pedestal. If you want to be with this man, open your arms wide to his family. To love a Cancer means to love his family (or in those rare cases, to hate them with equal venom).

# What He Wants from a Relationship

Have you ever had a guy just reach out and link his arm through yours, or throw his arm across your shoulders, making you feel totally safe, secure, and loved? Maybe he squeezes a little too hard, pulls you a little too close. But you don't mind. You feel like daddy's little girl, feminine in a primal way, maybe even swept off your feet.

Prepare the release forms and have your lawyer draw up papers. The possessive Cancer man wants ownership, and he's come to claim you. You will get a share of revenue and royalties, while he retains creative control, managerial rights and at least 51 percent of the partnership. You agree to walk by his side or two steps behind him; in return, he will valiantly shield you from paparazzi, street urchins, and other interested men.

The Cancer man knows exactly how to take a woman into his Crabby grip and keep her there forever. We may be setting feminism back a few centuries by saying this, but damn, it feels good to have a man take care of you like he does. Of course, there's a thin line between security and smothering. When he sidles up from behind and puts his arms around your waist, you'll either hope he never lets go, or make a mental note to page him if a choking victim needs the Heimlich maneuver.

Nothing fulfills a Cancer man more than a happy family, with himself at the helm. He rules the zodiac's fourth house of home and family. Lifelong security is his mission. On a horoscope wheel, the fourth house is located at the very bottom, representing the foundation of the chart. Indeed, the Cancer man builds his love life from the ground up, planting deep roots and nurturing them into a mighty, multigenerational family tree.

The Cancer man wants to build a legacy, and that starts with a wife and children. He's a proud papa who can't wait to raise kids and pass on his family ties. Fatherhood gives him a sense of duty and purpose. Cancer is a clique-y sign, and he treats his family like heirs to the throne, molding them to continue his legacy.

The Cancer man is dazzled by powerful women, and he may go through several marriages with beautiful, vibrant mates before he perfects his recipe for lifelong bliss. What's the deal-breaker? He needs to be needed. That's a tall order for a guy who's attracted to intelligent, independent women who already have their own full lives when he meets them.

He wants to have his cake and eat it, too. If that means baking it himself, hand him an apron and a Mixmaster. The Cancer man's ideal match is a woman who can make him laugh *and* think, who's outwardly simple with layers of depth, and—most important—who's always by his side when he needs her. He wants a willing companion who also has her own life, but not so much that it competes with his. A copilot won't work, but a sexy, solid first mate will do just fine.

The Cancer man needs to create dependents—and that goes for you, too. Are you willing to be fussed over, nagged, and mothered? You'll have to be to keep him.

Take the example of our Virgo friend Nancy, a self-made millionaire and world traveler. On her third date, she invited her Cancer beau Edward to her tasteful, art-filled New York City apartment. Rather than marvel at her rare book collection and African pottery, Edward noticed two things: that Nancy's living room air conditioner didn't work, and she didn't have an anti-slip pad under her tiny kitchen rug.

Nancy was irritated, but she also wanted Edward to be comfortable in her home. Before his next visit, she replaced the a/c unit, but their passion cooled along with her living room.

"What was the big f**king deal?" she throws her hands up, exasperated. "I just wanted to have a glass of wine and talk about life, get to know each other better. It was like he couldn't get over the damn rug. Who cares?"

Well, Nancy, you missed his Cancerian cues. Edward was testing to see whether Nancy needed him. Instead of fixing the air conditioner herself, she was supposed to ask him to help her replace it. According to the Cancer relationship rules, he's not only your boyfriend, he's also your handyman and caretaker. To Nancy, a little domestic discomfort was no big deal. She imagined their fourth date being cocktails at The Four Seasons, not appliance shopping at Circuit City.

And this is why it's so important to understand your man's sign. For some women, pretending to need a guy when you don't simply isn't worth the compromise. It feels like dumbing yourself down or, as our wise Aquarius friend Neda puts it, "dimming your lights so he can shine." You'll always feel a little bit… suburban with a Cancer man.

On the other hand, if you're willing to subdue your inner diva a little in exchange for his nurturing and guidance, to offer your appreciation and be wowed by him, he'll work his ass off to keep the stars in your eyes.

# Sex with a Cancer

It's the stuff of grocery store romance novels: the windswept damsel and the gallant hero who gathers her into his powerful embrace, carrying her into the throes of passion. Romantic Cancer knows how to "take" you, leaving you in a state of weak-kneed surrender. He's sensitive to your needs and loves to please you. This is no wham-bam-thank-you-ma'am lover.

Have you ever seen the astrological symbol for Cancer? It looks like a 69. Indeed, the Cancer man is talented with his tongue. The Cancer symbol also looks suspiciously like breasts, which makes sense since Cancer rules the chest. He's a boob man and he's not afraid to tell you. He worships your femininity and loves to caress your curves.

When the Cancer man wants you, he's "grabby." Those crab claws will circle your waist, and he'll pull you toward him in a primal, unga-bunga way. He's also gabby. He may seduce you with girl talk, listening raptly as you prattle on about your latest drama. He leans in close or touches your arm as he peppers the conversation with insightful questions. Before you know it, you're practically on top of each other, and well, you know how it goes from there.

Love a game of dress-up? The Cancer man will go for some light costumery. In fact, donning a new persona or role can ease his shyness. Many Cancers are great actors, since they feel safe revealing a wider spectrum of honesty when portraying an alter ego. Handcuffs or wrist-binding are a special favorite. After all, there's nothing that turns a Cancer man on more than knowing that you couldn't possibly leave him.

# Cancer: Turn-Ons & Turn-Offs

## Turn Him On

- Show off your curves—he's ruled by the Moon so if your butt, boobs, and hips are round and full, he'll howl for your heavenly body
- Play up feminine touches, like a flower in your hair, red lipstick, lace, flowing curls, dresses, and heels
- Have a wide-eyed innocence or wonder toward the world
- Be a foodie who loves to eat and cook
- Ask for his guidance on any life situation and put his advice to use
- Be vibrant, effusive, and full of life; he needs a bubbly, active mate
- Gush about your family and ask him all about his
- Have an interesting hobby
- Take classes that you can talk about with him
- Be well-read and culturally literate
- Believe in true love and fairy tale romance
- Gaze at him with a gooey, "you complete me" stare
- Have a Susie Homemaker streak and a dash of sporty spice
- Ask him to help you fix up your home

## Turn Him Off

- Be jaded, hardened or cynical
- Have a career or life that's too well defined so he can't see a way to contribute to you
- Insist on fixing everything around the house yourself
- Be jealous of his female friends or attempt to interfere with those relationships
- Declare chivalry dead
- Patronize or mother him—HE'S the mother in this relationship
- Talk smack about his mama, even if he says he hates her— you'll never replace the "other woman" in his life and you should never try
- Have zero interest in pampering, grooming, or self-care
- Criticize his taste in writing, art, or music... he'll consider it an attack on his emotions
- Cut him down when he's grandstanding, clowning, or showing off
- Refuse to go camping, sailing, hiking, snowboarding, etc., with him
- Tell him what to do—even well-meaning, unsolicited advice will cause him to rebel
- Blab his secrets or personal information (even innocently) to other people—Crabs HATE being exposed
- Laugh at his poetic sentiment... or mock him in any way
- Tell him you don't want kids
- Turn down invites to hang out with his family... especially his mother or sisters

# His Moves

## First Moves: How He Courts You

If the eyes are the windows to the soul, the Cancer man leaves the curtains open when he's feeling the love. His soft, tender gaze will melt your heart (or make you gag, if the interest isn't mutual). It's almost the way a mother looks at a newborn—radiating wonder and hope. Cue the violins! Toss the rose petals! Release the cherubs and their magical harps!

Not that he doesn't get misty-eyed over puppies, babies, and other sentimental moments, too. The Cancer man's heart is easily stirred. Still, there's something in the way he looks at you that will make his interest obvious. Courtship with a Cancer can be fun and romantic. At the very least, you'll enjoy a few lovely, carefully planned dates.

Here are a few signs that he's checking you out as a prospective girlfriend:

- He gets physical, touching your arm or wrist while he talks
- He puts his arm around you, hugs you, or pulls you close
- He hangs on every word you say and gets really involved in the conversation
- He calls you to "see how you're doing"—a gentle, well-being checkup
- He gets all gentlemanly—opening doors, kissing your hand, walking you home
- He offers his help with an issue or household project
- He listens to you vent about your loser ex (he's competitive and loves to one-up other men)
- He asks your friends about you behind your back (his "rejection protection" strategy)
- He asks deliberate questions designed to help him figure you out

- He invites you to join him for a cultural event or a well-planned date
- He offers to bring lunch over to your home or office

# He's In: How You Know He's Committed

Trust doesn't come easily to this tenderhearted sign, but once you earn his confidence (which could take years or an instant), he's eager to make it official. Once a Cancer decides you're the One, it's full steam ahead. Security is his obsession, and he tends to make prudent, calculated moves. Lest someone else claim you, he works overtime to close the deal. Here are a few signs that he could stick around longer than the flowers he delivers to your office:

**He tells you he's in love with you.** Romantic Cancer isn't afraid to let you know he's smitten. If he drops the "l-bomb," he's in.

**He talks about marriage and family.** On their first date, our Cancer friend and his now-wife sat outside Starbucks and spent four hours talking about weddings, baby names, and where they wanted to settle down. Some people would just have a latte. Not him. If he sees a future with you, he wants to make sure you share his vision.

**He seems to know you better than you know yourself.** Well, he's been studying you. Our Cancer friend Gary explains this strategy: "Know your partner," Gary says. "I like to establish what the other person needs in a partner, what's been lacking in her life, and that's what I become. I make strong in my persona what she lacks in hers." If he cares enough about your happiness to change himself this way, he's really, really interested.

**He draws a line in the sand.** Hardball? You bet. The Cancer man is not afraid to walk away from a wishy-washy woman who's toying with his emotions. This risk-averse sign needs to know that you won't go breakin' his heart.

**He tells his mother about you.** You know… the "other woman" in his life? Her opinion matters more to him than anyone's. So if she's gotten a good report on you, chances are you'll be meeting her really soon.

**He asks you to move in.** Home is where his hard-on is. If he wants to share an address, it's not just to save on gas and electric bills (though he considers this a plus).

## Unfaithful Cancer: Why He Cheats

Although a happy Cancer is a loyal family man, when in turmoil, his emotions can cloud his judgment. If that means finding comfort in the bosom of another woman, he may just go there. It takes a lot for him to cheat, but here are some probable causes:

**You hurt him.** Have you wounded your Crab in his soft underbelly? Cut down his ego or brought him to his knees? Never underestimate the Crab's retaliatory powers when he's in pain. If he thinks you don't care about his feelings, why should he care about yours? At least, that's what he tells himself as he's massaging some pretty young thing's shoulders while bitterly obsessing over you.

**You bored him.** With Cancer, there's a fine line between having too much edge and not enough. If you lack curiosity, he's out of a job. After all, he needs to dazzle you with his worldliness and finely honed cultural IQ. Too much "girl next door" will send him prowling down another block.

**You punked him.** The Cancer man guards his reputation carefully. Did you make him look or feel like a fool? Did he catch you sneaking around or flirting with another guy? He might just give you a taste of your own medicine.

**You took him for granted.** The Cancer man needs to feel appreciated for all the special care and sensitivity he gives you. If you treat his chivalry like it's no big deal, he'll find another lady in waiting.

## Dig the Grave: It's Over

Saying good-bye is one of the Cancer man's least favorite things to do. He fancies himself a gentleman, and he never wants to be the one to make a lady (or himself) cry. When it comes to breakups, he's a total wuss. The guilt alone could kill him. His departure could happen in such an indirect way, that you might not even be sure that he's left you until the papers are served, or you hear word that he's got a new woman in his life. Here are some of the signs that he might be making an exit:

**He retreats.** This man absolutely hates emotional confrontation. If you're locked in a battle with no resolution, he may just cut off contact. A cordial email or a Christmas card will arrive occasionally (he's Mr. Manners), but that will be as far as it goes.

**He gets really agitated or cranky around you.** One word: guilt. He's swimming in it because he knows he's about to hurt your feelings.

**He starts fixing everything in your house.** This is a tricky one, since it's often his courtship ritual as well. But if he sets up your WiFi, installs a home security system, and rehinges your closet door—then leaves with a lukewarm hug—he's giving you a parting gift. The Cancer man still wants to make sure you're well taken care of post-breakup. Maybe that's why his exes often turn into friends.

**His best girlfriends start calling even more than they already do.** No, he's not sleeping with them, he's being a girl with them. He's bitching about you, asking for advice, wondering what to do, and whining about how "bad" he feels.

**He systematically starts breaking the bond.** The Cancer man not only approaches you in a safe, non-threatening way, he leaves you like that, too. His emails become polite but distant. His calls are less frequent. Step by careful step, he'll back out of your life until he feels like your platonic best friend. Have you ever seen a crab scuttling sideways down the beach? That's how he creeps out of your relationship.

**Emergency Kit Remedy:**
**Demand a direct conversation.** Maybe he's making assumptions, or needs something that he thinks you can't give him. Rather than deal with direct conversation, he might just be retreating like a bitch. It could be worth a face-to-face, but you will have to initiate it.

# Interpreting His Signals:

## What does he mean by that?

| When he | It means... | So you should... |
| --- | --- | --- |
| Gets quiet | He's moody and brooding. | Go out with your friends and leave his bitchy ass alone. He needs his space. Take a hint and get away before he gets mean. He'll recover in a few hours' time. |
| Doesn't call | He thinks you're a nice girl and all, but he doesn't see this going anywhere.<br><br>You offended him or hurt his feelings. | Move on.<br>If you REALLY like him, see if you can sit him down to apologize and clear things up.<br><br>Warning: once bitten, he's twice shy, and he'll rarely give second chances. |
| Calls a lot | He's falling for you or thinks you're his new best girlfriend. | Ask him questions to draw him out of his shell. He needs to feel safe around you before he gets fully involved. |
| Doesn't make a move after a couple dates | He's intimidated.<br><br>He's not interested. | Show a little bit of your softer side, ask him for help with something to give him a point of entry with you. Don't rush him.<br><br>Move on; this guy knows what he likes. |

| When he | It means... | So you should... |
| --- | --- | --- |
| Doesn't make a move after a few weeks | If he's still calling you and taking you out on what could be considered a date, he's probably too shy or insecure to make a move. | Boost his ego and his confidence. Tell him why he's so much cooler than other guys. Compliment him so he knows you find him attractive. Schedule your next date over drinks to lower inhibitions. |
| Moves fast | Make no assumptions... he believes in love at first sight, but he can also be a horny bastard. | Slow him down if you want something real... he'll respect you for it. |
| Picks up the tab, gives flowers and gifts | He thinks you're worth real consideration... this guy doesn't part with his cash easily. | Swoon and gush over his gestures and fine taste. |
| Introduces you to his family and/or closest friends | You're being put through his litmus test for love. | Be genuinely excited to meet them. Ingratiate yourself—they'll be talking about you tomorrow and could be the deciding vote in your future with him. |

# Your Moves: Tips for Flirting and Everlasting Love

## Flirting with a Cancer

It's shockingly easy to flirt with a Cancer man. Flirting is one of his favorite activities, and he's always up for some playful banter with the ladies. This is the guy who will flirt with his mother's friends, or make the old ladies at the retirement home blush. He genuinely adores women's attention and company, so if you need a flirting fix, he's your man. Here are some good segues:

**Be obvious.** Bat your lashes and flirt shamelessly. Lean forward when you're talking so he can get a glimpse of décolletage, toss your hair, play to his camera. "I'm watching every little thing," says our Cancer friend. "I'll notice your haircut's new, you did something with your eyebrows, your shoes. I can tell when a woman's getting regular sex and when she's having sleepless nights because she's working."

**Complain about your boyfriend or a recent ex.** Competitive Cancer loves to play the sensitive-guy hero, one-upping all the other men. After all, understanding women is his secret weapon. Go ahead, tell him what a jerk your ex was. It just primes the pump for his favorite opening line: "If I was your man... "

**Ask for his advice.** Personal conversations (about you, not him) are the ultimate icebreakers with a Cancer man. Any opportunity for him to show his sensitivity help him avoid the small talk he hates.

**Talk about books, art, culture.** He loves a woman with a high cultural I.Q. Talk about your favorite CD, band, or a controversial *New Yorker* article and he'll be eating out of your palm.

**Be yourself—boldly.** Like a moth, he gravitates to the brightest light in the room. If you're the pulse of the party or the center of an exciting conversation, he may end up in your orbit.

**Be a little girly and giddy.** This is the zodiac's most likely guy to marry his childhood sweetheart, so flirt like the queen of the playground. He loves it when you giggle and blush like a schoolgirl—especially over him.

## Everlasting Love with a Cancer

For a Cancer, real love happens when he can feel it in his heart. Sex is just sex to him, and so is flirting. When his emotions get involved, that's when he starts to think of making your arrangement a little more permanent. Want to keep your Cancer around forever 'n' ever? Here are a few ways to lay the groundwork.

**Let him be your knight in shining armor.** Can he rescue you from your tower—even if it's an ivory one? He wants to make you a better person, pump you up, and be your champion. You don't have to be a damsel in distress, but you could be an overworked corporate queen who needs a little pampering. "If she purrs to my touch, there's no reason for me to leave her," says one Cancer man. If he knows that he can always bring pleasure and comfort to your life, he'll hop on his white horse, pronto.

**Be willing to play supporting actress.** Do you look good on his arm, and make him look even better? Do you make him feel like a god? This sensitive guy grapples with his own secret insecurities, and he needs your support, too. Give him his wings. Once it's firmly established that you're his, he'll push you into the spotlight and applaud from the sidelines.

**Earn and keep his admiration.** The Cancer man will sleep with anyone, but he certainly won't fall in love with a woman he doesn't respect. How could he bring you home to mama otherwise?

**Be super-wife and über-mom material.** Nothing keeps the Cancer man by your side more than picturing you as the ideal mother to his children, and the person with whom he creates a family.

**Give him space or companionship on demand.** The Crab needs to go in and out of his shell, depending on his ever-changing moods. Some days he needs you around constantly, other times he wants space. If you can remain cool and centered as his inner tides fluctuate, he'll anchor himself on your shores.

**Have a homebody streak.** The Cancer man's home is his palace. It's where he entertains, cooks, feeds, and nurtures his clan. It's where his all-important family gathers and where he gets to be "the lord of the manor." If you want to be with this guy forever, you've got to love a good Blockbuster night as much as you adore dinner and symphony tickets.

# Prep Yourself For...

## Your First Date

Alert: do not judge this man by a first date. He's a lifelong friend type who warms up slowly. Although he's a charming companion, there could be a few awkward moments during your first one-on-one encounter. The Cancer man can be shy or reserved, and he certainly doesn't bare his entire soul on the first date. He may overcompensate for his nervousness by being the loudest person in the room, cracking jokes, overplanning, making well-rehearsed small talk, or using other emotional armor to protect his tender feelings. "I always start with cocktails to loosen them up," says one Cancer man.

You can ease the tension with a little prep work. Think of a few things to talk about in advance. Prepare a mental list of "safe" but interesting topics to fill those awkward pauses: books or articles you've read, exhibits you've seen, places you want to travel. That can kick-start a dwindling conversation with Cancer. Or, just ask for his advice on a personal (but not too personal) matter. He feels a lot more comfortable talking about you before he opens up.

**The Basic Vibe:** Do you love a man with a plan? The Cancer man approaches first dates like a seasoned tour guide. He's an activity dater who likes to follow a well-researched (and often overpacked) itinerary. Although he's not exactly spontaneous, his midnight-oil energy makes up for it. This guy can stay out all night!

Feeling comfortable is his priority, since he wants to be at the top of his game. He'll probably take you to "his" places, where he feels most at home. Be sure to compliment his choices, because he's worried about pleasing you. He's eager to impress you, and he may also spend the week before your date finding a cool exhibit, concert, or club. Follow his lead.

The Cancer man will want to go everywhere and see everything. Even after a great meal and touring all twelve floors of the museum, he'll have a list of hip lounges in his pocket that he wants to check out. There's no limit to his cultural curiosity, especially when there's a pretty woman to share it with him.

The Cancer man is a foodie, so a restaurant will probably be part of the evening. "People are happy around food," says Gary, our Cancer friend. "Eating opens women up, starts the date relaxed. We need to get you to talk so we can figure you out, learn your needs so we can meet them." If you're equally uncomfortable opening up, we recommend starting your night with a drink, going to your movie/poetry reading/cultural event, then eating afterward. That way, if you can't find a conversational groove with him, you'll have something to discuss.

**What to Wear:** Femininity is like fine wine to this man, and he will lap yours up like a thirsty dog. The Cancer man loves a subtle whiff of perfume, your hair loose and flowing, pretty jewelry that doubles as a conversation piece. Most important to him, though, is that you're comfortable and at home in your body. Better to wear something simple that lets him notice your walk when you excuse yourself to the ladies' room. Cancer rules the chest, so cleavage is your number-one accessory. Can't fill an A cup? Wear a striking necklace and play up whatever boobs or curves you've got. Leave your stilettos at home, and wear your sexy bar-hopping boots, or ballet flats. He'll want to paint the town on a first date, so you'll need to be comfortable.

**What Not to Wear:** Down, dominatrix. Are you seducing him or competing with him? As a rule of thumb, don't dress like a total Alpha female. Avoid wearing anything too harsh or severe with this sensitive guy. He loves femininity, so take it easy on the tomboy touches, like complicated buckles, brass buttons, or hardware. Skip anything overly put-together that hides your figure, too. If you wear a suit or a jacket, soften it with a lacy camisole or a gauzy scarf. If your outfit doesn't make you feel like a total goddess, put on something that does.

**To Pay or Not to Pay?** Although he's usually too much of a gentleman, the Crab can pinch pennies in that claw. Bring cash just in case you want sparkling water instead of tap. He may be on a blind dating spree, and if it's been a busy week, he could have exceeded his budget. If you go to dinner (and you probably will), he'll tally up the bill to make sure no unnecessary charges were added. He'll want to keep the receipt for a tax write-off.

**Saying Good night:** The Cancer man knows how to play the gentleman, but that doesn't mean he won't grab you for a passionate farewell. He's probably gotten more touchy-feely as the night (and the liquor) wore on. He's usually a great kisser, so if you like him, enjoy. This is the guy who will make out with you and call in the morning.

## His First Home Visit

Pressure alert! The Cancer man will do anything to get into your home. Not just because he wants to throw you on the couch and make out with you (he does), but because he wants to "read" you. This guy is pickier than a British butler about his living arrangements, so your lifestyle is a major make-or-break factor for this domestic dude. More than anything, he needs to know that your décor won't clash or compete with his aesthetic.

You know the joke: What do lesbians bring to their second date? A U-Haul. So it goes with the Cancer man. He's always thinking about the "c" word (cohabitation). Tali went out with a Cancer who brought a disposable razor and toothbrush to their third date! Another friend ended up in a four-year relationship with a Cancer because, as she put it, "He spent the night after our first date, and he just never left." The Cancer man is ready to cozy up as soon as you are. Here's how to make sure your home is a welcoming space for him:

**Make sure something is broken.** We've said it *ad nauseum*: The Cancer man needs to be needed. If he can fix your pilot light or install a new dimmer switch in your bedroom, you've just given this eager-to-please man a job.

**Display your family photos and albums.** Unlike most men, this guy would love to see framed pictures of your parents, sorority sisters, and cute baby nieces. Believe us, he's got his share on the mantel, too. He's checking you out as a potential breeder, so he needs confirmation that you're into the whole family thing. Give him evidence. "I need to know: did she have a happy childhood?" says one Cancer man. "If she had a bitter and harsh upbringing, it's going to be hard to make her happy. She'll always go back to that person she was as a kid."

**Leave a lacy or silky bathrobe hanging on the bathroom door.** Feminine touches turn the Cancer man on big-time. He's into women who love to be women. The more your home feels like a Parisian parlor, the better. A bottle of French perfume on the vanity, some pearls and silk scarves draped over a chair, whatever. Create that hypnotic ambience.

**Don't have a house that's too "done."** Impeccable decor is less important to him than a homey feel. The moment he steps into your place, he's thinking about whether you could live together. If you're a pack rat, open up a can of Feng Shui on those piles and boxes before he comes. After all, where will he put his carefully curated music collection if there's not a square inch of free space? Make sure his cherished possessions could find a home among yours.

## Meeting His Family

If a Cancer man likes you, expect to meet his family sooner rather than later. At the very least, he has a dutiful relationship with his relatives. In most cases, though, he considers them his best friends. By the time you're sucking up to his parents (a must), you'll feel like you already know them, because he will have talked about them so much.

"Oh, Edna, it's such a pleasure to meet you. Let me give you a hug. Is it alright if I call you Mother?"

"Mr. Williams, it's an honor. Bryan has told me all about your model airplane workshop. I hear you just finished your 98th one this year. Amazing. Can I see the collection?"

If you're not into family, don't bother reading any further. Turn to the chapter on Sagittarius, Gemini, or Aquarius. None of them will give a rat's ass whether you want to summer at their parents' lake house, or spend Christmas dressed as an adorable elf delivering carefully chosen gifts to their fourteen nieces and nephews.

If you are, you could be on your way to a proposal. (He might just ask you to marry him in front of his family, too.) Jealous types need not apply here. The Cancer man may have children from a previous marriage, and you must embrace them as your own. Greet his family with open arms, and you'll win his loyalty. If his mother approves, it's a done deal.

# Saying Good-bye

## Breaking Up with a Cancer

So you want to get the hell out of this mess. Unless it's a mutual breakup, leaving the locked-up grip of a Cancer is no easy task. He fancies himself the gatekeeper and the keymaster of your relationship. This possessive guy is not going to make it simple for you to just walk out the door. He's feathered a golden cage for you, and it's not easy for a domesticated pet to return to the wild. Still, you want your freedom back.

Cancer rules the heart, so if you go breakin' his, prepare to pay. He will take full advantage of your guilt and emotions. Don't expect generosity from him. In fact, he'll have the bitterness of the Grinch.

If it's a long-term relationship, you've probably merged your lives enough to make this complicated. We're talking mortgages, credit cards, bank accounts, Costco memberships, pets. You will not want to deal. Suck it up and make it through the bitter negotiations and head games. Prepare to walk away from a few possessions. It's the price you pay to get your life back.

## Getting over Him: When a Cancer Dumps You

You want the unvarnished truth? He's a total wuss about ending things. The Cancer man isn't big on the open-faced breakup. He can barely live with the guilt he feels over hurting you. He'll either disappear, or invent an excuse to spend less time with you ("work has gotten really busy"). In your gut, you know what's coming. One Cancer man knew he wanted to break up with his girlfriend, but he still moved cross-country with her. Once she was all situated in an apartment and job, he made his graceful exit. Claiming incurable misery on the West Coast, he left the state—and her—in one shot. Read between the lines with this guy and trust your intuition.

### Have yourself one good last cry over...

- Having a best "girlfriend" and a boyfriend rolled into one
- His intense focus on you and only you
- The best hugs of your life
- The best oral sex of your life
- Getting to feel like a woman and a little girl
- His creative date-planning skills
- His cultural literacy—books, art, music
- Having someone to fix everything that broke
- Having to cook and clean for yourself again
- The security

### Praise the universe that you never have to deal with...

- His clinginess and insecurity
- Temper tantrums and those moody, broody spells
- The control freak you discovered that he could be
- Being nagged, fussed over, and treated like a child
- His occasional mean or critical remarks
- Itemizing every restaurant tab and doing things "for the tax write-off"
- The penny-pinching and Dumpster diving—did he really bring home *that*?
- His uncanny ability to piss on your parade
- Feeling like a suburban grandmother when you're only thirty-two

# Love Matcher:

## Can you find a common language?

| You are a(n)... | He thinks you're... | You think he's... | Common Language |
|---|---|---|---|
| Aries | Talented, but a little high-maintenance and a bit of a diva. | Sweet, intriguing, but too passive and hard-to-read. | You're both "extroverted loners" who enjoy the arts as much as a good night at home. |
| Taurus | Wife material. | Husband material. | Home and family are everything to you both. |
| Gemini | Intriguingly insane. | The mommy you secretly crave. | Dive bars, independent theater, video games, and eBay obsessions |
| Cancer | Sweet, but tough to please. | Killing you with kindness. Down, boy, down. | Nesting... you could set up a cozy little bubble together. |
| Leo | I'm supposed to introduce HER to my mother? | Romantic but a little wussy. | You're both hopeless romantics who'll let your lives go to hell for a shot of love. |

| You are a(n)... | He thinks you're... | You think he's... | Common Language |
|---|---|---|---|
| Virgo | Elegant, tasteful, sharp as a tack... but a little too much of a know-it-all at times. | Finally! A gentleman among the rogues. | Books, cooking, architecture, design... you foodies and culture whores will enjoy nights at home and on the town. |
| Libra | Hard to pin down and expensive to maintain. | Cheap, clingy and too much of a homebody. | Wining, dining, and dancing |
| Scorpio | His sexual fantasy in the flesh. | The rare soul you can actually trust. | The depth, intensity, and fragility of your emotions |
| Sagittarius | Nice curves, big mouth—an insensitive loose cannon. | High maintenance and oversensitive, but fun to talk to once you get past his shell. | Sex, gossip, work ethic, and raunchy sense of humor |
| Capricorn | The June to his Ward Cleaver. | Someone to bring out your softer side. | A house in the suburbs, 2.5 kids, white picket fence... |
| Aquarius | A fascinating head case. | An emotional basket case. | Sex, postcoital discussions about global politics (foreplay for both signs) |

| You are a(n)... | He thinks you're... | You think he's... | Common Language |
|---|---|---|---|
| Pisces | The damsel in distress he's been waiting to save. | Your hero. | An undying belief in fairy-tale romance |

# The Leo Man

Dates: July 23–August 22
Symbol: The Lion
Ruling Planet: The Sun—center of our universe
Element: Fire—passionate, dynamic, active
Quality: Fixed
Mission: Hunting for a Lion Queen

**Natural Habitat—Where You'll Find Him:** Producing, directing, and starring in his own independent film, swept away in a romantic escapade, running for president, sipping drinks in the V.I.P. section of a hot dance club, starting a high-powered company, planning the New World Order behind his computer, teaching himself how to speak Russian or a foreign language, playing Dungeons & Dragons, at a comic book convention, spending his last five dollars on cookies, eating dessert, in the front seat of a death-defying roller coaster, in the ivory tower of a university; at a lecture, poetry reading, or spiritual workshop; holding court as the host of his own blowout birthday bash, on his way to an audition, at band practice, scribbling song lyrics in a worn Moleskine notebook, reading classic literature, getting his chest and back waxed at a spa, getting a mani-pedi and massage, singing karaoke tunes on top of a bar

**What He Does for a Living:** movie star, world leader, bodyguard, lawyer, language specialist, coach or trainer, lead singer, performing artist, education director, department manager, filmmaker, director, dancer, politician, advocate, stuntman, bodybuilder, pro wrestler

**Noteworthy & Notorious Leo Men:** Ben Affleck, Matt LeBlanc, Daniel Radcliffe, Matthew Perry, Arnold Schwarzenegger, Robert Redford, Andy Warhol, Fred Durst, J.C. Chasez, Tom Green,

Scott Stapp, Ed Norton, Robert De Niro, Kevin Spacey, The Edge, Ashley Parker Angel, Billy Bob Thornton, Kevin Smith, Antonio Banderas, Wesley Snipes, Pete Sampras, Sir Mix-A-Lot, Omar Epps, Bill Clinton, Barack Obama, Chuck D, Fat Joe, Mick Jagger, James Cameron, Steve Carell

# Leo: How to Spot Him

- Intense eyes with a piercing gaze
- Small catlike nose, or a prominent nose that makes him look tough and sexy
- Resembles a lion or a cat

- Powerful body with sinewy limbs
- Distinctive hair—either thick and full or early baldness
- Wearing 007-style sunglasses at dusk

- Being the opposite of everyone else: the only quiet guy in a noisy room or the loudmouth breaking the silence
- Chest thrust out proudly

- Being the teacher's pet or eager follower of anyone he admires
- Flamboyant clothes—somebody was buying those fugly patterned shirts from Chess King. Mystery solved!

- Surrounded by a gaggle of women who just might be strippers, escorts, or a bunch of his ex-girlfriends
- Oversized coats and hats—the king needs his cape and crown
- Reading Tolstoy or an historical biography, with a furrowed brow
- Dancing flamboyantly and gracefully in tight clothes—rumba, cha-cha, merengue (think: Leo Patrick Swayze)

# Leo: How He Deals With...

### Money

Selectively cheap, impulsively extravagant. Money flies out of his hands quickly, especially on entertainment. Loves spoiling himself and you.

### Family

Loyal and close to his clan; very protective and affectionate. Often his parents' favorite.

### Love

A complete romantic idealist, in love with being in love. Wants to create a legendary love story together that will inspire envy and awe.

### Sex

Cat scratch fever! Hot jungle loving that might leave claw marks on your back. Meow!

### Children

The more, the merrier—can't wait to leave a legacy behind. An affectionate, playful dad who can also be strict and demanding.

### Pets

A total animal lover. Loves playing master to a hyperactive beast. Has a special fondness for cats and affectionate dogs who can be his sidekicks.

### Your Meltdowns

Pale in comparison to his. Defends himself ferociously if you attack his pride, ego, or honor. Otherwise, takes them in stride.

### His Meltdowns

Hello, drama queen. When the Lion roars, run! May go out and start a bar brawl or shouting match to release his anger. Stalks around in haughty, prideful silence.

### Breakups

Devastating events that inspire poetry, song lyrics, and brokenhearted mooning at the bar. While scribbling in his journal, he attracts the attention of the beautiful girl beside him. He pours his heart out and a week later, they're dating.

# Leo: What He's All About

The Leo man has a way of commanding attention, even without trying. Just walk into a room and see where your eyes fall first. The Leo man is the loudest, most animated person—laughing boisterously, brandishing a beer as he makes obnoxious jokes, starting a fight when someone challenges his supremacy. Or, he's a regal, quiet hottie smoldering on the sidelines, brooding and pouting until you notice him. Either way, he's impossible to ignore.

Leo is ruled by the Sun, the center of our solar system. Is it any wonder his sign has a reputation as being egotistical or self-centered? Like planets in orbit, everything revolves around this guy. In worst-case scenarios, he's a pompous narcissist driven by his own hedonistic desires. At best, he's a playful cub with boundless energy who needs constant action, attention, and entertainment.

Leo's zodiac symbol is the majestic Lion. King of the jungle he is—and he knows it. Whatever Leo does, he must rule at, or else he quickly loses interest. He plays to win, and he's not shy about bragging when he does, even if it makes him look arrogant. When he was awarded an Oscar for *Titanic,* Leo director James Cameron proclaimed, "I am the king of the world!"

The Leo man has so much in common with his iconic animal, that we turned to the wildlife experts to help you understand him better. Here's how the pros help us explain your Leo:

## Wilderness Behavior # 1

**Social groups of lions, called prides, are composed of one to three males, two to fifteen females, and their offspring.** (*Animal Planet*)

Wait a second, is there a celebrity here? Why are all those women gathered around that guy? It's just Leo, holding court with all his female friends. Most have either slept with him or hope to at some point, but there's no need to get vicious. He's got plenty for everyone.

With his high sex drive, monogamy is not a natural state for the Leo man, though he's capable of it as long as you've got the libido of three women. If anything, he tends to be a serial monogamist, never without a warm body by his side for long.

## Wilderness Behavior # 2

**When males are forced to leave the pride that they were born into, they form small bachelor groups and roam.**

The Leo man is pack leader among his male friends, too. As much as he adores women, he needs a roving band of brothers: his drinking buddies, Dungeons & Dragons posse, or Sunday football crew. With his backslapping bravado and infectious laugh, he makes every guy feel like "the man." After cowriting *Good Will Hunting*, Leo Ben Affleck and his Libra buddy Matt Damon became such a tight unit, they inspired tabloids to coin the term "bromosexual" to describe their brotherly lovin' bond.

### Wilderness Behavior # 3:

**Lions live in a matriarchal society. The lionesses work together to hunt and rear the cubs.** (San Diego Zoo)

There's no need to dumb down or dim your own lights with Leo. The Leo man is well aware of your power, and he embraces it. He's more than happy for you to play Supermom; in fact, he expects you to have a stellar career and be an amazing mother. There's nothing he loves more than a strong woman who can handle it all.

### Wilderness Behavior # 4:

**The males protect the territory and get to eat first; the lionesses do most of the hunting. While they do eat more than the lionesses and bring in far less food (they hunt less than 10 percent of the time), males patrol, mark, and guard the pride's territory.** (*National Geographic,* San Diego Zoo)

Yes, he's still king of the castle, even if you make twice as much money as he does. As self-appointed head of his household, the Leo man is incredibly protective and will destroy anyone who messes with his clan. He tends to have a strong sense of entitlement, which occasionally will make you want to kick his ass. He's prone to overindulgence, too—on food, alcohol, cigarettes, and other hedonistic pleasures. Leo Sean Penn smoked four packs of cigarettes a day before he quit at age forty.

### Wilderness Behavior # 5:

**Lions usually hunt at night and spend almost twenty hours a day sleeping or lounging with their playful cubs.**

The Leo man is an excellent, hands-on dad who loves to get down on the floor with the baby, and takes great pride in raising his children every step of the way. He has nonstop energy for playtime. The Leo man is far from lazy in most cases, but he can certainly do things at a languid pace, according to his own time line. This leisurely, catlike way is part of his charm. Most Leo men are nocturnal. Leo Barack Obama wrote his biography at night while his family slept. He likes to build his empire after dark.

## Wilderness Behavior # 6:

**They generally stalk and chase their prey, killing with a bite to the neck—although they can also kill with a single back-breaking swat of the paw.**

Ferocious Leo has a fighting spirit like no other sign. He's always ready to take down an enemy, whether with a verbal assault, his fists, or simply by proving his doubters wrong. The Leo man pursues his goals with the same warrior spirit and unflappable confidence of a jungle king. Leo Arnold Schwarzenegger was once an unknown Austrian bodybuilder who was mocked when he said he wanted to be an actor. According to childhood friends, "Ahhnold" often said his goals were to move to America, become an actor, and marry a Kennedy. He accomplished all three, and even became California's governor. Leo Andy Warhol's pop art was ridiculed, but he became an international icon with museums devoted to his work. Even Robert De Niro supposedly walked out of a movie theater at age seventeen and announced to bewildered friends that he was going to be an actor. When Leo sets his sights on a goal, he gets it.

## Wilderness Behavior # 7:

**A male's loud roar, usually heard after sunset, can carry for as far as five miles (eight kilometers). The roar warns off intruders and helps round up stray members of the pride.** *(National Geographic)*

The Leo man is incredibly vocal about his beliefs and values. Being a natural leader himself, he often gets involved in politics—or at least is up on current events. The Leo man is highly critical of leaders he doesn't like, and intensely supportive of candidates in whom he believes. Everything has to be a grand declaration for Leo: his favorite sports teams, bands, authors, and historical figures.

Like a cat with nine lives, the Leo man recovers from every setback with an impressive resilience. He dives headfirst into everything he does. If he can't do it passionately, why do it at all? While he may be underestimated, it only makes him more determined to show you what he's all about. The Leo man never really gives up. Don't be surprised if you look up one day and see his face or his company splashed across a billboard. What do you know? He did it. He made his dreams come true after all.

# What He Wants in a Woman

In the wild, it's all about survival of the fittest. The Leo man has his own version of natural selection in the game of love. In Leo's romantic Darwinism, he explores every possible mating option until he finds the best in breed. Along the way, he might earn a reputation as a womanizer, a lady-killer, a heartbreaker. *C'est la vie.* Leo refuses to settle. Once he finds his match, he begins the pair-bonding process, making her part of his family, creating a little love den just for two.

Lions live in matriarchal societies, and the lioness is in charge of hunting. You need to be strong, enduring, and fierce to be Leo's lady—quietly powerful so as not to upstage him, but a serious contender no less. Can you capture an antelope and drag it back to the lair? Are you available to mate and produce a litter of superior cubs? If so, he'll want to form a mutual admiration society. "He makes me feel like a smart, capable, adored, well-liked person," says one woman of her Leo husband. That's the gift a Leo man gives his woman when he anoints you his queen. You'll feel like the crown jewel… in his crown, that is.

Loyalty is one of the most important traits you'll need to keep him around. The Leo man has no tolerance for flakiness in his woman. Just because he roams the grasslands, doesn't mean you shouldn't be waiting at home when he arrives. Sure, he respects female power and autonomy. He just wants to come home to your open arms, to find you eagerly awaiting him and ready to play. He marries his best friend and ultimate confidante, someone powerful and successful whom he can brag about.

It's okay if you're a little bossy, as long as it's adoring and affectionate. And feel free to take charge of a few responsibilities, like shopping or budgeting. The king can't always be bothered with such menial tasks—and his spending can get out of control at times. "We have the same bank account and I am in charge of the money," says Lynn, a Sagittarius married to a Leo man. "He is a hedonist to a fault. Only when we are close to running out does he really pay attention to where his money goes."

The Leo man is ruled by his heart and his passion. He needs affection and touch, laughter and play. He wants to spoil and be spoiled, to have an eager recipient for his effusive romantic gestures. Simone, an Aries, recalls an elaborate surprise her Leo husband set up for their first Valentine's Day. "He told me we were going to the beach," says Simone. "It was 9:00 A.M. and he was rushing me. I was like, What is your problem? No one's at the beach this early. We get in the car, he blindfolds me and tells me we aren't going to the beach. We end up at a place where I hear nice jazz playing. Turns out I was in a spa and I got a full day of pampering—massage, facial, pedicure, manicure. I was crying when they took the blindfold off. By far one of my favorite memories!"

When a Leo man is in love with you, nothing stands in his way of letting you know. Money is no object when he gets the urge to be extravagant. Says Lynn, "I yelled at him the first Valentine's Day we were married because he had a $99 bouquet of roses— with the vase—delivered to the house. At the time he was making $725 a month in salary."

The Leo man demands a lot of energy, and he needs plenty of outlets for his passion. Stock the pantry with energy drinks, because you're going to need a serious attention span. When the Leo man gets started, he can keep going and going. While he can command the attention of a stadium or hold court with a crowd, he can be exhausting one-on-one. Encourage him to develop his hobbies and hang out with his buddies. Otherwise, he can be suffocating and draining—a full-time job you'll quickly regret taking on.

Leo loves to get engrossed in fascinating conversations with you (which he can monopolize unless you gently remind him that he's been talking nonstop for ten solid minutes). He can cover almost any subject, from politics to music to gossipy girl talk. He needs a high-intensity mate who hates good-byes and good nights as much as he does. The Leo man loves to stay up until dawn and see his ruler, the Sun, break over the horizon. If you hang out all night talking, he knows you're the One.

Believe it or not, the Leo man has a shy side, too. He can suffer from social anxiety and stifling self-consciousness (a symptom of being self-centered, but don't tell him that). Although he may act cocky or arrogant, he cares deeply what others think of him. He wanted to be liked and admired.

Your companionship helps him feel safer opening up—at least he knows there's a beacon of light he can always return to, even if others don't accept him with open arms.

Still, you'll need to regulate his needy side if you want to keep the flames burning. It can be hard to say "no" to Leo or shoo him away, but it's for the best. You don't want him hiding behind your skirt like a timid little cub. Pump him up and keep him feeling confident. Reassure him as much as you can, but don't let him smother you with his love.

# What He Wants from a Relationship

You know those staged pictures of adoring couples gazing tenderly into each other's eyes, holding each other with enviable affection? It's usually the manufacturer's photo that comes tucked into a picture frame—the one you remove and replace with your real picture. Well, Leo wants that "Kodak moment" kind of love. He wants conventional romance with all the trimmings.

When he's in love, Leo wants to celebrate your relationship. He's more likely to remember your anniversary than you are—and to shower you with all the Hallmark trappings. We're talking a dozen red roses right out of the florist's cooler, with stiff sprays of baby's breath tucked among the blossoms. Maybe a teddy bear clutching a balloon, a 14-karat gold necklace, or his favorite book of poetry. Some expensive jeans you've been coveting, or some sexy lingerie. Cheesy and sentimental is the Leo way—but somehow, it goes along with his effusive personality.

Like two lions forming a pride, the Leo man easily forms a unit with his woman. He loves if you command the spotlight together; in fact, he'll gladly court the paparazzi with you on his arm. Who could forget the legendary Leo-Leo coupling of J.Lo and Ben Affleck, otherwise known as "Bennifer"? During his presidential campaign, Leo Bill Clinton had Hillary so involved, the press started calling them "Billary." A headline is a headline, and he's glad to share ink with his devoted other half. (Of course, Bubba also shared ink with a fellow lion, Leo Monica Lewinsky. Two cats have a way of sniffing each other out!)

Of course, if that other half should outshine him or make him look foolish (remember the Bennifer box-office bomb *Jersey Girl* that began their downfall?), it's curtains for this royal production. A Leo man has to get burned pretty badly not to touch the hot stove again. After his fling with bling, Ben Affleck went back to his Leo roots: cheering on the Red Sox and his favorite political candidates, bumming around with Jennifer Garner in sweats, family bonding, and hanging with his loyal cronies.

Ultimately, the Leo man just wants an easygoing, fun relationship with a best friend who cleans up nicely. Like a lion lazing in the sun, he also wants his relationship to be a safe, comfortable space where he can kick back and let his hair down. He puts so much energy out in the world, he just needs a restorative sanctuary to recharge his batteries. The resting lion needs to be at peace, not nagged about how long he's been playing video games, how loud his music is, or when he's going to pay back his student loans.

Pride is a perfect term for the lion's family, because the Leo man takes plenty of pride in his. He wants to create a legacy, build an empire, to guide and teach his children and pass on wisdom to the next generation. If you've ever watched a male lion perched on a rock surveying his kingdom, that's Leo. He longs to sit at the top of the mountain with you, looking at the homes, cars, children, and years you've logged, to pull you close and whisper with awe, "Look what we've built together."

He wants to inspire others' admiration, too. The Leo man needs to be looked up to as a role model. His standards can be way too high, but try to tell him that—it will fall on deaf ears. Nothing is impossible in Leo's imagination. Even if he's got a new woman every week, it doesn't stop him from issuing a press release and parading you around town, introducing you as his girlfriend. He's a serial monogamist to the nth degree.

There are so many adventures waiting, and life with Leo will be full of them. Whether you travel the four corners of the Earth, or simply create a fascinating life in your domestic bubble for two, he's always bringing something new. "We started eating raw foods together, and we buy organic groceries," says Carol of her

Leo boyfriend. "We spend a lot of time cooking, and it's so much fun. He loves to do everything together."

Exploring the world is so much more satisfying to Leo with a fun, nurturing playmate by his side. Give him a wide-open playground for his hobbies, his ever-changing passions and interests, his romantic idealism. Cheer him on and let him champion you. Let your togetherness blossom into a romantic legacy, a love story that resounds through the ages, the kind your children will tell their children.

## Sex with a Leo

Sex is a grand performance for Leo, and he takes great pride in his prowess. The Leo man loves to set the stage for his regal romps, and may even design his bedroom like an elaborate movie set. One Leo man we know has a disco ball, black lights, and mirrored walls in his boudoir—plus a state-of-the-art sound system, since music gets him in the mood. (Every great performance needs a soundtrack.) Another Leo fashioned his room into a Moroccan-style harem tent, with burnt-orange walls, silk pillows all over the floor, and sensual fabric draped around the mattress. (Still, he'll take you in unfurnished quarters, too—anywhere, really.)

Leo is as playful in bed as anywhere else. He wants to roll around like two mating lions on the savannah, pawing and clawing at each other, tugging at your hair, biting and scratching. The only lube you'll need is ointment for the claw marks he leaves on your back. He'll throw in a few acrobatic stunts for flair, then lift you up and carry you into every room of the house. Stretch out beforehand—you'll need to be limber!

While Leo sweeps you away in passionate, romantic affection, he's still the star of this production. This is the guy who will take you from behind in front of the vanity, if only to admire his own sinewy body moving in time with yours. Or, you notice a tiny red light when you roll on your back: Leo has turned on the camcorder. (Fortunately, it's pointed at him.) Mirrors on the ceiling? Check. An element of risk is a turn-on for thrill-seeking Leo. He loves a hint of exhibitionism, and if he gets caught mid-act, so what? It just makes him feel like more of a stud.

In some cases, Leo can be a fat cat who's so focused on his own needs, you start to feel like a stage prop. "He was a little too impressed with his sexual performance," recalls Jessica of her Leo ex-boyfriend. "Yet, it was all for him. When he was done, that was it—whether I was satisfied or not." Don't give him any electronic competition, either. "God forbid I suggested using sex toys," adds Jessica. "He took it personally—like, 'Why would you need those? You have me.'"

Remember, Leo can have his choice of women, so he wants the pick of the litter. You can never "let yourself go" with this guy. To keep his attraction, you have to keep making an effort, even if he doesn't. You wouldn't walk the red carpet without full hair and makeup, would you? So if he rolls out his for you, he expects a proper presentation. Don't skimp on the bells and whistles. Every night has to be the Fourth of July with Leo. How better to celebrate than by setting off some passionate fireworks together?

# Leo: Turn-Ons & Turn-Offs
## Turn Him On

- Rub his head, run your fingers through his hair
- Spoil and pamper him with beauty treatments, spas, grooming
- Share an indulgent meal
- Dress in glamorous, sexy, risqué outfits
- Massage him (Leo rules the back)
- Cook elaborate feasts for him

- Sugar mama him a little—he likes to be treated as much as he likes to treat you
- Boss him around (playfully only)
- Challenge him to games—laser tag, anyone?
- Be intelligent and ambitious
- Be loyal and family-oriented
- Listen to the sound of his voice
- Mirror his greatness
- Go on "playdates": bowling, rollerskating, karaoke, sledding…
- Give him his daily dose of sex

## Turn Him Off

- Neglect your appearance
- Dress in frumpy, figure-hiding styles
- Embarrass him in public
- Compete with him and win too many times, making him look bad
- Act like an airhead
- Be overly submissive
- Be behind the times, especially when it comes to politics
- Be dull or old-fashioned
- Have no interest in the arts or current events
- Be overly practical or unsentimental
- Have a low sex drive
- Be a homebody or shut-in
- Have no sense of family
- Be too over-the-top or crazy (in a way that requires too much attention)
- Upstage him

- Laugh at his poetic sentiment or patriotism
- Be jaded and cynical
- Refuse to believe that dreams come true
- Rain on his parade
- Make fun of his action figures, comic book collection, Harry Potter merchandise, and other boyhood carryovers

# His Moves

## First Moves: How He Courts You

Lights, camera, action! The Leo man views life as a theatrical production, in which he naturally stars as the brooding empath, the tragic lover, the lone hero. There's a good chance Leo has seen every movie in his favorite genre, too—be it film noir, Turner classics, or 1980s teen dramas like *Say Anything*. A new love interest is just another chance for him to live vicariously as John Cusack or Humphrey Bogart, to act out his fantasies on life's big stage.

Leo loves the art of courtship; you could even say it's a hobby for him. The Lion is a predatory animal, so hunting is his game. It connects him to his prowess.

Just because a Leo woos you with three dozen roses, a case of champagne, and his own poetry doesn't mean he hasn't done this all before. You'll have to wait and see whether he's feeding his ego or genuinely wants you for his queen. Here are some of the male Lion's typical hunting behaviors:

- He sends you poetry, long emails about his feelings, or a favorite book passage
- He says it with flowers—enough to fill a small cottage
- He serenades you in the middle of the street
- He takes out an ad in the paper praising your beauty and talent
- He becomes your best friend

- He becomes part of your social activities and circles
- He insists that you remind him of his favorite movie star, and even starts calling you by her name
- He gushes about how amazing you are to anyone who will listen
- He starts a bar fight with another guy over you
- He parades you in front of all his friends
- He outright propositions you or sweeps you into a passionate kiss
- He asks you to dance
- He sends you concert tickets or a formal invitation to a black-tie event

## He's In: How You Know He's Committed

Here's some relieving news: You don't have to be Einstein to figure out that a Leo man is madly in love with you. Confident as he is, he's probably booked the reception hall before he even asks you on the first date. Unlike signs that keep you guessing and wondering "Does he like me?" the Leo man will never make you wait by a silent phone. He'd rather pick you up in his drop-top convertible, the wind blowing through his mane. When he's sure he wants you for his Lion Queen, here are some of his common mating calls:

**He says it with skywriting.** When the Leo man is in love, he wants to shout it from the rooftops, and make sure the world pays attention. Our Leo friend Ming proposed to his wife by having "Will you marry me, Debbie?" spelled out on a drive-in movie billboard. (And the Oscar for best marriage proposal goes to… Ming!)

**He's around you constantly.** Is the heat on in here? No, that's just Leo breathing down your neck again. Be careful what you wish for when you complain to your girlfriends, "Why can't I find a guy who wants to spend time together—is that so much to ask?" Constant companionship is still barely enough attention for the Leo man. Except, of course, when he's male bonding with his buddies. But since they usually do everything together, his best friend will probably start dating your best friend, and you'll soon be one big happy family.

**He gets all possessive and jealous.** When the Leo man claims you as his woman, that's it. Sure, his friends can tell him how hot you are (within limits), but if an obvious player type so much as glances in your direction, Leo will knock him out cold. Your life will turn into *West Side Story*, with turf wars and street fights staged in your so-called honor. Quick, get out before the cops come!

**He gets all "his-and-hers" on you.** "Oh honey, I'm so excited we're going to the amusement park today. And guess what I got us? Matching sweatshirts with our last name embroidered on them. I even got some for the kids! Isn't that awesome?" Or, "Close your eyes and follow me. I got you a very special surprise. Yup, it's a matching BMW—exactly like mine, except it's gold with hot pink interiors. Your favorite colors. Happy birthday, sweetheart!"

**He talks and brags about you to anyone who will listen.** When you're not around, the Leo man acts as your press representative, glowing with pride at all your achievements, boasting about what a wonderful mother you are or your latest work promotion. Leo Antonio Banderas says, "I admired [my wife Melanie Griffith] before I loved her." Of course, it only helps his image and inspires jealousy from other men when they hear that he's got such a great catch. But he's also genuinely proud.

# Unfaithful Leo: Why He Cheats

The Leo man takes great pride in his relationships, especially when they reflect positively on him. He makes chest-beating declarations of loyalty, sneers at other men who cave to their carnal weakness and stray. Then… his own animal nature gets the best of him. He's a demanding partner whose ego can be fragile, and when he's feeling down on himself, watch out. The Leo man is entirely capable of jeopardizing a long-term relationship with infidelity.

If he does cheat, the Leo man is careless and usually gets caught. He might even leave his diary or other incriminating evidence lying around in plain view. Jerry Hall remembers Leo Mick Jagger leaving other women's earrings and clothes in the bedroom from his extramarital trysts (yes, he cheated on his wife in their bed!). Is he trying to teach you a lesson? Either that or he's given in to his selfish side. Here's why Leo might play pet-the-kitty with another woman:

**Ego recovery.** He's defeated, humiliated, crushed by life. Oh, the drama! When the King of the Jungle feels like the Court Jester, he'll do anything—anything—to win back his throne. An affair can be the triage that stops his wounds.

**He's an attention whore.** The Leo man needs your admiration, praise, and focus like the rest of us need air. Red alert if he feels neglected, you've been away too long, or something else becomes your main concentration. He usually fires a warning shot: making a fuss, teaching you a small lesson, acting out in a way that snaps your attention back. But if the Lion's roars fall on deaf ears, well, perhaps another cat is listening. It's a jungle out there.

**You're an ice queen.** The Leo man needs affection, warmth, and tenderness, all wrapped in a beautiful package. If you're too cold or reserved, he might look for heat somewhere else. He doesn't mind if you're bossy—in fact, he welcomes it, as long as it's delivered in a loving, nurturing tone instead of a way that makes him look like a chump.

**Stupidity.** Limits? What are those? The Leo man doesn't know when to say "when." He may cross the cheating line every now and then as a result. After carousing about town with the fellas, having one too many beers and a little too much fun, he gets pumped full of drunken bravado and reverts to his bachelor ways. Before he knows it he's patting the barmaid's ass and roaring with laughter when she slaps him. Then he sidles up to the nearest female and slurs something about taking her home. Oh yeah, he can't, because you're there.

**He's hurt.** He wore his heart on his sleeve and you took advantage of it. A passive-aggressive affair will put you in your place.

## Dig the Grave: It's Over

Leo's loyalty is a gift he bestows on you, but make no mistake: He can always find someone else. The Leo man knows this instinctively, like the Sun knows it will rise every morning. The Leo man has a way of creating a legend around himself, a fan base that never stops growing. Even the most heinous, creepy Leo man always seems to have a few women waiting in the wings (how else to explain Leo Andy Warhol?). He always has a backlist of babes from his bachelor days, too. Here are some signs he might be looking for a new leading lady:

**Your lives no longer intersect.** If a Leo loves you, he wants to be around you as often as possible. If you work the night shift and he's on a 9-to-5 schedule, he's not going to get the affection and bonding time he needs. Ultimatum time! Change your lifestyle or he'll be changing partners.

**You shut down the amusement park.** The playful Leo can't stand when things get too serious. He needs a playmate. If you've become all stern and no-nonsense, rebuffing his flirtatious advances or romantic gestures, his spirits will be crushed. If every date doesn't feel a little like the first one, what's the point of calling this love? Might as well just be friends.

**You don't put out enough.** What, is four times a day so much to ask?

**He feels "emasculated."** It's a fine line between playfully bossing Leo around (which he likes) and putting him down (never disrespect the king!). If you no longer admire him, it cuts him right to the heart and he may not recover.

**He starts talking about a female "friend" or hanging out with her a little too often.** He's opened his casting couch for auditions, and the understudy is making a play for your role.

**You embarrassed him in public.** Play Leo for a chump in the public eye, and he'll quickly end the game. Make an ugly scene, yell at him, tarnish his reputation—he'll have none of that. If he becomes a laughingstock through his association with you, forget it. He's got a rep to protect.

**You've embarrassed yourself in public.** You're Leo's other half, and he's not going to walk around with a fool representing him. If you neglect your appearance, dress shabbily, act in poor taste, or do anything to taint your (and his) royal status, he'll oust you from the adjacent throne.

**Oops! He got another woman pregnant.** We've just heard this too many times not to mention it.

# Interpreting His Signals:

## What does he mean by that?

| When he | It means... | So you should... |
|---|---|---|
| Gets quiet | He's brooding. You've either insulted his pride or you're not paying enough attention to him. | Stroke him: his hair, his body, his ego. |
| Doesn't call | He's consumed with his life or whatever he's doing. What else is new? | Call him. He'll love the attention. |
| Calls a lot | He enjoys talking to you, thinks you're interesting, but it doesn't mean he likes you as more than a friend. | Hang out and get to know him better. |
| Doesn't make a move after a couple of dates | He's taking it slow, getting to know you as a friend. | Pump up the flirting and give him a clear signal that you're attracted. He might not be sure if you like him. |
| Doesn't make a move after a few weeks | He's either moving really slowly (Leo can) or he's sleeping with someone else. If he's not courting, flirting, or moving in a romantic direction at all, he either thinks you're not interested, or he sees you purely as a friend. | Go out for dinner and ask him playfully, "Have you ever thought of me romantically?" You'll get your answer. |

| When he | It means... | So you should... |
|---|---|---|
| Moves fast | He's infatuated or horny. | Pace him, unless you want to end up a pawn in his romantic saga. |
| Picks up the tab, gives flowers and gifts | He likes you, he really likes you. | Gush, swoon, and act as grateful as possible. Just don't assume you've got him wrapped up yet. He might be doing this with someone else, too. |
| Introduces you to his family and/or closest friends | Nothing—he introduces everyone to them. | Do your best to fit in—he wants a family-oriented type. Don't start picking out china patterns just yet, though. |

# Your Moves: Tips for Flirting and Everlasting Love

## Flirting with a Leo

It doesn't take much to strike up a flirtation with Leo. Just talk to him. Every conversation with Leo is a playful interaction, a game of verbal cat and mouse. It doesn't matter if it's appropriate or not; the Leo man could make filing income taxes feel like you've done something dirty and forbidden. Flirtation is sexual energy—life force energy—and that's the only fuel passionate Leo keeps in his tank. Dive right in!

**Hunt him.** Come on as strong as you want. The Leo man's not afraid of your feminine wiles and obvious advances. He's king of the jungle, so the wilder you are, the better.

**Pay attention to him.** Aim your adoring gaze his way and he'll soak it right up.

**Let him hang out with you and your friends.** The Leo man needs to feel like a VIP. If you let him into your inner circle, he knows he's in a privileged seat.

**Crack a raunchy joke.** Lusty Leo always has sex on his brain, so if you've got the mouth of a sailor, he'll only roar with appreciative laughter. Note: Don't dish this out unless you can handle his even cruder comebacks.

**Reveal your wild sexual experiences.** The Leo man loves to be privy to the kind of dishy "girl talk" featured on *Sex and the City*. Talk about your threesomes, outdoor trysts, the time you got fined for indecent exposure when you were knocking boots in the backseat of a car.

**Look him right in the eye.** Direct eye contact signals power and confidence, two big aphrodisiacs for Leo. He doesn't want to be with a woman who's intimidated by him. Match his gaze.

## Everlasting Love with a Leo

He may scoff or snarl at the idea, but don't be fooled: The Leo man believes in fairy-tale love and happily ever after. Loyal and honorable as he strives to be, the Leo man needs a noble purpose to serve, a love story that lives up to the legend in his mind. He wants to add branches to the family tree and make some cubs together. So if you're going to earn the privilege of sitting on the throne beside him, here's how to win yourself the crown:

**Be his best friend.** You're going to be spending all your time together, so you'd better love each other with the loyalty and affection of true, lifelong friends.

**Be his sounding board.** Listen to his dreams, read his short stories, watch him onstage and give him helpful feedback (only when solicited, and make sure 98 percent of it is positive). The Leo man needs to be with a wise woman who readily offers him a patient soul, a listening ear, and sound advice.

**Help him build his empire.** The Leo man usually has a grand life vision. Starting a family, running for political office, becoming CEO of a multinational conglomerate—it's usually a long shot from his starting point. With faith and a good woman, Leo knows that no dream is impossible.

**Make him fall in love with you over and over again.** The Leo man wants to feel like he's in a permanent state of courtship, even as the years progress. Keep it romantic—comfortable but never stale.

**Stand by him through trying times.** The Leo man's life is filled with dramatic moments that may require extreme endurance to get through: recovery from addiction, a public scandal, a major career transition. Can you tough out these trials and stand by his side as his loving, supportive champion?

# Prep Yourself For...

## Your First Date

Dating is pure fun for romantic Leo, a sign that thinks everything is better with company. Your first date is a good excuse to check out a movie or a concert with an attractive playmate. Leo might keep things casual and friendly at first. He usually has a lot of female friends, all harboring various degrees of crushes on him. He can't rush into narrowing down his options unless he's sure you're the best he can get.

The Leo man loves to make everything into a big event, but the five-star dates come later in the game, when he's certain you're the One. Of course, if he gets swept up in a romantic mood—or if your date happens to fall on Valentine's Day, Sweetest Day, or any other commercial holiday—he could show up with chocolates, carnations, and a teddy bear in tow.

**The Basic Vibe:** Activity dates are the Leo man's favorite kind. He wants fun and blockbuster entertainment, and he prefers to make plans in advance. Your date might involve tickets to something, like a concert, movie, or baseball game. (Confidently, he's already bought two in advance. If you said no, surely someone else would take your seat.) He loves any sort of "den" where he can kick back, be it a sexy lounge, a symphony hall, or a sports bar. Or, he might just take you dancing (salsa, flamenco, ballroom—whatever he's best at). He never outgrows those high school–era dating hotspots either—the bowling alley, karaoke lounges, or the video arcade. And why should he? They're fun and relaxing, a great place to let your hair down. You could fall in love sipping Budweiser at the billiard hall, throwing darts, or leaning sexily over your pool cue to line up a shot.

**What to Wear:** With a Leo man, it's always better to err on the side of overdressed. Dazzle him with your feminine glamour, but more importantly, flaunt your wildness and raw sexuality. Vamp it up and get creative. Don't be afraid of cleavage, heels, and bright colors, or big hair worn long and loose. Competitive Leo wants to inspire envy among other men, so be a hot head-turner. Throw on a little sparkle, faux fur, or velvet; wear your low-rise jeans and fake lashes. The Leo man's definition of "too much" is pretty broad. As long as you don't look like a member of the Gotti family or a fugitive from the Barbie Dream House (and maybe even if you do), he'll be into it.

**What Not to Wear:** Forget about that whole nice-girl code of conduct, that tongue-clucking spinster in your head that stops you cold at your closet door: "You can't wear that! You don't want him to get the wrong idea, do you?" Of course you do. If your style and attitude aren't memorable, you won't be either. Save those boring, plain, and unstylish pieces for the office—with Leo, you don't want to fade into the crowd. Victorian looks like high necks, ruffles, and long skirts will make him gag. Ditto for tunics, flowy shirts and Empire waists that hide your figure. Forget about covering up with pashminas or wraps—if you get chilly, he wants you snuggling up to him. So show some skin and get your heat from Leo; it won't be hard to generate.

**To Pay, or Not to Pay?** Prepare for anything, because the Leo man has issues with money. Either he squirrels it all away with unnecessary tightfistedness, or he blows it all on luxuries like NBA season tickets, CDs, computer gadgets, and organic groceries. The line between luxury and necessity is blurry for Leo. When he gets engrossed in conversation, the Leo man loses track of his limits. He might order round after round of drinks and appetizers, then when the check arrives, he'll reach into his pocket and realize, *Oops! I'm fifty dollars short.* Bring money along just in case.

**Saying Good night:** If the date goes well, he'll want to leave you with something to remember him. How about a passionate kiss… even a hickey? Don't expect this energetic sign to be gentle. When he's hot, the Leo man barely realizes his own strength. He could pounce on you like a lion tearing hungrily into a wildebeest. Down boy!

## His First Home Visit

There's nothing a Leo man loves more than lounging in a comfy, sensual, well-appointed lair. Style and home décor are important to many Leos—we know some Leo men who could put their fellow Lioness Martha Stewart to shame. To be fair, we've met plenty who are complete slobs and barely notice anything beyond their remote-controlled recliners (thrones for a civilian with Leo's royal heritage). If he's put a lot of energy into his home, he'll prefer to spend more time there. But if he's couch-surfing or temporarily crashing with his parents, you might gain an instant new roommate. Hope he's got enough left over for rent!

**Fill your lair with exciting toys.** Restless Leo needs something to tinker with; he might be the only man of the zodiac who can multitask. Leave out musical instruments, cameras, board games, a computer—if only to give yourself a break from having to pay nonstop attention to him. If all else fails, hang a full-length mirror. In high school, Ophira dated a Leo bike racer who used to pedal over in Spandex and shamelessly admire his calf muscles.

**Set up DVD player and surround sound.** Music and movies are always Leo passions. He wants to play you his demo, plug in his karaoke machine or iPod, show you a film he edited, introduce you to his favorite band or movie. If he's into something, it's got to be the greatest thing ever (even if he's over it next week).

**Trick out the love den.** If your bedroom looks like army barracks or a Cape Cod bed-and-breakfast, you'd best sex it up. Sensual Leo loves to feel textures, and he needs a space with lots of mood.

Go heavy on the ambience, even if you think it looks tasteless or over the top (it does—but not to him).

**Make a Costco run.** The Leo man is an indulgent snacker who can wolf down a family-size bag of Chips Ahoy in a single sitting. Stock up on beer, soda, and his favorite munchies. One woman says she and her Leo boyfriend have hours of wild sex, then gorge on ice cream. After the hunt, the Lion wants to eat, and he doesn't want to have to go out foraging in the wilderness for some damn Doritos.

**Throw a party.** The Leo man is a consummate entertainer, so you might as well push the furniture back and cohost salsa dancing or movie night for fifty of your closest friends. It could turn into an innocent group slumber party, since Leo never outgrows childhood pastimes.

**Strawberries and whipped cream, anyone?** Food is especially erotic for Leo, so stock your fridge with a few sexy edibles. Sticky, messy, and gooey are all fine with Leo.

## Meeting His Family

Family is a huge, huge deal for Leo—his pride and joy. Devoted to his clan with all his heart, he romanticizes his boyhood and loves to reminisce. The Lion king fancies himself part of a royal dynasty; he's fascinated by his family tree and lineage. It makes him feel so important, a part of history. He should only be so lucky to be named after his father or grandfather. Should he be privileged enough to put a Jr. or a III after his name, he'll try to live up to his namesakes' legend, and will likely name his own son after himself to carry forth the tradition.

The Leo man is usually spoiled and coddled by his family, an affectionate lion cub who reveres his parents. Don't be surprised if the Leo man's mom and dad are his best friends. This is the guy who may never have had an adolescent rebellion. Why would he, when his parents are the most wonderful, amazing, and generous people on earth? He can hardly wait for you to meet them! Especially since he's told you so much about them.

When you do meet Leo's parents, make yourself at home. Call them mom and dad, and help yourself to whatever's in the fridge. Like a Lion adopting another cat into his pride, he expects you to become part of his family—to learn their rules and traditions and participate with equal vigor in family events: reunions, picnics, holiday dinners, pumpkin carvings, Easter egg hunts... *ad nauseum*. That's where he'll be, so you might as well join him.

While you might feel strangled by his uncut umbilical cord, don't dare try to snip it. Blood will always be thicker than water with Leo, a fact you could discover in the heat of an argument, like our friend Elizabeth did. "My Leo boyfriend Jason would literally pick up the phone in the middle of our fights and call his mother!" she says. "He'd be like, 'Mom, Elizabeth's being mean to me again.' It was surreal. They would end up talking for an hour while I was like, what the hell?"

In most cases, though, you'll genuinely enjoy family time with Leo. He'll make sure you're comfortable, and will defend your honor if need be. If you hope to have a family with him someday, you'll be impressed by his tender affection for his elders, or his gruff, camp-counselor style strictness with younger siblings. It's a perfect preview into the kind of family you'll create together.

# Saying Good-bye
## Breaking Up with a Leo

The sky is falling, the sky is falling! To the Leo man, being dumped is not only rare, it's the end of the world. Total devastation. He weeps, torrents of anguished tears staining his cheeks; he's so fragile it breaks your heart. Angry poetry arrives via e-mail.

Mixed CDs with bitter songs are tucked into long ranting letters and slipped into your mailbox. You. Will. Not. Forget. Him.

Leo rules the heart, and when he gives you his, it's the whole thing, alive and beating. He falls in love with every ounce he's got, with passion and vigor and devotion. He can't live without you. You're his everything. On top of that, he's romanticized you beyond reality, infused you into the plotline of his personal movie. Now he has to scrap the manuscript and start all over with a new leading lady.

Which... he does. Quickly in most cases. While you're immersed in guilt, feeling like you just destroyed the sweetest man on earth, he suddenly begins romancing someone new. She receives a slightly altered version of the mixed CD he made when you started dating him, some barely revised versions of his best love poems. You wonder if he ever really loved you, or the image of himself in love. Oh well. At least you can be friends again.

## Getting over Him: When a Leo Dumps You

The Leo man is a serial monogamist. If he ends the relationship, he's probably lined up his next girlfriend, or has a few potential candidates in the wings. Things have got to be really bad for him to voluntarily drop himself back into stone-cold bachelorhood. That or he's going into enforced isolation (the military? rehab?) for an indefinite period and can't make time for a relationship.

You might be relieved. Maybe he got on your last nerve, with his excessive behaviors and selfishness. Let someone else deal with him, you figure. Or, you'll be shocked—because he's already started dating someone else and decided to leave you for her. This selfish type of Leo can be a real jerk about the breakup, casting you in an unflattering light. Take Leos Sean Penn and Madonna, who were married from 1984–89. In spite of their highly publicized physical fights and drama, Madonna has called Penn "the love of my life." On the other hand, Penn told the press, "It was a miserable marriage… and frankly, I don't recall having a single conversation in four years of marriage. I've talked to her a couple of times since, and there's a whole person there. I just didn't know it." Translation: She stole my spotlight, and now I'm taking it back.

**Have yourself one good last cry over…**

- Losing your best friend
- The romance, poetry, and flowers
- His affection
- The loyal, loving, and tender gazes
- How well he really knew you
- How admiring he could be

**Praise the universe that you never have to deal with…**

- His wild overspending
- Catering to his ego
- His arrogance and entitlement
- His lack of any sense of limits, that put your life in jeopardy
- Being embarrassed by him in public
- His neediness and demands on your attention
- His refusal to realize that the world doesn't revolve around him

# Love Matcher:

## Can you find a common language?

| You are a(n)... | He thinks you're... | You think he's... | Common Language |
|---|---|---|---|
| Aries | Sexy, but possibly too much competition for the spotlight. | Passionate, exciting, and someone who can handle you. | Being the star, creativity, entrepreneurship, a need for one-on-one attention and praise |
| Taurus | His secretary (zzz...) | Impractical and immature. Really bad with money. | Love of luxury goods, fine dining, and music |
| Gemini | Great to talk to, but a little too independent and scattered to give him the attention he needs. | Needy and demanding, but good for fun or conversation. | Partying, socializing, political debates, long conversations |
| Cancer | A good keeper of his lair, but a little too reserved or stingy with affection, warmth, and praise. | Irresistibly sexy, but has some growing up to do. | Books, art, film, music, home, family, tradition |

| You are a(n)... | He thinks you're... | You think he's... | Common Language |
|---|---|---|---|
| Leo | The other half of his romantic fairy tale. | The king to your queen. | Romance, love, affection, over-the-top spending and gift-giving, showing off, basking in the spotlight, dressing up, courting attention |
| Virgo | A stick in the mud. | Embarrassingly expressive and too emotional. | Taking everything personally |
| Libra | A beautiful, romantic goddess, but a little bit of a diva. | Hot, sexy, but not gentle enough. | Overspending, vanity, dressing up, romance, museums, flowers, poetry, art |
| Scorpio | Sexy and respectable, even a little intimidating. | The wild man you've been waiting to ravage. | Sex, passion, intensity, loving the nightlife |

| You are a(n)... | He thinks you're... | You think he's... | Common Language |
|---|---|---|---|
| Sagittarius | His perfect playmate. | Fun, sexy, but a little dependent. Sometimes needs more attention than you're willing to give. | Fun, laughter, raunchy jokes, travel, adventure, sex, starting businesses, karaoke |
| Capricorn | A status symbol, but a little cold or reserved. | Fun and exciting—just what the doctor ordered. The bad boy who makes your life interesting. | Clubs, VIP lounges, business, formal wear, executive titles, prestige, ambition, social climbing |
| Aquarius | In possession of self-control he wishes he had. | A high, maintenance drama king who also excites you. | Politics, social issues, socializing, performing |
| Pisces | A dreamgirl worthy of his cheesy poetry. | Your hero and knight in shining armor. | Romantic fantasy, getting swept away, creating a bubble for just the two of you, family, tradition |

# The Virgo Man

Dates: August 23–September 22
Symbol: The Virgin
Ruling Planet: Mercury, the "messenger"
planet of communication and the mind
Element: Earth—grounded, traditional, stable
Quality: Mutable
Mission: Master and Commander

**Natural Habitat—Where You'll Find Him:** Cleaning and organizing, driving around for hours lost in thought, saving a damsel in distress, arguing a point, hosting a party at his home, reading a book, solving a crossword puzzle, watching CNN, engaged in an intimate one-on-one conversation, hiking or doing something outdoorsy, tending a garden or plants, at a family event, holding a baby, gossiping, analyzing a situation, worrying, working out, juicing or shopping for organic ingredients, in the kitchen, mixing up a home remedy for a sick friend, visiting elderly relatives in the hospital, on the phone, helping wherever help is needed

**What He Does for a Living:** Therapist, social worker, nutritionist, religious leader, accountant, database designer, computer programmer, horticulturist, botanist, critic, office manager, journalist, lawyer, architect, interior designer, acupuncturist, industrial designer, music producer, attorney

**Noteworthy & Notorious Virgo Men:** Ryan Phillipe, Keanu Reeves, Luke Wilson, Jack Black, Ludacris, Kobe Bryant, Marc Anthony, Michael Jackson, Macaulay Culkin, Jimmy Fallon, Adam Sandler, Chris Tucker, Sean Connery, Richard Gere, Julian Casablancas, Xzibit, Paul Walker, Mario, Nas, Liam Gallagher, David Arquette, Jonathan Taylor Thomas, Rich Cronin, Prince Harry, Mystical, Harry Connick Jr., Tony Kanal, Guy Ritchie

# Virgo: How to Spot Him

- Soulful, puppy-dog eyes
- Cute baby face—often looks younger than he is
- Nice hands with well-shaped, long fingers
- Neat, well-tailored, usually preppy or simple style
- Wearing gear from a high-end outdoor line (Patagonia)
- May wear glasses
- Moves with precision, quick on his feet
- Geometric or severe hair—crew cut, angular spikes, or perfectly smooth bald head (he may even cut his own hair!)
- Often well built and fit, especially in the arms, chest, and pecs
- Heading to the bathroom at a pre-scheduled time, newspaper tucked under his arm
- Making or carrying a list
- Scribbling his ideas in a notebook or on scraps of paper
- Shopping for vitamins and supplements to add to his collection
- Scents and sensibility: shopping for aromatherapy kits, bath goods, soaps, hair care products, essential oils
- Taking care of animals or a garden
- Planting his own herb garden or crops
- Perfectly seasoning a steak for the grill
- Working out, especially outdoors: soccer, hiking, biking
- Tweaking or editing something for the millionth time
- On his soapbox, passionately crusading for his beliefs
- Drumming, deejaying, or mixing beats (Virgo is a very rhythmic sign)

- Performing community service
- Babysitting the neighbors' kids or pets

# Virgo: How He Deals With...

### Money

Frugal, with refined tastes. Likes to live simply and be in control of his finances, but can also splurge on a few expensive, well-chosen pieces.

### Family

Loves it, lives for it. Very connected to his ancestry. Gets along especially well with older and younger relatives. If he's estranged from his family, can be completely self-righteous and bitter, cutting off all contact.

### Love

Believes in soul mates and won't settle for less. Wants to love you slightly more than you love him so he knows he's scored a real prize.

### Sex

Loves to be the caretaker, and is a total giver in bed. Excellent technique, especially with his hands. Your pleasure is his pleasure.

### Children

Fatherhood utterly completes him as a person. May have kids with more than one woman, or become a father young.

### Pets

Sensitive to their dirt and smells, but adores animals and is great at training them. Often adopts or takes care of his friends' pets.

### Your Meltdowns

Where he shines. Holds you, listens to you for hours, coaches and counsels you. You could fall in love crying on his shoulder.

### His Meltdowns

Mostly internalized. He shuts down, bottles up, and disappears into his own little world. May engage in subversive or addictive behavior during extreme incidents.

### Breakups

Does not handle them well. Becomes bitter, outraged, and will trash you to anyone who will listen. Wants you to pay for hurting him.

# Virgo: What He's All About

If you don't make passes at men who wear glasses, you might miss out on Virgo. And you *will* be missing out. With his handsome baby face, sexy voice, and thoughtful gaze (think: Virgos Ryan Phillipe and Hugh Grant), intelligent Virgo is the guy who will truly listen to your rants, your dreams, your big ideas. He loves a woman with vision. Although he may shoot back a sharp opinion or judgment, his feedback is honest and often hits the mark. The Virgo man is one of the best listeners around.

Virgo's zodiac sign is stereotyped as a neat freak, a nerd, and an anal retentive. Indeed he can be all of these things. But don't let his minimalist décor, starched and dry-cleaned shirts arranged by color, and perfectly folded "tighty-whitey" briefs frighten you. Virgo still lives on earth, and he's far less likely to blur the lines between fantasy and reality than signs like Aquarius or Leo. If anything, Virgo is a hardcore realist, even a cynic. He might indulge in escapist hobbies, but if anything, it's because he needs a break from his constant worrying. And while he's fastidiously clean, he's also a pack rat. The Virgo man hates to waste, and doesn't like throwing anything away. He might need it someday! One Virgo we know is constantly finding stuff, repairing it, and selling it on eBay.

The Virgo man can be an intellectual or he can be a jock, but whatever he does, he strives for excellence and mastery. This is the zodiac's most detail-oriented sign, and he's all about patiently developing his technique. Remember Virgo Keanu Reeves in *The Matrix*? Many Virgo men excel at martial arts for this reason. At times, he may take things way too seriously, or go too far striving for perfection. Virgo Michael Jackson, with his plastic surgery addiction and mask-wearing kids, is an example of what happens when this sign's neurotic tendencies go too far.

A couple months ago, we visited our longtime friend Bill, an archetypical Virgo. Bill and his Scorpio wife Zora live in a beautiful Chelsea loft, which Bill purchased for peanuts in 1977, when New York was pronounced a hopeless war zone. Gifted with Virgo foresight and craftiness, Bill renovated the loft from floor to ceiling, transforming it into a gorgeous space worthy of an *Architectural Digest* spread. Decades later, they still live in this art and light-filled space, now on one of New York City's prime blocks. A couple of years ago, Bill ripped out the floors and laid new ones by hand. Detail-oriented to a fault, and a proud control freak, the Virgo man takes extreme pride in what he builds.

That particular evening, Bill had just returned from the gym (Virgos can be fastidious about health and fitness). He served himself a bowl of pasta and joined us in the sitting area. Then, he did something very curious—and totally Virgo. Carefully selecting two sheets of the *New York Times*, he folded them precisely and placed them on the hardwood floor under his feet. Then he tucked into his spaghetti carbonara and ate it "safely," so that any stray pasta might fall on the Sports section rather than on his pristine oak planks.

Virgo is the sign of the helper, and he's at his best when serving others, making a difference, or being productive. He can't stand sitting still with nothing to do. If he's lounging, you can bet he's watching TV with a critical eye, or reading five different books. Like Gemini, Virgo is ruled by Mercury, planet of communication and the mind. He loves to analyze things, and can be rather bullheaded, even forceful, when making a point. Yes, the Virgo man can be preachy, and he keeps a soapbox handy for his anti-smoking or anti-whatever tirades. At times, he can get a bit of a God complex, and his rants will be too much to take.

He can also be hilarious. Mercury gives Virgo a quick, impish mind and linguistic gifts. Witty repartee is his specialty, and he can make the cattiest, snarkiest comments. He also makes a great journalist or social worker, since his whole essence in life is striving to understand, to analyze, to make sense of everything. Regimented to a tee, he may even schedule his bathroom time (Virgo rules the intestines). One Virgo man we knew planned his meals around when the office john would be the least crowded. We kid you not!

Being an Earth sign, the Virgo man loves to commune with nature. Organic foods and hemp products can compete for shelf space with his vitamins, supplements, books, and building supplies. His weekends may be filled with nature hikes or river rafting trips. In college, we knew a horticulture-obsessed Virgo who collected seeds from the nearby nature trail and actually grew full-size trees in his dorm room!

Then, there are other ways that the Virgo man brings the outdoors inside. Can you say… pothead? The Virgo man can be found packing bowls of marijuana and lighting up, especially when he's anxious (which is most of the time). Nervous by nature, it can take a joint or three to relax this dude. With his green thumb, his cannabis may even be homegrown. (What—

it's cheaper that way!) Of course, they don't call pot a gateway drug for nothing, and sadly, some Virgos, like River Phoenix, can lapse into addiction. This man is prone to stress, and he needs to manage his—namely by turning off his mind. The Virgo man always suffers from a terminal low-grade anxiety. Therapy, tai chi, or meditation can help Virgo build essential coping skills. Many Virgo men are practicing Buddhists, or highly spiritual. Chanting his "oms" and going Zen are far better than working and drinking himself into the ground.

If you're comfortable with his tics and hang-ups—or if you're bad at setting limits for yourself—his regimented lifestyle could be a steady source of comfort. Your life might become a lot less public or social, but sometimes, spending time in an insular world for two can teach you a lot about love's finer points. With Virgo, that's where the best parts of life reside.

## What He Wants in a Woman

Let's start by clearing up this whole "virgin" myth that surrounds his sign. The Virgo man doesn't need to be your first lover, although he'll gladly accept the honor. You don't have to "save" yourself for him or invest in a chastity belt. He's an Earth sign, deeply in touch with his senses and lusty nature. He knows sexuality is natural, and embraces that.

Rather, the symbolic essence of virginity is what the Virgo man adores—namely, an overarching sense of purity. We mean that literally, since your hygiene and grooming will not escape his hyper-observant gaze. Our somewhat messy Libra sister invited a Virgo boyfriend to her home for the first time. While she ran down to the grocery store, he washed all her dishes and scrubbed her sink to a sterile gleam.

Purity of spirit, above all, will enamor him. Childlike wonder, hope, faith, and a belief that anything's possible—these are traits that Virgo deeply admires. It's fine if you're a little loony, too ("a little nutty, but not psycho," is how one Virgo put it). The Virgo man needs you to loosen him up, to make him laugh with your kookiness. He doesn't care for naïve or clueless women. Virgo prefers you with life experience and a few well-storied scars.

If you've survived a difficult past and emerged believing in the fundamental goodness of humanity, the Virgo man will elevate you to heroine status. The martyr figure comes to mind, someone whose spirit can't be broken by any amount of suffering. "She's gotta be strong, not ready to crumble at the slightest breeze," says Steve, a Virgo computer programmer, about his ideal woman. It's an attitude, an orientation. In most cases, this sort of angelic radiance comes naturally. You've either got it or you don't—and Virgo can tell.

To the prim, dour Virgo man, such optimism is a rare and precious commodity. He lapses too easily into gloom, clucking his tongue and shaking his head at the sorry state of our world. His glass is usually half-empty—by exactly .00864 ml according to his calculations, but he could be off by a thousandth of a point. As the zodiac's critic, Virgo sees the flaws first. He is precise and aware at all times. This is the guy who notices the single dandruff flake on your shoulder, the micro-speck of parsley in your teeth, the tiny polish chip on your pedicure. One Virgo man recalls being turned off by a girlfriend's "lopsided bikini wax."

Cynical as his earthly existence may be, he yearns to be restored to his own pure, original state. He longs to believe, to hope, perchance to dream. The woman who inspires this in him is the one he'll stay with forever. Perhaps that's why Virgo men like Marc Anthony and Guy Ritchie married Leo powerhouses Jennifer Lopez and Madonna. Each woman came from humble beginnings, but believing in her vision, she created an empire.

Another aspect to the Virgo man's purity is his deeply private nature. He wants a lady in the streets, a hooker in the sheets. Behind closed doors, the earthy wild man within will let loose, and he wants you to let your hair down. However, you must know how to conduct yourself in public, how to turn it on and off. The Virgo man has a thing about propriety, and projecting an image of civilized control. Inside, he beats himself up mercilessly (his perfectionist standards are cruelest when unleashed on himself). The Virgo man fears judgment and criticism. He can dish it out by the truckload, but taking it is a whole 'nother story.

The Virgo man is complex, and he needs you to be, too. While he likes his women with spunk and sass, there's a limit. The Virgo man will not be dominated. He's a "top" masquerading as a "bottom." Virgo by nature is a giver, so he needs a receptive mate—someone who will appreciate and savor what he offers. He doesn't trust readily, and it's rare that he really opens up. If he shares his life history or private details, you're among a privileged few. His emotions and heart live in a gated community, heavily fortified with maximum security. Like a therapist, he's more likely to listen to your problems, help you, and probe deeper into your history. The Virgo man is always observing you, and he'll remember everything from your childhood pet's favorite trick to the name of your elementary school.

If you want to know how a Virgo man feels about you, just look at his eyes. They may be hidden behind glasses, but if they shine with tender affection, or get that puppy-dog look—watch out. Virgo has fallen and he can't get up. If he's smiling, laughing, and lightening up, he's yours for keeps. Just handle him with care. Believe it or not, he's as fragile as you've become in his nurturing keep. How else would he recognize your sweet inner child if he weren't so well acquainted with his own?

Once the Virgo man realizes he's been dominated, played, or used? Game over. He may be an abundant giver, but that doesn't mean he wants to be taken for a fool. The giving Virgo bestows his way of honoring you—and in a way, controlling you. If it turns out you're up to petty, selfish games, or that you didn't really hand him your beating heart on a gilded platter, he will snatch back his generosity so fast your head will spin.

So handle him with absolute care. Cherish him. You don't have to gush—in fact, he'd prefer you didn't—but let your actions show honor, loyalty, and respect. If you think something doesn't really matter, think again. It probably matters to Virgo. The little things mean everything to him.

# What He Wants from a Relationship

As the zodiac's sign of selfless service, he needs to be needed, to serve and protect. Relationships give Virgo a sense of duty and pride. This guy is rarely single for long, unless it's by choice, since he does have incredibly high standards. Still, the Virgo man is lost without a project, so he tends to be hands-on, even controlling, about the direction of his love life.

Are you tired of raising your boyfriends and teaching them how to act like grown men? Hang up your metaphorical nursing bra. The Virgo man needs none of your mother's milk, thank you very much. Self-sufficient and self-directed, he's no Oedipus or mama's boy. However, he can dig in his heels like a headstrong child. Like all Earth signs, he's stubborn. Virgo can plant himself firmly in a position and refuse to budge. "You can't make me!" he might as well say. On the upside, he's as doggedly loyal to you as he is to his stubborn beliefs.

Still, with Virgo, you can channel your maternal energy where it belongs: toward the children. And he'll want at least one or two, if not a gaggle. Hillary Clinton may believe it takes a village to raise a child, but to Virgo, it takes a child—his childlike spirit, that is—to raise a village. He'll spread his seed far and wide, and he tends to start young. Don't be surprised if your Virgo already has kids from a previous partner or two!

Since he's naturally stern and fatherly, the Virgo man makes a devoted dad. He doesn't mind playing papa to you, either, though he has his limits. It's alright if you're a little needy, as long as you're smart and ambitious. His Earth-sign nature makes him stable and grounding, a favorite among daddy's girls and women with absentee fathers. From his melodious voice to his tender gaze, there's something soothing about the Virgo man. With his firm, athletic body, he can hold you in a way that makes you feel completely safe.

Codependence is the Virgo man's copilot. Many of his relationships start while he's helping a "friend" get back on her feet. He has a knack for finding women who've fallen on hard times: divorce, death of a loved one, recovery from abuse or alcoholism. He loves to be there, comforting and shepherding you through the grieving process, holding your hair back as you puke up your soul. He'll listen to your troubles with a therapist's patience, knowing that his foolproof strategy will work once again. The damsel in distress always falls for the noble knight. And if the knight just happens to gallop off once she's restored to well-being, that's just how fairy tales might end. He never promised you Happily Ever After just because he picked you up on a white horse. But he'll never throw you off the horse before shepherding you safely back home.

The other night, we met a Virgo man (let's call him Phillip) and an Aquarius woman sitting at an adjacent restaurant table. They were incredibly friendly—within five minutes, she was spilling her whole life story—she'd had a difficult pregnancy, followed by breast implants and a tummy tuck in an attempt to regain her pre-baby figure. It became clear she was either drunk or on the verge of a nervous breakdown—probably both. Phillip just watched quietly, as Virgo men do, letting her chatter away and order a $25 cosmopolitan "for all of us to share."

When she teetered off to the smoking lounge in her seven-inch Louboutins, Phillip leaned in conspiratorially. "She's not really my wife," he announced matter-of-factly. "She's just going through a hard time. She had a baby a year ago and fell into some really bad postpartum depression. She's married to someone else. We're seeing each other on the side while she gets through it."

At first, we were baffled. How could a sign as preachy and judgmental as Virgo sleep with another man's wife? Not to mention the risk of diseases—a four-star alarm for the germ-phobic Virgo.

Then it struck us: A woman searching online for an affair is either a) horny, b) bored, or c) (ding ding ding!) sending out an SOS. She's crying out, "Help! I'm done with this marriage and I don't know how to get out. Somebody save me!" Bingo. It's the Virgo man's soft spot, and he rushes in for the save. In his own way, the Virgo man feels that he's performing a public service helping a woman leave a bad marriage. He'd never fancy himself a homewrecker. After all, she was already sniffing around for a side dish. He was just being… helpful.

Ultimately, the Virgo man needs a bigger cause than patching up strays. His astrological duty is to serve humankind. He must find his mission, his life's work and calling. Unless he is contributing to the greater society, or at least a noble cause, the Virgo man is adrift at sea. He will squander his gifts by playing the enabler and codependent hero. He'll take on women's problems, when he should really march them to the nearest therapist's couch. And he will walk away from amazing women—with whom he is highly compatible—simply because they don't need his rescuing.

Until this control freak learns to let go and trust, he can never receive. Giving without receiving (and vice versa) makes for a one-sided relationship. With lots of practice, Virgo might finally loosen his grip and enjoy a healthy relationship, one based on companionship rather than control.

# Sex with a Virgo

Finally, a man who doesn't skimp on the foreplay! Virgo is the zodiac's caretaker, and he knows how to take care of you in bed. He's tender and earthy—this is the guy with whom you can truly "make love" and understand what that means. If you've been through trauma, as many women have, sex with the Virgo man can be incredibly healing. He's patient and nurturing, a safe space for you to relax and express your sensual side.

Generous as he is, Virgo likes to remain in control of your sexual dynamics. He'll never dominate, but he will hold back, always remaining just a little more in control than you. Surrender isn't his thing. The Virgo man can have a cold, clinical air, like a doctor or detective assessing a crime scene. But what he lacks in mushiness, he more than makes up for in technique. Virgo rules the hands, and he has an incredible touch. Just ask him for a massage and he'll gladly give you one. Oral sex is a particular talent, one he's glad to share. He might even study Tantra or Taoist sexual techniques.

We always think of Richard Gere, a Virgo, in his unforgettable *Pretty Woman* role. He portrayed a powerful executive who picked up a Hollywood Boulevard hooker and Cinderella'd her into a classy goddess. Although he was enchanted by her beauty and made rapturous love to her, he kept her at an emotional distance. He would hand her thousands of dollars, expensive dinners, and clothes—anything but his heart.

Virgo is the sign of the Virgin, a misleading icon for him. He's not exactly chaste, but he can be reserved and deeply private about his sexuality. When it comes to hardcore fantasies, Virgo is a purist in this way: should a fetish pop into his imagination, he's not likely to explore it with a long-term partner. The Virgo man classifies women into groups—it's just how his orderly, analytical mind works. The kinky stuff is for a certain "type" of woman, as far as he's concerned, and she's rarely the one he marries—unless she hides it well.

Some would call this naïve and hopelessly old-fashioned, but that's Virgo. Too much judgment and repression can cause him to act out with perverse, odd sexual behavior, driven by the urge to be "bad." On the downlow, he may patronize massage parlors, escort services, and strip clubs. Virgo Charlie Sheen was a notorious client of Madame Heidi Fleiss; Virgo Hugh Grant was publicly caught with a prostitute.

One married Virgo confessed that he'd secretly like to have an open relationship. Duty prevented him, he explained. And since disappointment is a fact of life that Virgo accepts, even savors, he'll probably do without those extra trimmings. Still, he could stand to bring more fantasy into his stark reality. Don't be afraid to suggest a little of that either.

# Virgo: Turn-Ons & Turn-Offs
## Turn Him On

- Be sophisticated, classy, and a little bit wacky
- Need him to help, save, or rescue you
- Be an adventurous eater, even a foodie (bonus if you know about wine)
- Be a hygienic hottie: Keep your home, laundry, and yourself springtime-fresh and spotlessly clean
- Make stimulating conversation about a range of issues

- Stay by his side all night at a party or gathering
- Show interest in analyzing human nature and psychology
- Value healthy living, be into the outdoors and fitness
- Get a great mani-pedi, wear beautiful shoes, carry a finely crafted handbag
- Grow your own food, or be connected to the earth in some such way

## Turn Him Off

- Criticize or judge him (never mind that he'll do that to you…)
- Be too much of a Superwoman—he needs to be needed
- Have too many bad habits that disrupt his sense of order
- Do, say, or eat the same thing over and over again
- Offend his sense of propriety or dignity
- Try to make him the punch line of your joke
- Put him down or disrespect him, especially around other people
- Be too much of a social butterfly at parties, neglecting him
- Flirt with other men, even the tiniest bit
- Refuse to have long, drawn-out conversations about your issues
- Have bad taste in clothes, music, food, TV, books…
- Waste anything: money, time, electricity, water, natural resources
- Try—just try—to make him stop smoking (and we mean whatever he's puffing on)
- Whine, complain, and take him for granted

# His Moves

## First Moves: How He Courts You

Ruled by communication planet Mercury, the Virgo man connects through conversation and mental chemistry. Although he may have a mischievous twinkle in his eye and loves to flirt, the Virgo man prefers to be straightforward about his interest, rather than play evasive games. Underneath the sarcastic jokes and catty comments, he's a serious guy looking for a serious girlfriend. He wants to make sure all the basics are there—chemistry on every level, friendship, and other elements of a solid relationship. So courtship is really the Virgo man's research laboratory, his way of testing whether you'll suit his particular tastes well enough to keep around. Here's how he might approach you:

- Makes a sly joke, showing off his intelligence and wit
- Comes on strong, drawing you into intimate conversation and overwhelming you with attentiveness
- Writes you long letters or leaves you little notes
- Becomes your best friend, and works his way into romance
- Shows up consistently; he's just always there, and thus becomes an indispensable fixture in your life
- Comments observantly on a detail of your outfit or style
- Talks to you about movies, music, or his favorite social issue
- Offers to help you with something—homework, housework, errands, whatever
- Wows you with great conversation and keen listening skills
- Does simple but sweet little things—drives you to work, brings you lunch, walks you home, cleans up the dog poop in your yard

- Plays Trivial Pursuit, asks all about you and remembers the details
- Makes you funny, clever little gifts and cards
- Tries to kiss you right away (he needs to check the merchandise)
- Pursues you relentlessly, calling you at all hours or several times a day

## He's In: How You Know He's Committed

Virgo has a formal and traditional side, and he likes to be ceremonial about special occasions. This is a get-down-on-one-knee kind of guy. He may fly by the seat of his pants in some instances, but if he's giving his word to a commitment, he wants to make a big deal out of it. He loves marking these moments, and will often bring along a special treat, like a bottle of wine or expensive massage oil. Don't expect skywriting or a full-page newspaper ad declaring his devotion (that's Leo territory). Rather, the Virgo man will create something intensely intimate for just the two of you. Here are some of the other ways he shows that he's all yours:

**He starts acting like he's your husband.** The Virgo man is a serial monogamist. He likes intimacy, one-on-one connection, and quality over quantity. Once he's set his sights on you, he simply starts behaving like you've been married for twenty years.

**He turns into a "stage mother."** He fell in love with your free spirit and wacky ways, but Virgo keeps his own future under tight rein. If he's going to merge his life with yours, the days of blowing your paycheck on Prada are over. You're getting health insurance, a 401(k), and an allowance. The flashy outfits are toning down and you're going to conduct yourself like a proper lady in public.

**He shows up for you again and again.** Reliable as your favorite pair of slippers, the Virgo man is your rock. He's consistently there whenever he's needed, and even when he's not.

**He calls all the time.** Conversation is Virgo's aphrodisiac. He never runs out of things to talk about, and he loves to analyze, ponder, and share for hours. He'll blow up your cell phone with text messages and phone calls.

**He looks at you with puppy dog eyes.** We used to jokingly call a Virgo friend Kind Eyes, because his tender gaze when he looked at his girlfriend made his feelings so obvious. If a Virgo man watches you adoringly, there's not much to worry about.

# Unfaithful Virgo: Why He Cheats

Although the Virgo man is capable of great loyalty, his sign can also become CEO of Infidelity, Inc. As with everything for Virgo, his motivation is usually control. The unpredictable natures of love and relationships make his restrained sign feel deeply out of order. He tends to overreact, desperately grasping at the first thing that restores his sense of command—be it a prestigious work assignment or the firm double-Ds of another woman. Here are some reasons Virgo might cheat:

**He's freaking out.** No stranger to neurotic, compulsive behavior, the Virgo man may sense that he's getting attached to you and flip out. Once his inner control freak takes the wheel, the Virgo man may cheat just to prove to himself he's not "whipped." (Especially if he senses he's more into you than you are into him—watch out.) Regrettably, he soon discovers he *is* whipped, and no amount of sleeping around can change that. Way to make a mess, buddy.

**He needs to be naughty.** It's true: the Virgo man can be as tightly wound as a rubber band on a slingshot. When this controlled, controlling sign veers too far into rigidity, it's only natural that he'll rebel. That's when the Virgo dark side emerges, sampling fetishes that you will not want to know about—900 numbers, massage parlors, escort services…

**Your relationship is too domestic and motherly.** You used to be playful, and now you're practical. Help! You've turned into him! This *Freaky Friday* business can bring out the Virgo man's sleazy side. He loves if you make a good wife and mother, but you'd better not lose that temptress edge. The Virgo man would rather take over the cooking and cleaning (he's probably better at them anyhow) than lose the vampy vixen he fell for in the first place.

**You're boring.** Again, you've taken over his job (um, only kidding, Virgo!). Actually, Virgo is a mutable sign, which mean he needs variety and change on a regular basis. If he senses you're stagnant or lacking experience, it's a total turnoff.

## Dig the Grave: It's Over

With a Virgo man, it's never really over. Like a bad rash, he won't go away. He likes the comfort of being in a relationship, and may keep calling you for years—even if it's just a booty call. Here's what it will take for him to nail the coffin shut:

**Mission complete.** The Virgo man's role as your unofficial guru/healer/therapist/daddy has run its course. You are now a whole person, scars faded, childhood wounds healed. You don't need him anymore. It's time to move on to his next case.

**You bossed him around or dominated him.** You've crossed the line from gentle prodding and mothering to henpecking control. He will not put up with being told what to do. No indeed, he'll show you who's boss—and he'll show that other woman he's now screwing, too.

**Your hygiene is sub-par.** The only dirt Virgo is interested in is topsoil (for planting a lovely spring garden) and gossip (he's always up on it). If it lives in bacterial form on your shower tiles, under your nails, or in your unwashed hair, bedding, and clothes, he will be utterly repelled.

**He starts to get sick.** Virgo is the zodiac's health sign, so when his well-being breaks down, he's reached the end of his rather long rope. You've now stressed him out, and taxed his resources. He's got nothing left to give.

**You took a little too much space.** So you needed time to clear your head, to be on your own and reevaluate your priorities. Hope it wasn't for long. If you break the bond once with Virgo, it's hard to get him back. He's a sensitive soul and will put the protective wall up quickly if he fears you'll break his heart.

**He caught you flirting or cheating.** Cheating on him? Stealthy as a Ninja, Virgo will catch you in the act. We know a Virgo man who could creep into a room without anyone hearing him. He's possessive of his women. If you pay more attention to other males, he'll brood and ruin your night. Nobody plays this sign for a fool and gets away with it. He has far too much pride.

**You try to make him change one of his OCD habits.** Listen; if he wants to wash his hands twenty times in an hour, it's a free country. And while we're on the topic, aren't you due for a manicure?

# Interpreting His Signals:

## What does he mean by that?

| When he | It means... | So you should... |
| --- | --- | --- |
| Gets quiet | He's analyzing and observing you, or processing something. Something's on his mind, as usual. | Ask him what he's thinking about. He might need to talk. |
| Doesn't call | Passive-aggressive backlash. You've offended him and he's letting you figure it out on your own. | Call him and find out what you need to apologize for. |
| Calls a lot | He's into you. If he's interested in a woman, he loves talking to her for hours. | Pick up the phone and say hi. Don't worry if you can't talk; he'll understand. |
| Doesn't make a move after a couple of dates | He's still analyzing you and making sure he knows you well enough to gain the upper hand.<br><br>He thinks you're fragile and doesn't want to offend or scare you. | Reveal a little more of yourself to build his trust.<br><br>Touch him lightly to signal it's okay to make a move. |
| Doesn't make a move after a few weeks | He's scared you'll break his heart. | Ask yourself if he might be right. If he's got you pegged wrong, reassure him that you take him seriously as a person. |

| When he | It means... | So you should... |
|---|---|---|
| Moves fast | He wants to lock you in as his next monogamous girlfriend. | Move at your own pace. He's cool with that. |
| Picks up the tab, gives flowers and gifts | He's considering you as a girlfriend. He might go Dutch otherwise (Virgo can be penny-wise). | Thank him several times, even if he waves it off with "It's nothing." It's actually a big deal for him. He's sensitive to being used or taken for granted. |
| Introduces you to his family and/ or closest friends | He'll be soliciting their opinion later on. It's an audition. | Act natural and a little demure. Follow his lead and stay by his side as he shows you around. Be flattered. |

# Your Moves: Tips for Flirting and Everlasting Love

## Flirting with a Virgo

Flirting is relatively easy with Virgo, who's always up for a little provocative banter. You may have to initiate it, though. He can be shy and self-protective at first. Before approaching you, Virgo will "read" you. He'll lock eyes from across the room to see if you look back. Or, he'll observe you unnoticed before making a well-calculated move. Then, he'll pick the ideal moment to engage you in conversation. He's crafty, that Virgo. Here's how to make it safe for him to approach you:

**Talk about your dreams.** Virgo loves a dreamer and a grand idea. Being such a good planner, he imagines himself as the practical grounding force that will help you realize your lofty goals. He also has dreams of his own, but his pessimism and skepticism can interfere. Your optimism boosts his faith.

**Engage in lively conversation.** Virgo is ruled by communication planet Mercury. He loves to text, talk on the phone, and share pop culture trivia and witty banter. Analyze a topic together and express a strong opinion. He loves women who are feminine and feisty, and know where they stand. Wishy-washiness is a turn-off.

**Be yourself.** The Virgo man appreciates honesty and realness. He's not big on fake conversation or guessing games, and he likes a tough-talking woman. With Virgo, it's okay to be direct when you flirt with him, even a little raw—as long as your body language exudes femininity and a nondominant stance.

**Ask him about his favorite TV shows, movies, or books.** The Virgo man is up on news, pop culture, and celebrity gossip. He always has a favorite movie, show, or newspaper. Bonus if you know the character lineup of his favorite TV series, remember past episodes, or have theories on upcoming plotlines.

**Get him alone.** Virgo's private nature makes flirting best when it's one-on-one, away from prying eyes and listening ears. Pull him into a corner or a hidden area. Your words can make him blush, but don't make a scene.

**Be receptive.** He's a giver and a pleaser, and he wants to be part of your everyday life, providing a helping hand. He just needs you to open the door. Make it safe for him to extend his generosity and he gladly will.

## Everlasting Love with a Virgo

The Virgo man loves to have a steady woman in his life. The only thing that keeps him from lifelong serial monogamy is his own fear—mainly of getting attached and hurt. Still, he usually finds the gumption to go for it. Although he may not propose to you with skywriting, he can definitely get swept into romance and puppy love. Here's how to make sure he doesn't start sniffing around for new tricks once he becomes an old dog:

**Take it slow and steady.** The Virgo man is eager to lock things in, and he moves decisively. Don't feel pressured to go along at his swift pace, though. He respects boundaries; to him, they show self-respect and dignity. Just be clear and direct. Don't play games.

**Give him his space.** The Virgo man is an introvert who needs downtime to recharge. He needs to be left alone with his thoughts, worries, and hobbies. Have a life of your own.

**Be available to talk throughout the day.** The Virgo man might need time to himself, but he still keeps you on speed dial, calling and sending text messages all day. He's a worrier and he wants to know where you are. He also just likes to connect, or bounce ideas off of you. Our friend Stephanie's Virgo husband leaves her little notes in unexpected places, which she loves to find.

**Encourage him to take risks.** The Virgo man can be very Type A and risk-averse, even if he works in a creative field. Left to his own devices, he can get too rigid, and easily comes up with reasons not to take a chance. A little push from you can go far.

**Make him laugh.** The Virgo man has a rich sense of humor, but he gets way too serious and lost in his head. He needs a playmate to restore levity.

**Bring calm into his world.** The Virgo man loves to get into a peaceful groove with you by his side. His favorite thing is for you both to be "in the zone," doing your own thing but in each other's company. If you can just "be" with each other, no talking required, he'll think he's found bliss.

# Prep Yourself For...
## Your First Date

Relax. You've got nothing to worry about, kiddo. Even if there's not a love connection, this date is a breath of fresh air to Virgo. Make that a gulp of oxygen when he's asphyxiating, really. The Virgo man is a perfectionist who spends his alone-time replaying conversations, wishing he'd said this or done that. Self-critical to masochistic proportions, he beats himself up constantly. Being with you is a vacation from his overactive mind. He should be thanking you just for showing up.

**The Basic Vibe:** The Virgo man likes to connect through intimate, one-on-one conversation. He'll take you somewhere quiet and romantic, date-worthy but never flashy. He wants to be comfortable, not showy—and he needs to make sure you're not a gold-digging player (his big fear). He might take you to a movie, a lecture, a comedy show, or a concert. If he likes you, he'll want to keep talking. He loves to be outside, so you could sit at a rooftop bar or somewhere under the stars if the weather's nice. You might even end up taking a long walk, losing track of time while you get caught up in conversation.

Many Virgo men are foodies who know a lot about gourmet ingredients and wine (restaurateur and chef Mario Batali is a Virgo). They love spicy food and high-quality preparation, and love to savor a good meal. The Virgo man can be a food snob, and he's very picky—he'll want his food done just right. It's best to let him pick the place, since he's so particular. You'll earn big points with him for being an adventurous eater with well-honed tastes. "I knew a girl who ordered the same dish every date because she never had anything else at this spot," recalls Virgo Steve. "It was a total turnoff for me."

**What to Wear:** It's all in the details, so don't neglect the little touches. The Virgo man will notice your hands, your teeth, your toes, and your perfume. He'll see that your shoes are scuffed, your hems frayed, a button coming unthreaded. Polish it up, sister. He loves if you emphasize your girlishness, so femme yourself up and show some skin—think classy with cleavage and curves. He doesn't mind if you're teetering around on stilettos. It's just a convenient excuse to give you his arm.

**What Not to Wear:** The Virgo man needs to feel like he's with a "lady." Just say no to anything too power-suit, tomboyish, or menswear-inspired. Boxy shapes that hide your figure will get you nowhere. Rumpled is unforgivable—a slap in the face. Don't you own an iron, girl? Show him that he's worth it by taking that "dry clean only" dress out of the plastic.

**To Pay or Not to Pay?** The Virgo man wouldn't dream of letting you pay on a first date. If he goes Dutch, it's because he's either out of work, or it's not clear that you're really on a date (in other words, you had a prior friendship that's evolving into something more). He can be a little cheap later on in the relationship, but never upfront.

**Saying Good night.** Down, boy! With his high sex drive and tendency to repress himself for far too long, the Virgo man gets into horndog mode quickly. He can be a little too eager. (You'll have to forgive him: The male Virgin is always nervous and overly excitable before the first time.) He'll try to kiss you, but it might be best if you give him a flirty farewell—provided you can resist.

## His First Home Visit

Dirt alert! The fussy Virgo man is the sign that rules home and hearth. Cleanliness is next to godliness. Neat and orderly, his home is his sanctuary, and he doesn't want to imagine you filling it with dust bunnies and clutter. Sorry to report: He will notice every little flaw in your house. If he doesn't comment, he'll keep glancing at them. Soon, he may start itching and twitching. Before you know it, he's picked up a power tool or a scouring pad to take care of it. Here's how you can minimize his annoying observations and enjoy his company:

**Declare war on bacteria, dust bunnies, and grime.** Remember back in the 1980s when Michael Jackson (a Virgo) took up residence in an airtight bubble so that no germs or diseases could permeate? Yeah, we know. Spotless is just barely clean enough for Virgo. Sterile would be better.

**Get a good bottle of wine.** Anything that helps Virgo relax is good. Of course, he might be a health purist who doesn't drink. Then again, he might be a foodie who knows a lot about wine. Take a chance and pick up a decent grape. He'll be impressed, even if he doesn't imbibe.

**Create a homey, comfortable ambience.** Pay attention to details. Include good music, hors d'oeuvres, and comfortable seating for conversation and kissing. Generally, though, the Virgo man prefers his own home to yours, even if it's minimalist or barely furnished beyond the basics.

**Make dinner together.** The Virgo man is often equally talented in the kitchen and the bedroom. It's all about technique for him, and he's great with his hands. It's getting hot in here... and the oven's not even on yet!

**Nurture him.** Throw him a little mother energy, but not in a belittling way. Just give him a preview so he can imagine you as the mother of his kids, a nester, someone he could bring home to his family. A home-baked cookie, a kitschy apron draped over the kitchen door, a recipe book left casually on the table... just a detail will do.

**Have something he can fix.** The Virgo man loves to help. Do you have pictures to hang, a hinge to fix on your closet door? Hand him the drill.

## Meeting His Family

A word upfront: Before you meet Virgo's parents, you might actually be meeting his children. In fact, his kids might even live with him, since Virgo is a hands-on dad who often has full custody (the mom's probably a narcissistic nut who ran off with the postman). If your Virgo's not a father yet, he's probably got nieces and nephews who are very special to sweet Uncle Virgo. Not to mention the latchkey kids from down the block who look up to him as a father figure, the youth group soccer team he coaches, and his students from the Kung Fu academy...

If a Virgo introduces you to his family, treat them like gold. That's what they are to him. You've got to be polite, proper, and parent-approved. Keep your wacky side in check. He prefers that you share his family values and religious beliefs, but it's not a deal-breaker as long as you play along well. The Virgo man needs you to show interest in his family. Ask a lot of questions, be intrigued by their history, flip through photo albums and listen to stories about every picture. Show that you're family-oriented (especially since you might inherit a few kids in the deal). Never miss a holiday dinner.

The Virgo man loves family gatherings, traditions, and reunions. There's a certain innocence to these connections, in his mind, a nostalgic boyhood mythology Virgo cherishes. One Virgo man we know listed his favorite hangouts as "bookstores, barbecues, family events, and baby birthday parties." He wasn't kidding. He'll take a dirty diaper over dirty talk any day. He absolutely adores cradling an infant in his arms, photographing a toddler's first steps, listening raptly to ninety-nine year-old Aunt Sadie recall her life in war-torn Europe, eating dinner with his grandmother before he goes out drinking with his boys. He's big on lineage, ancestry, and family trees—probably because he loves flow charts so much.

You could say that the way to Virgo's heart is through his family. Since they are among the few mortals he trusts in this lifetime, their opinion of you counts. If they take an instant liking to you, sweet. If they don't, he'll stick by you, but with a lingering sadness. And if his family was dysfunctional, he could be bitter for the rest of his life. In a perfect world, the woman of Virgo's dreams fits neatly into his clan, allowing him to seamlessly blend his past, present, and future into a timeless masterpiece.

# Saying Good-bye
## Breaking Up with a Virgo

Let's make one thing clear: This is not going to go well. Once the Virgo man opens his heart—after long and careful consideration—he plays for keeps. He is far too much of a control freak to embrace surprises, much less the bombshell of a breakup. He'll want to know why—WHY?—and he'll have a retort for every answer you give. There could be tears to dry (his) or an angry emotional outburst. He'll pace, stalk like a tiger, park outside your house until you come outside and talk this out like "sensible" adults.

If he finally surrenders to the realization that you're not coming back, things could get ugly. The Virgo man will hate you for doing the unforgivable: pulling the rug out from under him. He can be vicious, catty, as mean as a teenage girl—he'll talk trash about you to your friends (to anyone who will listen, really), spill your secrets, let it slip that you have herpes or drunkenly "ménaged" with him and another woman. He will hate you for months, even years afterward.

As the saying goes, resentment is like drinking poison and hoping the other person dies. His bitterness may fill him with toxic sludge, but he will resent and resent until he's completely knocked you off your pedestal and demolished your reputation so badly you skip town. Either that, or he stonewalls you until you beg him pitifully to take you back. Then, he'll scorn and reject until you've suffered adequately and assured him that you'll never, ever, ever break his heart again. Make sure you're certain of this decision before you call things off.

## Getting over Him: When a Virgo Dumps You

Oh, the pain... the PAIN. When a Virgo leaves you, it's worse than a breakup. It's like losing a family member—a father or a favorite uncle. It's nothing short of devastating. Largely, this is because the Virgo man swoops in during a vulnerable time in your life, when your sense of self is wobbly at best. Along he comes like a codependent super-savior to "give you" your identity and lead you to salvation. He may have crafted such dependency that you have no idea who you are without him. Your guardian angel has abandoned you, and you're falling far, far down.

You could be outright shell-shocked by his decision, barely able to get out of bed. One friend of ours was catatonic for six months after a Virgo boyfriend left her. He was the first man she'd dated in several years, her first foray into trust after leaving an abusive ex-husband. When he sensed that she was fully healed, he took her for a walk through the neighborhood and gently explained that their lives were going in different directions, and he needed to be on his own for a while. She wanted to know why—WHY?—and he stood firm, the way an Earth sign can remain so infuriatingly rooted once he makes up his mind. Of course, she and the Virgo still slept together every six months for the next seven years. He can never really break an attachment all the way, the Virgo man. But he sure can break your heart.

**Have yourself one good last cry over...**
- His tender gaze
- His gentle, healing energy
- Feeling like daddy's there to make it all better
- The great, long conversations you shared
- The sweet little ways he showed his love and affection
- Being led around by someone so in control of the situation
- Having a decision maker to handle all the things you prefer to avoid
- His cooking and/or cleaning (damn, you have to hire a maid and a private chef now?)
- Losing your personal Mr. Fix-It
- Losing the person who listened to your hopes, dreams, and fears without laughing
- The way he championed you and believed in you more than you believed in yourself

**Praise the universe that you never have to deal with...**
- His inflexible, rigid personality
- His neurotic, OCD habits
- His love of the ganja and other controlled substances
- Being nagged and lectured

- The way he pouted when you didn't pay attention to him
- His need to be in control of everything
- The excruciatingly nitpicky behavior
- His catty, critical comments
- His annoying soapbox preaching
- His ability to notice every little detail that was out of place
- The times he got cold, withdrawn, and shut you out
- Having to groom, pluck, and de-flaw yourself like a post-airbrushed fashion magazine photo

# Love Matcher:

## *Can you find a common language?*

| You are a(n)... | He thinks you're... | You think he's... | Common Language |
|---|---|---|---|
| Aries | A brilliant fireball who needs his guiding wisdom. | Too controlling and nitpicky—acts like he's your father. Chill, dude! | Him taking care of you, OCD habits, germophobia, picky appetites |
| Taurus | A sexy, sophisticated mate who makes him look good in public. | Compatibly cultured, but a little cheap. | Food, wine, highbrow or fussy tastes, culture, budgets |
| Gemini | Whip-smart and fun, but too hard to tame. | An intellectual equal who needs to pull the stick out of his ass. | Books, music, ideas, conversation |
| Cancer | The future mother of his children. | Your hero (sigh). | Family, food, nesting, financial security, living happily ever after |
| Leo | Incredibly over-the-top and egotistical, but inspiring, too. The lioness he loves to tame. | Disciplined in a way you admire, a grounding force that won't compete for the spotlight . | Family, children, tradition, health and fitness, hard work, old-fashioned romance, religion |

| You are a(n)... | He thinks you're... | You think he's... | Common Language |
|---|---|---|---|
| Virgo | A fellow fussbudget who might make a better friend. | A stick in the mud, but a kindred spirit, too. The perfect, patient gentleman, especially to be your "first". | Health, hygiene, family, kids, low-key living |
| Libra | Beautiful, enchanting, but your social butterfly nature makes you seem hard to pin down. | A perfect captive audience for your beauty and charms. A little controlling. | Music, art, long conversations, food and wine, taking your sweet time to finish a project, a critical eye |
| Scorpio | His sexy best friend. | Arrogant and needs your help bringing him back down to reality. | Analyzing everything, obsession with control and details |
| Sagittarius | Great for long walks and long talks, but too independent and blunt to be tamed. | Your favorite person to talk to, but way too serious and introverted—loosen up! | Philosophical conversations, clever jokes, marveling at your own intelligence, agreeing that you're smarter than the rest of the world |

| You are a(n)... | He thinks you're... | You think he's... | Common Language |
|---|---|---|---|
| Capricorn | A refined earth angel who's as loyal and practical as he is. | The man you should marry. | Tradition, friendship, family, OCD habits, just about everything |
| Aquarius | From outer space. | The controlling authority figure you want to rebel against. | Sex, love of animals and kids, instant attraction that devolves into fiery wreckage, mutual hatred of each other after your often inevitable breakup |
| Pisces | Sweetly in need of his help, but inevitably drives him insane. | The daddy type you've dreamed about, but a little controlling. | Health, healing, compassion, spirituality |

# The Libra Man

Dates: September 23–October 22
Symbol: The Scales
Ruling Planet: Venus, the planet of beauty, art, and romance
Element: Air—grounded, realistic, wants material security
Quality: intellectual, changeable, social
Mission: My Fair Lady

**Natural Habitat—Where You'll Find Him:** At a networking mixer, befriending strangers at the bar, ballroom or salsa dancing, following his favorite band around the country, at a stadium watching a sports event or concert, organizing his file cabinet, getting fitted for a custom suit; shopping for brand-name clothes, household goods and grooming products; organizing his dress shirts by color, living at home until his mid twenties, taking his sweet time to do anything, listening to music dreamily, ambling through a gallery or museum, philosophizing about life at a coffee shop, wooing everyone with his natural charm, driving somebody home from an event, offering a sharp opinion or criticism, elegantly dressed at a wine tasting, dining at a large, airy restaurant

**What He Does for a Living:** Engineer, diplomat, mediator, art dealer, artist, food/music/wine/culture critic, judge, fashion designer, interior decorator, photographer, salesperson, insurance broker, novelist, model, actor, strategist, all-around "company man"

**Noteworthy & Notorious Libra Men:** Matt Damon, Tommy Lee, Usher, John Mellencamp, John Mayer, Snoop Dogg, Wyclef Jean, John Lennon, Sting, Clive Owen, David Lee Roth, Bernie Mac, Ralph Lauren, Michael Douglas, Eminem, Jermaine Dupri, Will Smith, Sammy Hagar, Simon Cowell, Zac Efron, Christopher

Reeve, Meat Loaf, Bryant Gumbel, Johnny Mathis, Yo-Yo Ma, Paul Simon, Jean-Claude Van Damme, Jeff Goldblum, John Lithgow, Hugh Jackman, Luke Perry, Jim Henson

# Libra: How to Spot Him

- Deep, adorable dimples (at least one)
- Impossibly cute, even pretty, face with soft features
- Well-maintained physical fitness—never bulging muscles, but well-defined shape
- Dressed to the nines, with everything coordinated
- Dressed like a cute, metrosexual emo boy: button-down shirt, round glasses, linen trousers, a tie or pocket square
- Taking photo after photo with his expensive camera equipment
- The only guy in the nail salon/home décor department/ Pilates class
- Tastefully selecting jewelry or an outfit for a female friend
- Handing out his business cards at a corporate networking mixcr
- Grossly overtipping the valet or concierge to make himself look and feel like "the man"
- Flirtatiously attempting to charm every woman he meets, even those half his age
- Wearing upscale accessories that nod to his semi-developed spirituality: a sterling silver Om necklace, a Kaballah red string, a Hebrew "chai" pendant
- Wearing quirky accessories that maintain he's still "down with the people" even though he's gone corporate: a tie designed by Jerry Garcia, patterned socks or boxers
- Playing wingman to a charismatic but less classy friend
- Kissing the CEO's ass in hopes of getting ahead

# Libra: How He Deals With...

### Money

Needs to make lots to support his love of material goods and upscale living.

### Family

Dutiful and devoted to his. Has a hard time cutting the cord with his parents, which could annoy the hell out of his girlfriends.

### Love

In love with being in love.

### Sex

Can be a total horndog, but can also fall into a rut. Doesn't mind doing the same technique/trick/position over and over again. Loves a good lapdance or being "serviced." Other times, tender, nurturing, eager to pleasure.

### Children

Affectionate, doting, and very hands-on. Spares the rod and spoils the child. Prays to the Goddess for a daughter so he can father the ultimate "daddy's girl."

### Pets

Yes, he has a teacup Yorkie/Maltese/miniature Poodle. No, he's not gay. Why do you ask?

### Your Meltdowns

Completely freaks the second you slightly raise your voice. Your upsets tip his scales waaaaay too out of balance. Turns into a defensive, pouting, shouting six-year-old boy. Will discuss matters "sensibly" with you later.

### His Meltdowns

Complete and utter drama that will suck you in like a funnel cloud or a deadly cyclone. Head to the tornado shelter, Dorothy, unless you want to be dropped into his insane personal Oz.

### Breakups

Throw his life completely out of whack. Takes twice as long as anyone else to recover.

# Libra: What He's All About

Picture, if you will, a pastoral scene from the idyllic 1950s. A perfect little nuclear family, all dressed in their crisply ironed Sunday best, piles into the family automobile for a pleasant drive through the country. Cruising along the new Route 9 at a gentle 15 mph, Father pulls over occasionally to point out the wildflowers and dairy cows. The children crowd at the window to see. Hours later, the family completes their ten-mile journey to the next town, where they'll stop for hamburgers and milkshakes, perhaps stroll down Main Street. The family's in no rush. It's Sunday in the glorious new suburbs, and life is grand.

That sweet, bucolic glow of simpler times past is the essence of the Libra man. He's all about leisure, harmony, and the first blush of spring. His lens on the world is set to soft focus and warm tones. While few of us even notice the roses, he stops to smell them all. Daydreaming is one of his favorite hobbies, and he has quite an imagination.

Life must be beautiful around a Libra man. And if it isn't, he's the first to notice—and comment. Actually, he can barely tolerate discord. This man has keen senses, especially for colors, scents, and sound. *American Idol* judge Simon Cowell is the quintessential Libra. He considers his harsh contestant critiques a public service: He's saving the planet from bad music. To Libra, ugliness is the ultimate pollution.

A social Air sign, the Libra man thrives in human interaction. Whether he's an investment banker or a bricklayer, he's the guy you want to put in front of the customer. All dimples and savoir-faire, he brings a courtly flair to even the most mundane occasion (although his occasional blunt remarks may offend). The Libra man can and will talk to anyone. Drop him in a networking event or an annual board meeting, and he lights up the room. Sit next to him at the local bar, and he'll treat you to cocktails and conversation.

The Libra man excels in presentation. His desk may be a disaster zone, and his private paperwork could be fraught with frantic scribbles. However, when he turns in a finished product, it's excruciatingly neat and impeccable. Of course, it may be hours past due—or perhaps he stayed up all night hand-lettering a cover for his monthly expense report. For this reason, Libra can unfairly be branded a procrastinator.

*Au contraire.* It just pains him to produce anything that's less than aesthetically perfect. This is the man who needs a workshop—if only to hide his unfinished projects that he's dawdling over. To Libra, symmetry is bliss. One Libra friend makes sure the spines of his entire books are all lined up perfectly, pulled away from the wall at the exact same distance. He'll spend hours arranging his shelf, instead of reading!

Libra brings these same discriminating standards to his looks. Okay, he can be a vain little pretty-boy about his clothes, hair, and shoes. This über-metrosexual dude is often mistaken for gay—and will gladly accept compliments from every queen on his finely tailored wardrobe. Many Libras love to dress like old-fashioned gentlemen: custom suits and ties, designer shoes. He cleans up nicely, and often speaks in a harmonious tenor pitch, neither too high nor too low. Moderation is his sweet spot. He's not a top or a bottom; he's a middle. Indeed, he often finds himself playing moderator or diplomat, the peacekeeping fulcrum between two warring factions.

As talented as Libra can be at settling conflict, he'd rather avoid it. In his typical "man of leisure" style, Libra will spend hours at the gym. He can be very disciplined about fitness and diet, and he likes to do the whole workout circuit with proud precision. Afterward, a soak in the Jacuzzi, a sauna, maybe a massage—he's never in a rush. Marathons and triathlons are right up his alley. With his raging sweet tooth, the Libra man can pack on pounds, and if he gets out of his workout habit, his whole life gets thrown off balance.

Although the Libra man is a total softie, if push comes to shove, he's got bite. He can be delightfully snarky—and you'll love meeting the bitch that lives within every Libra man, as long as the claws aren't aimed at you. He's cattier than a teenage girl. With his adorable dimples and pretty features (think: Zac Efron, Matt Damon), he probably has lots of admirers. This guy was born to steal teenage hearts and pose as a pin-up centerfold.

If you're looking for Prince Charming, Libra could be your guy. Debonair Libra is ruled by Venus, the planet of beauty and love. Of course, he may act like a spoiled little prince who demands his way. But he's just as eager to spoil you in return, which can make his fussiness worth all the trouble.

# What He Wants in a Woman

The Libra man's romantic checklist is basic: He wants elegance. Femininity. Edge. Beauty. Someone to call "my little love monkey." What, is that too much to ask?

The Libra man may seem indecisive, but he's crystal clear about what he wants in a woman. Nothing short of the mark will do. He's looking for a graceful goddess with the Libra "holy trinity": beauty, truth, and justice. He wants to be captivated by your radiance, awed by your honesty, and dazzled by your sense of equality. He needs a fair maiden—in every sense of the word "fair"—someone who will call it like she sees it, but who can also dazzle him with her ladylike allure.

Although Libra loves to be in love, the zodiac's Prince Charming will rarely settle. He can be incredibly judgmental, even catty, pointing out a tiny stain on your collar, or sniffing at your framed Ikea "art." Never mind that he may still live with his parents, amid unfolded laundry, Southwestern tapestries left over from college days, and shelves of high school trophies. Whether or not the Libra man exercises his fine taste, he's got it.

The Libra man wants to admire you, even put you on a pedestal. Ideally, you should be somewhere between a saint and an angel in his eyes. If he resigns himself to marrying a woman who doesn't fit his romantic dreams, he'll never be happy. He'll wait until his late thirties or forties to marry (or remarry) the right person. Being a "late bloomer" is his best insurance against divorce.

There's a catch, though: Libra is ruled by Venus, the planet of romance and beauty. Cupid makes him stupid. He'll go gaga for a gorgeous creature, even someone five to ten years younger than he is. If you're attractive enough, his normally solid judgment can go right out the window. He may gloss over the glaringly obvious mismatched traits that normally raise his red flags.

Once the ego boost of "getting the girl" wears off, the Libra man will deeply regret his imprudent lapse. This man should never rush to judgment about a woman, one way or another. If he lets himself fall down the rabbit hole, he won't enjoy digging himself out—and it won't be fun for you, either. The wise woman doesn't let her Libra have the milk without paying for the cow. You must both take time for his infatuation to ripen into real love. Common ground is essential. He needs a woman who can share his hobbies and values, and earn his heartfelt admiration.

Michael Douglas and Catherine Zeta-Jones, both Libras, are a great example. "As soon as I met Catherine I told her I wanted to have babies with her, and the moment I found out that she had the same birthday as me—tadaah!" Douglas said of their connection, "Then when I discovered she loved golf, I realized all my fantasies had come true. I've lucked out at this time in my life. I just lucked out. I'm so impressed by her intelligence, sense of humor, and work ethic."

Ladies, practice your swooning. You must believe in old-fashioned romance to enjoy the best of Libra. He needs a muse, somebody who inspires him to paint, compose lyrics, buy flowers, pen love letters on fine linen stationery with an ink-dipped quill. Bonus points if you can waltz, tango, and rock some formal wear. He loves a woman who knows how to dress up and paint the town.

But wait... there's more. For Libra, everything must be counterbalanced to keep his scales even. You'll need to have a practical side, too, since he can float off into the ether without enough substance. Libra needs you to be an iron fist in a velvet glove, strong enough for a (girlie) man, but made completely like a woman.

# What He Wants from a Relationship

He loves you, he loves you not. With the Libra man, your relationship can feel like a pendulum, swinging wildly until it finally settles at a comfortable point. Why can't he just make up his mind?

More than anything, what the Libra man wants from a relationship is to be sure—a hundred million trillion percent sure—that you're the One. If that takes him five minutes or five years, so be it. You could already be his common-law wife by the time he drops to one knee.

Of course, it doesn't have to take that long. It depends on how well you complement each other. The Libra man craves an interdependent, equally balanced relationship. He wants you to be autonomous and capable of finding your own happiness, with or without him. At the same time, he likes to feel like you're the missing piece in his romantic puzzle, to create an even higher state of bliss together. A slight contradiction, but that's Libra. If you provide the counterweight that balances out his bad habits and shortcomings, he'll gladly join forces.

Libra is the sign of the judge, so he subjects prospective mates to a lengthy evaluation before committing. During his weighing and measuring process, he'll examine whether he's "settling" by being with you. This guy has a breathtaking sense of entitlement—only the best for Prince Libra! Years can pass between his relationships, and he often marries late. Unfortunately, he also has a case of verbal diarrhea, and will babble out his whole messy thought process well within your earshot. Hello, insensitive. You'll need to develop a thick skin to tough out those times.

The Libra man craves peace, and if you're better at making war than love, you'll only delay his evaluation process. If your demands, temper, or unexamined emotions tip his scales too far, he'll wisely draw back and let you reconfigure your own system. He can only handle so much drama, especially since he's often staging his own. After reboot, you must return mature and self-possessed if you want to regain his favor.

Although his tough love pays off in the long run, it's also infuriating. Even though he can be a spoiled brat, he has little tolerance for your being pouty, clingy, or childish. Of course, he may foster that very dependence with baby talk, silly voices, and cute nicknames. It's all about moderation and proportion with

Libra. If you're going to be a little girl today, he wants you to be a sophisticated woman tomorrow.

Equality is a big deal for Libra. He needs you to play fair, and although he denies it, he's always quietly keeping score. When he needs to win an argument, he'll pull out his arsenal: "Well, I did the laundry last time and the dishes, so you should take out the trash." Or, "We went to your favorite restaurant last time, so tonight we have to go to mine."

Anything too extreme throws Libra out of alignment, turning him into a grouchy ogre, even a tyrant. Our Libra grandfather had two favorite sayings: "Too much!" (when we served him an overfilled dinner plate) and "Q-U-I-E-T!" (he'd bellow out this warning before taking his daily nap). He needs to retreat and refresh himself, and has a few regular routines that must not be denied. For our grandpa, it was a 1:00 nap, followed by a cup of Lipton tea and two crumbly Pecan Sandies—every single day of his thirty postretirement years. Our friend Amanda has grudgingly accepted that at 7:00 P.M., her Libra husband will be meeting his cyber-buddies online to play *World of Warcraft*, a multi-player computer game. Whatever the Libra man requires to unwind and rebalance—a cold beer, a run on the beach, an hour in his model airplane studio—the wise woman learns to let him have it.

As much as he may take the long side roads to the altar, Libra is the sign of partnerships, contracts, and marriage. Ultimately, he's at his best when he teams up with his equal partner. The right relationship can be a wonderful canvas for him to express his finest qualities of diplomacy, love, and harmony. Just don't rush him, okay?

## Sex with a Libra

Nice guys finish last, and in the Libra man's case, it's a good thing. Unless you're the "wham, bam, thank you Sam" type, you'll enjoy this man with a slow hand. He'll rub and caress you, love you tender, kiss you slowly for hours. In fact, the Libra man may even seduce you by offering a skillful massage. He can Shiatsu your defenses away so well, you'll be begging for his sweet, sweet lovin'.

There's a bit of a hippie in every Libra (no matter how clean-cut he looks), and he can be a free-loving swinger in his exploratory days. You might even find him in the midst of a threesome, enjoying his role as the middleman (read: being pleasured from all sides). Bonus: He can avoid committing or making a permanent choice, and still get laid. When it comes to sex, the Libra man is glad to multitask.

The Libra man loves beauty, and he has a voyeuristic side. Perhaps he'll want to paint, sculpt, or photograph you in the nude. Or, like Libra Tommy Lee famously did with Pamela Anderson, he might even switch on the camcorder. The Libra man can get off by watching you dance around in a sexy, lacy thong, especially if you give him a rear view. He might even enjoy a light spanking, or a side of dirty talk.

Libras are the zodiac's "gourmets," and we've met a few Libra men with highbrow fetishes and fantasies. Usually, he has the sense to explore these in downloadable or DVD format, rather than request that you act out these demeaning scenarios. He's just such a "nice guy" in real life, that fantasizing about women being dominated, even humiliated, balances out too much of his submissive yes-man posture. Of course, he feels terribly guilty about enjoying his chosen smut. But hey, only you will ultimately benefit, since he'll overcompensate by pleasuring for you an extra hour.

Sure, your Libra could look a little buttoned-up or preppy. But rip off his pastel Brooks Brothers shirt or expensive beefy white T. You could find a shiny set of nipple rings, or a sexy tattoo. It's all about balancing the opposing forces for Libra. And since he's usually such a good boy by day, imagine how naughty he can be once the lights go off.

# Libra: Turn-Ons & Turn-Offs

## Turn Him On

- Be a well-balanced, even-tempered woman with a little bit of edge
- Share his taste in music, books, art
- Play up your natural beauty and femininity—like an elegant goddess
- Be a sweet, angelic saint that his family adores
- Call him on his s**t while sparing his dignity: He loves an iron fist in a velvet glove
- Swoon at his romantic gifts—the oversized flower arrangements, the framed photo of you two, the poetry you inspire him to write
- Be the woman he pictures as the mother of his children
- Spoil him, especially in bed
- Let him play "daddy" and drive you home or call you cutesy nicknames
- Embrace your diva side—spend quality time on pampering, grooming, and choosing your outfit
- Know your name brands, and be something of a label snob
- Take full responsibility for your part of the relationship (he needs you to play fair)
- Listen to him wax philosophical for hours

## Turn Him Off

- Rush or pressure him to make up his mind about anything
- Have bad manners, hygiene, and taste
- Grow body hair like your name was Rapunzel
- Talk in a loud, obnoxious voice that he can't tune out

- Be showy and attention-hungry (he says it's tacky, but he really just wants the spotlight to be on him)
- Wear anything too bright, revealing, or over-the-top
- Put your needs before the family's or children's—he wants a team player
- Argue or cause unnecessary conflict
- Clash with his parents and siblings
- Demand a ring or a proposal before he's ready (What? It's only been eight years!)
- Be overly practical, especially about clothing, or deny him access to luxury goods
- Kill the magic by scoffing at romance
- Shop anywhere that rayon or other synthetic fabrics predominate
- Be rude or indifferent to animals, children, homeless people, service workers
- Think "your s**t don't stink," as one Libra man put it

# His Moves

## First Moves: How He Courts You

It's all sweetness and light when a Libra man pours his honey-coated charms on you. Gentlemanly rituals and courtship are in the Libra man's blood, and he makes an art form out of the slow buildup to love.

With women, he loves to spoil and be spoiled. You might find him holding court amid a gaggle of giggling beauties. Although he may seem to be flirting with all of them, the Libra man is surprisingly decisive about the kind of woman he wants. Should you be "his type," he may turn up the charm a notch higher to signal his pursuit.

Here's how a Libra lets you know he's interested:

- He walks up to you and hands you his business card
- He flirts shamelessly with you, flashing his dimples and batting his long lashes
- He stays on the phone with you for hours
- He takes you out for a "lovely evening"
- He gives you a ride home, or walks you to your door
- He sends you a huge bouquet of flowers
- He writes poetry about you and reads it to you
- He tells his mom about you
- He takes you out and keeps the night going and going…

## He's In: How You Know He's Committed

Ah, the old "C" word. Not one of Libra's favorites, since this guy hates to be rushed into a decision. He operates on his own time line, usually about half the pace of everyone else. Libra likes to weigh each factor before making a decisive move. Meantime, you're getting bored and anxious—is he wasting your time? Here's how you'll know he's in:

**You gave him an ultimatum… and he chose you.** For Libra, the courtship phase can stretch for decades before he actually feels "ready" to fully commit. His worldly possessions may be in your closets, his mail delivered to your address, and still he drags his feet. You may just need to break it down for him: s\*\*t or get off the pot. If you've been casually dating for years and you want a ring, he may need time in the pressure cooker. (Be firm but kind if you try this.)

**He buys you thoughtful gifts.** The Libra man really likes to understand the woman he loves. If he starts bringing over presents that reflect your tastes and interests, he thinks you're worth his precious attention. He might even make you something:

a painting, a poem, a hand-sculpted piece of art. Libra is the sign of beauty, so if he starts beautifying your life, he wants to be there to enjoy it.

**Flowers arrive on a regular basis.** Romantic Libra can be a little slow to say "I love you," but he doesn't mind saying it with flowers. If he follows up a "lovely evening" by delivering a huge, tasteful arrangement to your office, his heart's going pitter-patter. Our Libra grandfather brought our grandmother fresh gladiolus (their favorite flower) every Friday afternoon.

**He's still there.** This is not a rock-solid indicator, since Libras are just as slow to end a relationship as they are to begin one. But the longer he stays, the harder it is for him to leave. If you want to take it to the next level, you may need to deliver an ultimatum (see first item).

**He looks at you like he just saw a unicorn.** Is he gazing at you with eyes of wonder, like you're the most magnificent, rare creature he's ever seen? When a Libra man gets "unicorn goggles," it means he's gaga for you.

**He sees you as the woman of his dreams.** Fantasies are important to this idealistic sign—equally as important as reality when it comes to love. Your fitting his ideal picture (somewhere between a saint and a goddess) is the one reason a Libra man might rush to propose. If you're a tall, leggy model and he's a short, square accountant, he may think to himself, "It's never gonna get any better than this." Vanity—it's a bitch. A bitch named Libra, that is.

# Unfaithful Libra: Why He Cheats

The Libra man is an honorable dude, not one to go around breaking women's hearts on purpose. Once he finally makes up his mind to commit, he's gone through a lengthy internal process of weighing and measuring every scenario. He probably won't want to turn back after all that work! The odds of you cheating on him are much higher, since you may mistake his slow pace for a lack of interest. Or, you just might get bored waiting for him to come around. Should he stray, here are some possible reasons:

**He's too much of a wuss to end things.** The Libra man hates, hates, HATES conflict. He's too much of a nice guy to break your heart—at least, to your face—so he concocts a passive-aggressive exit strategy. By cheating, he sabotages your relationship to force your hand. How convenient: You get to be the bad guy dumping him!

**He was never really sure about you in the first place.** Maybe you rushed him. Maybe he chose you against his better judgment. Maybe you insisted on being together, even though he told you he didn't see you as the One. If he doubts his decision, he may test its soundness in the arms of another woman.

**Pure vanity.** He felt "fat" and he needed to feel beautiful again. Nobody ever admired him like that before. Okay, girlfriend. Whatever.

**You've killed off the romance.** You've gone from Bergdorf Blonde to Supercuts Susan. Curse words and cynicism have tainted your once-poetic lips. Furry slippers have replaced Fendi pumps. You must not love him anymore.

## Dig the Grave: It's Over

Libra men can be stubborn once they've made up their minds. It takes a lot for him to walk out the door—permanently, anyway. It took him years to get here, so why would he want to leave? Here are a few indicators that his Libran scales could be tipping out of your favor:

**He saw your "other side" and couldn't deal.** So you got angry and lost your temper. Maybe you exploded, sobbed uncontrollably, threw an object. Anything short of even-tempered can set Libra off. If you need emotional highs and lows, turn on *Days of Our Lives*. He has no capacity for your soap opera. (After all, he might just be busy with his own.)

**He comments unfavorably on your hygiene.** Skip your deodorant once, shame on you. Twice, well… he's too sensitive to chance a third strike. Beauty and cleanliness are priorities for Libra. If you've got bad breath, ripe pits, a dirty house, or unwashed hair, he'll find someone who understands the meaning of "power shower."

**He dresses down.** He was Mr. Microfiber, Italian sport coats, and imported silk. Now he only wears fleece, flannel, or drawstrings around you. Uh-oh.

**He stops courting you.** He stops for takeout on the way home instead of taking you out. Flowers and gifts are a thing of the past, and it's not like he's broke. The gentleman has left the building, and chivalry is dead. He won't be holding the door for you anymore—except to escort you out.

**He withdraws or stonewalls you.** Am I talking to a brick wall? I said, AM I TALKING TO A… yes, you are. The Libra man hates fighting and repeating himself. He aims to be direct and polite, so you'd better listen to him the first time. If you make him get ugly or lose his cool, he'll drop the conversation—and you.

**He pouts.** It looks like grouchiness, but watch closely: He's getting ready to throw a full-on "man-trum" (as our Libra friend Ben coined it). He has had it up to here, and he's gonna show you what drama really looks like.

# Interpreting His Signals:

## *What does he mean by that?*

| When he | It means... | So you should... |
|---|---|---|
| Gets quiet | Mantrum alert! He might be pouting or brooding. He needs to decompress NOW and something's holding him back. He's gazing at you dreamily. | Get out of his way and let him do whatever hobby or activity he needs to unwind (a run, a nap, a cigar... ). Gaze right back, but make sure you break eye contact first. |
| Doesn't call | He lost track of time—once again. | Leave him a message. Your voice will snap him out of his daydreams. |
| Calls a lot | He admires your opinions and intelligence. He enjoys talking to you. | The Libra man has lots of female friends, so this may not mean anything until he puts his ass on the line and asks you out for a bona fide date. |
| Doesn't make a move after a couple of dates | Nothing to worry about, really. He's a don't-rush-me kind of guy. | Give it a few more dates before you start wondering if he's "just not that into you." |

| When he | It means... | So you should... |
| --- | --- | --- |
| Doesn't make a move after a few weeks | He may have some hesitation about your compatibility, but then again, this can still be Libra's standard pace. He likes to extend the courtship phase for as long as possible. | Ask him what's up. Better to find out where his head and heart really are. |
| Moves fast | He's horny and not thinking about anything serious. | Enjoy a fun fling, or slow him down. |
| Picks up the tab, gives flowers and gifts | This is business as usual for chivalrous Libra. He does it for his sisters, mom, and 20 best female friends. It makes him feel like a man. | Let him treat you (he'll insist, anyway). Don't make assumptions about his interest level. |
| Introduces you to his family and/ or closest friends | You've made it to the semifinals. Now, you have to pass their litmus test. | Do what it takes to make them love you. Suck it up and pour on the artificial sweetener. |

# Your Moves: Tips for Flirting and Everlasting Love

## Flirting with a Libra

To charming Libra, flirting is as natural as breathing. He loves the whole mating dance, and he'll shamelessly flirt with anyone who looks in his direction—bank tellers, cashiers, the dog walker. Want to wind this seductive sign around your finger? Try this:

**Be a little immune to his charms.** Nothing reels in a Libra man more than the dynamic tension of a woman playing slightly hard to get. Giggle at a couple of his jokes, then ignore the next one. Let him gaze into your eyes, then walk off and work the room. That push-pull thing will really rev him. Tip his carefully balanced scales back and forth and stir up some friction.

**Share a deep, one-on-one conversation.** There's nothing the harmony-loving Libra man loves more than connecting through a talk that lasts for hours… and hours. He loves a woman with brains and beauty, so let your golden tongue captivate him.

**Mirror him.** Libra is the sign of partnership and equality, and he responds to subconscious cues that signal you're in sync with him. Mirror his gestures, or "speak" to him with harmonious body language. Like perfectly balanced bookends, he'll feel totally in tune with you. (Besides, there's nothing this metrosexual pretty-boy loves more than his mirror.)

**Make him laugh.** Cleverness is a Libra passion (think of sharp-witted Libra Oscar Wilde), and it turns him on big-time. Crack him up with a shrewd little comment. He may be the only person in the room to catch your smart, sly sense of humor—and he'll appreciate it. The inside joke will be the beginning of your bond.

**Dress elegantly and impeccably.** The Libra man is easily charmed by a beautiful, sophisticated woman who carries herself with grace. Delight his senses with your fine taste in fabric.

# Everlasting Love with a Libra

So you hope to reach the altar with your Libra. Like New York City, if you can make it there, you can make it anywhere. Sure he may shower you with poetry and romance, but truly walking his talk takes a lot longer. You may need to ride his indecisive waves to the point of seasickness. Do you think he's worth those stormy seas? If so, here's how to inspire his eternal devotion:

**Always look like you're on your first date.** Hair, makeup, nails—check. The Libra man loves to dress up and hit the town, so you'd best keep a closet full of lovely outfits to accompany him.

**Mind your manners.** We know that after being together for a while, you relax and "let yourself go." Not so fast. To keep the Libra man fantasizing about you, you might pee with the door closed for the rest of your life, or wait until he leaves the house to take a crap. One woman we know never farted in front of her Libra husband, and they'd been married for eight years! In his mind, a goddess doesn't have gas. Besides, once you open that can of worms, you'll regret it. He thinks everything he does is sacred, including his own bodily functions. Do you really want to hear his bowel report? He'll be glad to share. Don't ask, don't tell.

**Share his hobbies.** So he loves ballroom dancing, photography, and traveling on guided tours. You have two left feet, no patience for camera equipment, and would rather take a spontaneous getaway than follow an itinerary of sightseeing. Better warm those hips up for the fox-trot and prepare to tour the Eiffel Tower—from top to bottom, huge camera around his neck, in the company of thirty new "friends."

**Create a beautiful home together.** The Libra man is sensitive to his environment, and he loves to bask in ambient beauty. The more furniture, *objets d'art*, and real estate you jointly own, the less likely he is to ever go anywhere else. In fact, building a collection of pretty possessions together can be great "baby steps" for the commitment-shy Libra.

**Invest in rose-colored glasses for two.** Libra wants that magical "life is beautiful" vibe to follow him everywhere. Let your inner Merry Sunshine pull him out of his occasional gloom, and keep him looking at the world through dreamy eyes.

**Be the woman he admires most.** Don't bother hiring a publicist! If the Libra man admires you, he'll toot your horn wherever you go. He wants to be utterly enchanted by you, a fan of your talents, awed by your natural grace.

**Get knocked up.** With this indecisive dude, you may need to force his hand. We don't recommend secretly puncturing the condoms, or skipping your birth control pill. Dishonesty will kill your relationship. But if you accidentally find yourself "with child," he may go from boy to man in record time. The Libra man makes a devoted dad, and he wants to do the right thing. Nothing kicks his ass off the fence more than the responsibility of kids.

# Prep Yourself For...

## Your First Date

Ah, the Libra man in his element: on a date. He loves to court women, so just enjoy whatever charming itinerary he cooks up. The more patient and self-possessed you are, the more you'll guarantee that every date feels like the first.

**The Basic Vibe:** You know those guys (weenies, we call them) the kind that ask you out, but you're not really sure if it's a date or they just want to hang out as friends, so you end up doing something casual and non-datelike, feeling awkwardly tortured the whole time? Well, thank God the Libra man won't subject you to that. He loves to date as much as any girl, and he'll want to make your time together romantic and special.

The Libra man can be a thoughtful planner, so let him choose the restaurant, wine bar, museum, concert, whatever. His taste is probably far more upscale or decadent than yours. Just show up, look beautiful, and enjoy being taken on the town. Not so much to ask, is it?

**What to Wear:** Err on the side of overdressing with Libra. Look good, smell good, and dress like a lady. If your nails are chipped, get a mani-pedi on your lunch break, 'cuz he'll notice. He responds to pastels and soft femininity, so save the shocking fuchsia or cobalt blue for another evening (unless you wear it in proportion; it's all about symmetry with Libra). Go upscale and elegant. Even if you met him at a college sports bar wearing jeans and a baseball cap, you probably won't be going back to Scorekeepers Campus Grill on your date. Chances are, he's planned an itinerary, so you'll probably know where you're going and can dress appropriately.

**What Not to Wear:** The tomboy look is not his speed. The Libra man wants to date a classy lady. Your army jacket, scuffed shoes, black nail polish, and Goth gear might make him your best buddy, but they probably won't win his heart. Take a trip to the dry cleaner before your date, since you'll want to skip the wash-and-wear or rumpled clothes.

**To Pay, or Not to Pay?** Not on your life. The Libra man loves to play the caring gentleman, and he might even be offended if you pull out your wallet. He's the sign of equality, but he'd rather have you even the score by dressing up and looking like a goddess.

**Saying Good night:** If the Libra man is truly interested in you, he'll take care of you until the very end. Like a gentleman, he'll drive you home or walk you to your doorstep. Or, he may put you in a taxi, pressing a bill into the cab driver's hand and ordering him to "get her home safely." Chances are, he'll have built up the romance gradually all night, so you won't be going home without a good night kiss. Depending on how slowly his internal clock ticks, it will either be a polite peck or a full-tongue press.

## His First Home Visit

All hail, the Prince is coming! The Libra man takes pride in his home, and some men of this sign could put Martha Stewart to shame. Our Libra friend Ben once walked into Ophira's house, pointed out all the sharp corners and declared, "Don't you know about Feng Shui? This apartment is filled with poison arrows!" The Libra man loves a balanced, tasteful home. Neatly stacked rolls of toilet paper, well-framed fine art, perfectly folded towels that smell springtime fresh—now we're talking. So if you want him to feel at home, create a little balanced, feminine elegance.

**Freshen it up.** The sensual Libra man is strongly affected by "everyday household odors," as advertisers call that funk from last night's roasted garlic soufflé, or your miniature schnauzer's Wee-Wee Pad. Make sure he's not assaulted by a blast of scent, even if it's from potpourri, a strong candle, or bleachy cleaning products. A mist of designer household spray in a classy, mild scent like aged teak or cedar will do.

**Tone it down a tad.** If your house is painted in bold or shocking colors, that's your right. But if your Libra man walks in and asks for sunglasses and a tab of Excedrin—or starts offering unsolicited decorating tips—don't say we didn't warn you.

*Vive la femme.* Pretty up your digs with fresh flowers, art, coffee table books, and a few girlie touches. Make it pleasant and comfortable, and he'll want to linger for hours.

**Have dessert ready.** Don't like to keep sweets in the house? Well, you won't be keeping his sweet ass in yours. Sugar will get you everywhere with a dessert-loving Libra man. Have some confections in the pantry, along with a few snacks. He likes to munch on finger foods. Some of them can be healthy, like hummus and chips, as long as you don't give him raisins when he wants Chips Ahoy.

**Highlight your important relationships.** Libra is the sign of relationships, so feel free to display albums and framed photos of your family and closest friends. He'll want to know that you have important connections, since he values his own. Don't be surprised if he starts paging through your scrapbooks, even asking about your relatives and later, remembering the sentimental stories.

**Put "pairs" on display.** Got two pretty wing chairs, a matching set of vases, a café table for two? Make these a prominent focus. The Libra man subconsciously responds to "pair-bonding" clues in the environment, and he'll gravitate there. Arrange your seating area in a social configuration, one that allows you to face each other for intimate conversation and gazing.

## Meeting His Family

The Libra man is the crown prince of his family. Chances are, he was spoiled and coddled by his parents, maybe he was even Mama's favorite. Still, he rarely faces rivalry, since he's a caring brother who usually has an affectionate, even fatherly, relationship with his siblings. Libra is the sign of dependence, and it can take him years to move out of his family's house. Even then, he often settles nearby, where he can take advantage of mama's cooking and family gatherings.

Cutting the cord is extremely difficult for the Libra man. Since the separation process often comes with an "ugly" rebellion, he may avoid it altogether. He hates conflict and unpleasantness, and would rather compromise than fight. Part of his commitment-phobia is a latent teen rebellion, misdirected at his girlfriends rather than his parents. This can take a toll on his relationships unless he's willing to grow up—or dates someone with an equally childlike parental bond.

Several years ago, Ophira went on an Internet date with a Libra guy. At twenty-eight, he'd just moved out of his parents' house into his own apartment a few miles away. Still, he revealed (without a trace of shame) that his mother cooked a week's worth of food and brought it over in Tupperware, along with his freshly starched laundry. After following the band Phish to 138 concerts (including through Europe), he just started his first "real" job at a dot-com, and was now eager to blow his paycheck on the dating scene.

Dinner and conversation were lovely, and Mr. Libra generously followed up the expensive meal with a live performance by his favorite band. Then… it all went south. As the band started their first number, Mr. Libra threw his arm around Ophira's shoulder, pulled her too close and cooed, "My parents are bringing bagels over in the morning. Want to be there to meet them?"

In most cases, the Libra man is married to his family, so you'd better learn their rules and play by them. In other words: suck up, sister. Bring gifts, flowers, girlish gratitude, and a willingness to call his parents "mom" and "dad." Be a sweet, kind angel that they adore. The upside is, he'll usually ingratiate himself to your family, charming them like he does everyone else. He's sentimental about family, and is always on his best behavior with yours.

Being Mr. Equality, he expects the same of you. Even if his mother drives you crazy and his father all but shuns you, don't even think about airing any grievances. Beware the temptation to fight his battles, too. He may rail about his father's narcissism behind closed doors, but in daddy's face, he plays the meek little solider-boy. Don't get involved. Bite your tongue and exclaim over his mommy's cooking instead. If you can't think of anything nice to say, say nothing at all.

# Saying Good-bye
## Breaking Up with a Libra

Please—be gentle. Go easy on his tender emotions. He's the sweetest guy you'll ever meet, even when he's being a jerk. While the Libra man may infuriate you with his languid pace and ten-year delay to the altar, if you break his heart, he'll take years to recover. Libra is the sign of dependence, so once he's really let you in, losing you will be agonizing. He'll get weepy and sentimental, suddenly showing you all the emotions you never knew he had.

Heed our words: never, *ever,* break up with a Libra by phone or email. Playing fair is important to this courtly idealist, so respect him enough to end things face-to-face. You can soothe the blow by breaking up poetically ("Let's be friends forever"), though he may bitterly reject any sentimental gestures. Bottom line: He's the sign of fairness, and he doesn't think it's fair for you to dump him without a damn good reason.

Even though you've got every right to move on, the thought of hurting Libra could make you feel guilty forever. Ophira broke up with her first boyfriend, a Libra, at age fourteen—on a random teenage whim (and over the phone, no less). He'd just gotten out of the shower after his fast-food job when she blindsided him. "I feel like someone just punched me in the stomach," he told her, then started to cry. Ouch! Who can bear to hurt a sweet, tender Libra? Twenty years later, his words still haunt her, and make her cringe with guilt.

## Getting over Him: When a Libra Dumps You

The Libra man hates conflict, and he usually takes a back-door approach to breaking up with you. He's the unofficial king of the "passive exit." Rather than dump you cold, he'll make conditions so unbearable that you end up ditching him. He usually does this by flip-flopping and being suddenly indecisive: "I don't know if we're right for each other." Or, "It's not you—it's me. I just don't know what I want." Or the favorite, "I'm just not ready for something this serious" (uttered after nine years—or minutes—together). Of course, if you take him seriously and leave, he may panic and run back a couple times. It's no easier for this sign to commit to a breakup than to a long-term relationship.

The Libra man hates conflict, so by being indirect, he hopes he'll hurt you less. Sadly, he usually ends up hurting you more. Eventually, if you put the metaphorical gun to his head and demand a clear answer, you may only get a partly cloudy "adios." Usually, you'll need to read between the lines. In an ideal scenario, you'll have a friendly, mutual breakup and remain pals forever. Then again, you might also believe in unicorns, too.

Once you're sure it's over, detoxing your home will be top priority, since it's probably filled with his sentimental gift items. Pack away all the cutesy objects, crying as you engulf each in bubble wrap… or flames. Rearrange your furniture, paint, and change the energy as much as possible. You might even need to redecorate, since he may have had a hand in your current interior scheme.

**Have yourself one good last cry over…**

- The sweet, sentimental gestures
- His fine metrosexual taste
- The gifts—wasn't it fun to be spoiled?
- Feeling like daddy's little princess
- His appreciation of your femininity
- His silly, sarcastic sense of humor
- The way he took the time to get to know your whole family, their stories and interests
- Losing his family in the breakup, if you got along with them

**Praise the universe that you never have to deal with…**

- His total domination of the bathroom mirror, shelves, and closet space
- Sugar shock: playing the nice, sweet, accommodating angel—when you really want to scream

- His gooey, sentimental side
- His indecisiveness and wishy-washy backpedaling
- Having to watch him schmooze, kiss ass, and charm the room—come on, nobody's THAT nice

- His moments of spinelessness when you wished he'd be assertive
- His earnest, unblinking hero-worship of daddy, his boss, the company president…

- His gruff, grouchy moments—who's the bitch here, anyway?

# Love Matcher:

## *Can you find a common language?*

| You are a(n)... | He thinks you're... | You think he's... | Common Language |
|---|---|---|---|
| Aries | His dream diva. | Your knight in shining armor. | Romance, pampering, indulgence |
| Taurus | Pretty but a little too practical at times. | Handsome and charming, but might make you jealous. | Wine, food, highbrow tastes, sensuality |
| Gemini | Fun, wild, but a little chemically unbalanced. | Cute, sexy, but a little too soft. | Parties, conversation, flirting, fun |
| Cancer | The mother of his children (but a little clingy). | A handsome knight in shining armor who will sweep you off your feet. | Affection, family values |
| Leo | A romantic and passionate siren, but kind of demanding and bossy. | Sweet and sexy but moves too slow. A little too cool for your warm-blooded style. | Living out romantic fairy tales, overspending on luxury goods, bingeing on expensive chocolate |

| You are a(n)... | He thinks you're... | You think he's... | Common Language |
|---|---|---|---|
| Virgo | Admirably refined, but a little too practical for his liking. | A dreamer who needs a reality check, but also brings magic to your earthbound life. | Your anal-retentive habits, obsession with hygiene and grooming |
| Libra | A goddess. | Your romantic soul mate. | Love, sweet love |
| Scorpio | Intense—and intensely fascinating. He could do without the jealousy and power games, thank you. | An incurable flirt who will activate your hair-trigger jealous alarm. | Investments, money, high-end material goods, making everyone jealous of you, fashion and power dressing |
| Sagittarius | Hilarious, spontaneous fun, but in need of better style and grooming skills. Might embarrass him in public. | Fun, but a little bit stuffy. Reminds you of your grandpa sometimes. Loosen up, dude! | Sarcastic, spot-on jokes and observations. Spontaneous fun. Deep-seated fear of commitment. |

| You are a(n)... | He thinks you're... | You think he's... | Common Language |
|---|---|---|---|
| Capricorn | Controlling, dominating, but a real trophy girl that can boost his status. | Vain, shallow, flighty, and full of s**t. All talk and no action. | Making money, status, social climbing, corporate ass kissing |
| Aquarius | The kind of free-spirited soul he adores. | A grounding, stabilizing force—believe it or not—and totally your kind of guy. | Ideas, adventure, art, music, travel, life, everything |
| Pisces | The sexiest, most enchanting mystery he's ever tried to solve. | The Prince Charming your fairy tale's been waiting to cast as its leading man. | Escaping and avoiding reality, living out romantic fantasies, blowing your budget on pleasure |

# The Scorpio Man

Dates: October 23–November 21
Symbol: The Scorpion
Ruling Planet: Pluto, the planet of transformation (coruled by warrior planet Mars)
Element: Water
Quality: Fixed
Mission: Soul mate Patrol

**Natural Habitat—Where You'll Find Him:** Soaking up the arts at an indie concert or snooty gallery opening, geeking out at a computer conference, rebalancing his energy at a yoga or spiritual retreat, behind the velvet rope of a restricted V.I.P. area, at home cleaning and spending quality time with his kids, in front of his computer at 3 A.M., working after hours in a dark studio or lab, at band practice, working at the office after everyone's left, hiding from the world in a secluded waterside cabin, deep in nature, sitting at the bar or the corner booth of a trendy restaurant, obsessing over an ex or love interest, plotting his next major life quest

**What He Does for a Living:** Media mogul, artist, musician, real estate agent, private investor, computer programmer, energy healer, body worker, dancer, fashion designer, chiropractor, lawyer, security director, detective, novelist, cop, agent, celebrity

**Noteworthy & Notorious Scorpio Men:** Ted Turner, P. Diddy, Matthew McConaughey, Ryan Gosling, Leonardo DiCaprio, Owen Wilson, Ethan Hawke, Nick Lachey, Anthony Kiedis, Bill Gates, Gavin Rossdale, Kevin Kline, Pablo Picasso, Truman Capote, Larry Flynt, Charles Manson, Kurt Vonnegut, Neil Young, Martin Scorsese, Prince Charles, Art Garfunkel, Ike Turner, Danny DeVito,

Larry King, Kevin Kline, Dennis Miller, Nelly, Billy Graham, Richard Burton, Sisqo, David Schwimmer, Auguste Rodin, Gerard Butler, Chris Noth, Ryan Reynolds, Dylan McDermott

# Scorpio: How to Spot Him

- Hypnotic voice
- Hawklike eyes and a slightly protruding brow—his "shield" for gazing intently at the world
- Medium-length, nimble fingers
- Finely structured face, usually heart-shaped
- Dark sunglasses
- Carrying equipment—he's the guy with the drumsticks, guitar, tripod, or three laptops strapped to his body
- Effeminate, flowy gestures, which occasionally make you question his sexual orientation
- Lurking presence—he's the guy at the bar who hasn't taken his eyes off of you
- Standing with crotch thrust forward, probably pointing at you
- Preppy Scorpios like P. Diddy dress in fussy white sneakers (and may carry a toothbrush to clean them periodically)
- B.O. assault! Grungy Scorpios like Matthew McConaughey and Ethan Hawke give new meaning to "bring in the funk"… but his pheromones might just turn you on
- Streaker alert! He's prone to random acts of public nudity
- Charming chubster: he's the guy with the big belly surrounded by a gaggle of admiring girls half his age

# Scorpio: How He Deals With...

## Money

Loves it, needs it, will spend all of his (and yours, too) if you let him. Prone to credit card debt; may max out his Visa trying to impress you in the courtship phase.

## Family

Love/hate relationship with all his relatives, particularly his mother. Longs to be back in her womb but harbors a deep-seated resentment at his dependency on her. Can be more Oedipal than a Cancer.

## Love

Believes in soul mates and won't settle for less. Wants to love you slightly more than you love him so he knows he's scored a real prize.

## Sex

Sex is a spiritual experience for him. A "lights on" guy who wants to see every micro-millimeter of your body, then describe it in poetic—or excruciating—detail later on.

## Children

Hello, Mr. Mom. Loves kids, wants to be involved in every aspect of parenting. A great dad who can be overprotective or controlling.

## Pets

Hello, Mr. Cat Lady.

### Your Meltdowns

If you're upset about something other than him, he'll make you tea and give you a hug as you vent. Warning: He has a half-hour limit for indulging histrionics before he loses interest and starts talking about himself.

If you're upset about HIM...he'll become instantly defensive, especially if you start crying or raging. He'll follow up with a cold shoulder and screen most of your calls. Behind the scenes, he may read self-improvement books and articles to bolster his argument against you, or remedy the shortcoming you're complaining about.

### His Meltdowns

File a missing person's report. The Scorpio man's meltdown is dark and depressing and in extreme cases may involve an extended disappearance. Our friend's Scorpio boyfriend once flew to the Philippines alone, then asked the locals to row him out to a deserted island and pick him up two weeks later. And this was his idea of paradise...

### Breakups

Ices you out completely but rages/obsesses about you for months, even years. May Google you for life.

# Scorpio: What He's All About

Do you long for the predictable? Fear the unknown? Then stop reading now. The Scorpio man is a complex, often confusing creature who thrives on life's extremes. There is no such thing as moderation with this intense, all-or-nothing guy. He's as infuriating as he is addictive, fascinating yet exhausting—a sexually and domestically gifted man-boy who can put the "ho" in "homemaker."

He's also one of the most creative signs in the zodiac. This man has a knack for stamping everything he touches with his own personal flair. Although he can obsess on a subject, his powers of concentration are unrivaled. What Scorpio lacks in breadth, he makes up for in depth. The Scorpio man will plunge into his passions, studying and experimenting until he's a walking encyclopedia on the topic. Mastery is his ultimate goal.

It's said that there are two types of Scorpios: the Scorpion and the Eagle. The first is the "lower" form of Scorpio—the vengeful, easily threatened ground-dweller with a deadly sting. When Scorpio overcomes this darker nature, he can achieve spiritual elevation and become a powerful, world-transforming force. Like a soaring eagle or hawk, he gains a sweeping command of the world beneath him. Rather than control, he uses his power to elevate others to their highest spiritual plane.

To truly understand the Scorpio man, just study a really butch lesbian. She looks like someone you'd never want to meet in a dark alley. She intimidates the hell out of you. But underneath the sneers, leers, and pomade, there's a woman in there.

*Et tu,* Scorpio. He's an emotional Water sign, uncontrollably rocked by his powerful feelings like a ship on stormy seas. It's why his closest friends are usually women—and contrary to his sign's reputation, he's not actually sleeping with them (at least, not yet). Although he can be caustic and cranky, he can also be deeply compassionate—a best-girlfriend kind of listener who cuts to the core of your issues with a single, laserlike observation. Scorpio rules psychology, and he understands human nature well.

Of course, you'll always feel a bit exposed as you share secrets with a Scorpio. Emotionally naked is more accurate. He's always undressing you in some way, and he has a gift for getting you to show your hand while he keeps his cards close to his chest. Be careful what you wish for, though. In typical extreme fashion, he can be as self-absorbed as he is silent. It's easy to find yourself playing therapist with a Scorpio man, and once you start, you'll regret it. He can be a bottomless, obsessive pit of need. It's best to let him work out his own issues.

There's a dark side to this guy, and he can be a real energy vampire when he fixates on negative thoughts. He needs to do a lot of "processing" to unsnarl his turbulent emotions. He may do it privately: reading spiritual books, calling psychics, or channeling his powerful emotions into music, art, or sex. Or, he'll navel-gaze out loud, assuming his audience is as fascinated by his emotional landscape as he is. (Usually, they just want to sleep with him, and hope he'll finally shut up and get naked.)

Although he may "settle down" domestically, the Scorpio man is on a lifelong inner quest. Satisfaction equals death in his mind, because it means he's stopped growing. Yet, he's always seeking the very thing he doesn't want: an easy answer. As a result, there's a tortured air to the Scorpio man—at least, until he learns to set ever-higher goals for himself and rest in between.

Channeling his angst into a creative project is highly cathartic, and essential to your relationship's survival. The Scorpio man is always obsessed with something—be it his job, his guitar, his fitness, or balancing his checkbook. Every Scorpio guy we know has his "thing," and his hobbies will often cut into your quality time together. Forget about him cheating on you; his camera or computer will be the real "other woman." Scorpio is a night creature, so he can keep late hours, and is often most productive while the rest of the world sleeps. The woman who keeps him knows how to lay down the law while still giving him room to roam.

If you want the bills paid while you live out your caviar wishes, a Taurus or Capricorn is your guy. Scorpio is no sugar daddy. Though he talks a good game, the Scorpio man is not necessarily a provider. In fact, he's happy to play stay-at-home dad, since he cherishes his sacred alone time. Scorpio is the sign that rules other people's resources, so he's best off with a corporate expense account—or your checkbook. If you bring home the bacon, he'll make a breakfast fit for kings. He can be surprisingly tight with his own cash. Even wealthy Scorpios are busy investing, so don't expect regular Madison Avenue shopping trips with this guy. He wants you to have your own passions, pursuits, and bank account.

If you need constant togetherness, switch to a Leo or a Cancer. You'll need to have your own life to survive Scorpio's erratic schedule. If you're a secure woman who craves excitement, he's got plenty, though. Scorpio is a curious prowler who loves nightlife, arts, and culture. He remains eternally young and hot, and often gets hotter with age. He may eat or drink too much, but he usually takes good care of his body—and he'll take even better care of yours. This guy will take you on mental, spiritual, and sexual adventures you'll never forget. Like riding a roller coaster, you'll feel on the edge of losing control, but the highs can be thrilling, too.

# What He Wants in a Woman

Do you love a good game of master and servant? Can you handle him with kid gloves one day, steel-toed boots the next? There's a sadomasochistic vibe to every Scorpio man's love life. He's the sign of power and control, and the woman who innately understands this game will keep him. Rule number one: Never, ever, EVER kiss his ass. Rule number two: Never show that you want him more than he wants you.

If you're a little bit mommy, a little bit rock 'n roll, the Scorpio man will set up camp at your breast forever. He'll raise the kids; you'll raise him. Of course, your reformatory efforts will be in vain, since nobody controls the zodiac's most willful child.

Fortunately, he knows how to follow your fury with sweet lovin', reeling himself back into your good graces.

The biggest turn-on to a Scorpio man is your self-respect. After all, it's the rare woman who can keep hers intact around him. With his "come to daddy" hotness, he's accustomed to women falling at his feet. Dozens of sexy young thangs lie brokenhearted in his wake, wondering why their exposed thongs, lap dances, and obvious cleavage couldn't win over the zodiac's "sex sign."

Sure, looks matter to Scorpio—way too much, in fact. Scorpio is a highly physical sign, and he can be a body-obsessed modelizer who likes his women shaped like prepubescent boys. Many Scorpios are tall and fat-free, and they're often obsessed with their own bodies. If his idea of a trophy wife is a 5'11" rail-thin underwear model (P.S.: she has to be brilliant, artistic, and the envy of all his friends, too), prepare to spend time on the rack. If juice fasts and grueling triathlons aren't your thing, choose a Taurus or a Cancer, who love a curvaceous babe.

But he needs more than a hot body to keep him interested forever. When he gets on bended knee for a buttoned-up Birkenstock babe who pushes him around, jaws drop below sea level. What the hell was her secret? In addition to having the steely composure of a dominatrix, she probably has the patience of Mother Theresa.

The Scorpio man loves powerful women—but it has to be the "right" kind of power. In a nutshell, you have to be a little too good for him, just out of his league. Though Scorpio rails against the system, he can be a name-dropping fame whore in counterculture clothing. His screening process is simple: *would the people I envy be jealous of me if I'm with this woman?* You must have suitably impressive credentials—Academy award–winning actress, prima ballerina, native Italian—that he can mention every time he talks about you.

"You know that Elite model I was dating? Yeah, we broke up," he'll brag. "She wasn't intellectual enough. Now I'm seeing Sabrina, the art history professor. Did you know she's the youngest person to be considered for tenure in her department?"

Go ahead, make more money than he does, as long as it makes him look good. He needs to feel like he's scored an upgrade from coach to first-class by dating you. One Scorpio we know started an "affair" with his English teacher a week after graduating high school (he claims she was hot). Desperation gives Sir Scorpio hypothermia of the crotch. Another Scorpio friend iced out his Cancer love interest when she baked him a birthday cake after their first makeout session. Good thing she had the wisdom to back off; they're together five years later.

Masochistic as it sounds, the threat of rejection turns him on. Could you dump him cold and find someone richer and hotter tomorrow? Sold! Once you prove you've got the cojones to walk, it's game on. Now, he'll quietly observe (through an additional series of tests or clandestine Googling) whether you're soul mate material. The detail-oriented Scorpio man is particular and uncompromising in this quest. He wants a cultured, classy, edgy woman who makes him look good in public. He could be flat broke with love handles and half his teeth. No matter. He sets his sights at the top of the food chain, and pursues until he gets the girl. This could take a long time, since he's often secretive and self-protective. One Scorpio man we know sent several flower arrangements anonymously to his crush before working up the nerve to sign the card! Lucky for him, she wasn't too weirded out.

Because Scorpio is a secretive sign, he can come off as accidentally creepy. Like a laser beam, he's forever honing in on his exact target, then zeroing in for the kill. The woman who holds his interest must fall within his scope, while occasionally darting out of his reach. If a lifelong game of cat and mouse excites you,

you'll never be bored with a Scorpio. He loves that edge of danger and mystery, of striving to be part of the "in crowd," while still remaining undiscovered on its fringes.

Although we've stressed the Scorpio man's need for space, he has a double standard. He may demand the right to be seen as a separate person, but he doesn't readily grant that to you. When he needs you there, you'd best come a-runnin'. A friend recently ran across her Scorpio ex's online photo album. She saw him with his new girlfriend, racing bikes in color-coordinated spandex. On Christmas, she dressed up as a sexy elf to complement his Santa costume, and on it went. In the pictures, she appears perfectly content being a female extension of him—and he looks over the moon. To some Scorpio men, this is a dream come true.

Ultimately, he longs for a spiritual and sexual soul mate, someone to "become one with" on a truly intimate level. The Scorpio man's greatest fear is also his truest desire. The woman who can patiently remain unrattled through his turbulent cycles and many rebirths will keep Scorpio around for a lifetime.

# What He Wants from a Relationship

Bonnie and Clyde. Sid and Nancy. Brangelina. The Scorpio man is looking for an iconic relationship, a hall of fame soul mate story—and he refuses to settle for less. He may give his body, even his name or DNA. But until he finds his mythic other half, the person who makes him look and feel like a god, he'll never give his soul.

The Scorpio man needs to be part of a power couple. He needs a trophy wife and a soul mate in one. Here's his idea of nirvana: He's the king of his empire, and you're the queen of yours, and together, you're the envy of the world. It's rumored that Scorpio P. Diddy will never get over Jennifer Lopez—even the model who bore his children can't keep him faithful.

Although he's a classic family man, Scorpio isn't overly traditional about marriage. In many ways, he's a feminist here. He loves a powerful woman with her own life, money, career, and interests—and he won't try to change you once you get married. He doesn't mind if you keep your own last name, or even out-earn him, as long as you keep your salaries private. He'll gladly pick the kids up from school, make dinner, and scrub the bathroom with a toothbrush if it means he can be left alone to pursue his passions.

When it comes to his home and family, the Scorpio man demands creative control. Protective and possessive, he'll set up a utopian family structure under his tight supervision, even home schooling his kids. He wants everything he does to be the "ultimate"— and molds his family according to his uncompromising vision. Scorpio rules the reproductive system, making him a natural father. He longs for a close-knit family filled with love and open communication, and he'll do what it takes to get that.

Behind every Scorpio man's relationship style is... his mom. He has a complicated, love/hate relationship with his mother that can border on Oedipal. Cutting the cord isn't easy for him, and his resulting behavior pattern can be tricky to navigate. He fears that every woman wants to "engulf" him, yet he constantly creates situations where he needs to be mothered by his mate. You may have to endure a "come-here-now-go-away" drama until he realizes you're not trying to control him. He'll need to take baby steps to let you in.

Scorpio is the sign of deep bonding and extreme detachment, making him a bit schizophrenic about intimacy. Closeness frightens him, because deep down, he fears separation. Abandonment issues? He's got 'em for days. While he longs to merge souls with you, another part of him is terrified to lose control. He feels pain at a deeper level than any other sign, and breakups can haunt him for decades. To protect himself, he'll try to keep some sense of "space" in the relationship—having a long-distance relationship, working late, or keeping his own apartment. If you push him to take a step before he's ready, he'll draw back. This could go on for years until he feels "ready" (read: safe enough) to come a centimeter closer.

The Scorpio man needs space, but he also needs you to lay down limits. Don't give him an all-access pass to your life (are you listening, Sagittarius, Leo, and Gemini ladies?). He needs an edge of mystery, some part of you that he'll never figure out. Dancing this fine line can be exhausting and unrewarding for some women, and we don't recommend it unless it comes naturally.

Once you're in, should you make it that far, you'll feel like a goddess. The Scorpio man is a wholly different creature once he surrenders to trust. He lets you be totally sexually expressed while feeling fully respected. There's no Madonna/whore conflict. The more you fly your freak flag, the more he pledges allegiance.

Scorpio is the sign of death and rebirth, the mythic phoenix rising from the ashes of destruction. You may have several breakups or relationship phases en route to fully committing. Though they will be harrowing for you, he considers these fiery emotional trials a purification ritual. In his mind, the more your relationship withstands turmoil, the more "real" your connection is. Hardcore? You bet.

Although he can seem commitment-phobic, he takes marriage and relationships more seriously than mafia initiation. He cherishes trust and honesty—at least your honesty. On the other hand, you may never quite know where he stands. But that's part of the adventure with a Scorpio. Just when you think you've got him figured out, he throws you a curve. Stay on your toes, and he might just sweep you off your feet.

# Sex with a Scorpio

Like a drug, sex with a Scorpio man can be addictive, a dragon you'll chase for years after the first high. He might be a little rough or jerky at first, but it won't matter. Scorpio knows the art of seduction, of blasting you with his full attention, then abruptly snatching it back. This awakens a primal part of women's brains and makes us want him even more. The overall experience of being with him can cause your brain to release addiction-forming chemicals, making him a hard habit to shake. It's the way he looks at you, like you've changed his life, and nothing else matters but you. He's confident in his sexual prowess; after all, his sign rules the crotch and reproductive system.

Sex is a spiritual experience for Scorpio. Although he'll have his flings, he prefers to give his entire focus to one partner, body and soul. He wants to experience oneness on every level, to transcend his body while also being completely immersed in physical pleasure. Genevieve, a Gemini, says that sex with her Scorpio boyfriend "varies between being really grinding and dirty, and also being more spiritual and sensuous."

Like many Scorpios, Genevieve's boyfriend is interested in sexual technique, and he brought home a book on tantric sex. "He learned all about breath," she says. "He wanted to be multi-orgasmic. He really took it seriously. He would practice during the day—it was really enjoyable to him.

"He also got this book on sex and Kaballah," continues Genevieve, "and they teach you that when you have an orgasm, you give off all this energy to the universe. So he visualizes these Hebrew letters when he's coming. It kind of magnifies the sexual energy and makes it into a cosmic spark." Only a Scorpio.

Whatever his pleasure, the Scorpio man will tell you. He can talk objectively about his fantasies, almost like a research scientist. He'll never judge yours. In fact, he may expand your sexual comfort zone significantly. He's fascinated by his desires, and wants to worship you like a goddess. If you want to explore your sexuality with a safe partner, the Scorpio man is an amazing teacher and guide.

## Scorpio: Turn-Ons & Turn-Offs

## Turn Him On

- Dress in racy (but never trashy) clothes: high heels, short skirt, La Perla lingerie peeking out of your top.
- Lose all but 8 percent of your body fat: this guy is the most shameless "modelizer" of the zodiac.
- Name-drop about your rich, famous, and fabulous friends—Scorpio men want to be down with the hippest of the hipsters.
- Hold your own in conversations about world issues, music, literature, and art.
- Be up on the latest cultural events, especially concerts and gallery openings.
- Read… the paper, poetry, novels, cultural criticisms, biographies of presidential candidates… and quote the books in conversation.
- Have your own domain that he can brag about. His lust for power includes a powerful woman.
- Tell him in graphic detail about your sexual experiences, especially if they involve other women.
- Show him that you're a good friend with a solid character—trust is everything to Scorpio.
- Be a world traveler.
- Remain unfazed by his harsh or critical remarks: He's testing you to see how vulnerable you are.

- Innocently pepper conversations with "secrets" about your lingerie collection, bikini waxing, or self-pleasuring preferences. He will be fantasizing... and taking notes immediately.
- Be slightly rejecting or distant at times—he loves the thrill of pulling you close again.
- Bond with his friends—they are his unofficial family and their seal of approval could make or break you.
- Side with him when he complains about his relatives. That "us against the world" thing is one of his secret fantasies.

## Turn Him Off

- Remind him a little too much of his mother or get too chummy with her—you'll stir up his secret shame about his Oedipus complex.
- Show that you like him more than he likes you.
- Wait too long to return his call. He loves to talk and will find another conversation buddy if you're not around.
- Cry in public or make a scene. He'll feel like you're humiliating him and making him look like the bad guy.
- Cross the line from sexy into trashy. He might be a flasher, but he doesn't want you to be.
- Make him look like a chump in front of his friends: instant deal-breaker.
- Refuse to visit him at his place. Scorpio men are nesters and like to control the environment.
- Stir up his abandonment issues by walking out on him during an argument. He won't be home when you come back.

- Act high and mighty, like you're more important than him—he'll make it his mission to knock you off your pedestal.
- Gain weight.
- Expect him to pay for every date, or forget to say thank you when he does.

- Get too excited when he starts musing about marriage and children—he likes talking about it, but unless he directly says he sees you as wifey, don't assume he thinks you're the One.
- Interrupt him when he's pontificating about music, politics, or any of his obsessions. And no, not even if he's been talking about the subject for two hours.

- Make fun of his hobbies or his art.
- Refuse to talk about sex.

# His Moves

## First Moves: How He Courts You

Is he staring at you, or at the painting behind your head? With a Scorpio, it's hard to tell. Sure, you may feel an undercurrent of sexual chemistry with him, but so does everyone. He likes to keep people guessing. Scorpio men have lots of female friends, and he's affectionate with his. Nobody gives a better hug than this guy, and he enjoys risqué banter. You may always wonder whether he's hitting on you or just making playful conversation.

Scorpio is the "detective" sign, and he begins every courtship by studying you from a safe distance. If you have the unsettling sense that somebody's watching you, you either forgot to take your meds, or a Scorpio man is checking you out.

Here are signals that this astrological "man of mystery" might be interested in you. (That said, the line is always blurry with him at first, so don't get your hopes up too high just yet.)

- He pulls you away from the crowd into a one-on-one conversation
- He stares at you intensely and smiles, making you blush and look away
- His "do-me" body language: hips loose, crotch subtly pointed at you
- He invites you to drinks or dinner at his favorite spot
- He tells you he has two tickets to a show or event
- He shares a journal entry or highlights from his therapy session
- He blurts out that he has a crush on you at a completely awkward, inappropriate moment
- He asks around about you
- His hug lingers just a little too long

## He's In: How You Know He's Committed

Let's get something clear: This is not going to be an overnight relationship. The Scorpio man takes longer than a flight to Tokyo before he trusts you. He knows that he'll get deeply attached once he lets you in, so you may endure several breakups and massive resistance before he finally caves to commitment. By the time you get to this point, if you still give a damn, there won't be much gray area left.

**He brings up the "m" word—monogamy.** Scorpio is the sex sign, so if he deems you worthy of an exclusive, he's probably not planning to spend the night elsewhere.

**He brings up the other "m" word—moving.** The Scorpio man's home is his shrine, and he doesn't share it readily. Moving in together is a huge step for him, and a total sign of trust. Caution: Make sure you're ready, because once he takes this leap, you've got a permanent roommate.

**He gives you a shockingly well-researched gift.** If he's stopped showing off long enough to study your interests and tastes, he's into you. The gift may not be expensive—he might even have found it in an obscure eBay shop—but the love is in the details. He's giving you a token of your connection, and showing how well he knows you.

**He lets you hang out with his friends on a regular basis.** Private Scorpios have a tight inner circle that they guard from outside invasion. He likes to keep an Alpha position in his posse, and doesn't introduce girlfriends unless he's sure he wants to be with you. If he invites you to see his band play, or includes you in his personal life, he thinks you're impressive enough to show around.

**He wants to be with you all the time.** One woman says of her Scorpio boyfriend, "He's so into me. He doesn't have a roving eye at all. When he's with me, he gives me all his lust and attention, makes me feel like I'm the most important person in his life. I feel like I'm his woman and he wouldn't want to be with anyone else."

## Unfaithful Scorpio: Why He Cheats

Flirty and sexy as he is, the Scorpio man isn't a big cheater. If he is, he's damn good at keeping it under wraps. Because of his strong sexual energy, you may wonder whether he's hiding something from you, but don't get too paranoid. As one Scorpio guy put it, "If I've gotten to the point of actually being in a relationship, that means I trust and respect the person enough not to do that." If he wants to sleep around, he'll set up an open relationship, or just avoid committing to you. In rare cases, though, he'll live up to his lothario reputation. Here's why:

**You've lost your edge.** Have you become too conventional, or turned into a Wal-Mart wifey? This guy needs a sophisticated soul mate with all the sexual trimmings. If you want to take the safe road to suburbia, try a Cancer or a Capricorn instead.

**He thinks you cheated on him.** Although he'll usually just dump you cold, Scorpios also have a vengeful streak. If you hurt him deeply enough, he may fight fire with fire.

**He meets his "soul mate"—and she isn't you.** Deep down, the Scorpio man will never rest until he's met his spiritual partner. Should she suddenly come along when you're, say, eight months pregnant with his child, c'est la vie. Although he may not sleep with her until your official breakup, he might start an emotional relationship.

## Dig the Grave: It's Over

With Scorpio, no relationship is ever really over. He has a powerful memory, especially for pain, and he can't stand to let go of anything. Although he may obsess over you for decades, his modus operandi is usually to ice you out faster than a Subzero freezer. Scorpio is the zodiac's surgeon, so like a doctor removing a tumor, he thinks it's best to take the pain all at once, even if it means taking drastic measures. How do you know your steaming hot affair with a Scorpio has gone from sizzle to fizzle? Here are some telltale signs.

**He stops answering your calls.** Have you pissed off a Scorpio? The sound of silence will tell. Rather than fight, he just freezes you out. If he doesn't take your calls for more than three days, you've hit the iceberg and the *Titanic* is going down.

**He tells you.** The Scorpio man doesn't mince words; he minces you with them. If he tells you "it's over," it is—at least for now.

**He starts hanging out with a new female friend, and doesn't introduce you.** It's probably just platonic, but he's on a soul mate search. You're no longer the goddess he worships, and he's planning his exit.

**He rips you to shreds in an email.** The Scorpion's tail delivers a deadly sting. If you hurt him where he's most sensitive, prepare to take the poison. Although he may not say it to your face, the Scorpio man can be brutal. He'll tell you exactly what he thinks is wrong with you in no uncertain terms, pushing your emotional buttons.

**He makes plans to pursue his dream lifestyle—and you don't want to join him.** Opening a massage school, having kids, living in Nepal—whatever his dream is, if you don't share it, consider it a deal-breaker. Scorpio is a "come to me" kind of guy, and you either fit his agenda or he'll find someone who does.

**Emergency Kit Remedy:**

**Stage an intervention to talk about it.** Let him know that you're willing to try things his way (read the books he likes, have children, not have children, go vegetarian). If this feels like selling out, don't do it!

# Interpreting His Signals:

## What does he mean by that?

| When he | It means... | So you should... |
|---|---|---|
| Gets quiet | He's developing his next brilliant idea and needs to be quiet so he can obsess and think. | Shut up and leave him alone. If you stick around, go into an adjacent room and work on your own projects. Bonus points if you create a nurturing space by ordering dinner or passing him a drink. |
| Doesn't call | He's either overwhelmed or underwhelmed by you. | Get on the horn with other friends and make your life as cool and enviable as possible. When he does call, he'll kick himself for being left out by the in crowd. |
| Calls a lot | He's intrigued. | Answer all his calls, stay on the phone for half an hour max (even if he wants to keep talking). Then, have somewhere to go. He likes attention but he wants his woman to have a life. |
| Doesn't make a move after a couple of dates | He's questioning your character and isn't 100 percent sure that he can trust you. | Cool out the wild child antics and show him your stable side. Trigger his memories of mama with a home-cooked meal. |

| When he | It means... | So you should... |
|---|---|---|
| Doesn't make a move after a few weeks | He's enjoying your femininity but has shuffled you to the friend category or is still afraid you'll reject him if he makes a move (his biggest fear). | Flat out ask him if he's attracted to you. He'll tell you the truth and you might just like what you hear. |
| Moves fast | He's horny and is ready to end his abstinent spell. | Enjoy the most intense sex of your life but remember that Scorpio is the sign of extremes. He'll pull back as quickly as he pounces and may go AWOL after your hookup. Call him a week later if he hasn't called you. Scorpios can be "girls" in relationships and he's probably waiting for you to make the next move. |
| Picks up the tab, gives flowers and gifts | He thinks you're the real deal—this dude doesn't spend money on just anyone. | Show heartfelt appreciation. Odds are, he's put a lot of thought and research into the gift. Never, ever criticize what he gives you or forget to say thank you. |

| When he | It means... | So you should... |
| --- | --- | --- |
| Introduces you to his family and/or closest friends | Bottom line: He trusts you now, which is a big deal to this suspicious sign.<br><br>Friends...he thinks you're cool enough to impress them.<br><br>Family...he's trying to impress them too, and quite possibly to make them stop wondering if he's gay. | Be self-possessed, confident, and warm—extend yourself without trying too hard.<br><br>Make him look like The Man.<br><br>Never, ever tease him in front of his relatives! |

# Your Moves: Tips for Flirting and Everlasting Love

## Flirting with a Scorpio

The Scorpio man is a greedy attention whore who loves to be admired. He's a total tease who wants everyone to want him, even if he has no intention of delivering in return. Just about everything he does counts as flirting. He can't even pick up dog poop or take cash out of an ATM without making some come-hither gesture. Want to seduce the master of seduction? Here are a few ways to beat him at his own game.

**Name drop.** We used to joke that Scorpio men's sexual orientation is "celebrity." Quietly ambitious, he's always angling for a seat at the big, mahogany executive table. Know a famous artist or sports figure? Got box seats to the playoffs or a regular table in the VIP section? Mention it like it's no big deal, and you'll have his attention. Hint that he could possibly join you in the future, or that you might introduce him to one of your high-profile contacts. Leave him subtly feeling like he's not quite good enough to make it past the velvet rope. He'll ask you out tomorrow.

**Talk to him about his passions.** The Scorpio man is always revved up about something—music, art, books, travel—and he loves to share. Be sure to interject your own opinions and challenge him a little. Don't pretend you're interested just because you want him to ask you out. He won't. He'll just talk you to death.

**Talk to him about your passions—with extreme passion.** What do you love? What makes you leap out of bed in the morning? It doesn't matter what you're into, as long as you love it unabashedly and aren't afraid to say so. He responds eagerly to inner confidence. The Scorpio man wants a soul mate, so show him your soul.

**Lock eyes.** Scorpio's penetrating gaze is both unsettling and thrilling. The minute he pins you to the wall with an intense look, the sexy power play begins. Do you have the guts to stare right back? Attraction and power dynamics go hand in hand for him. Match his penetrating gaze with a confident, equally intense look.

**Be the rock star in the room.** Although he may act low-key, inside he considers himself a rock god, entitled to the best. Make him clamor for an autograph.

**Touch him.** The Scorpio man is incredibly physical, but he can be shy about breaking the touch barrier. Believe it or not, he's terrified of rejection. A gentle but firm touch, a hug, or an accidental brush of your bodies signals that you're safe. From there, it's all systems go.

## Everlasting Love with a Scorpio

Although he may kick and scream his way to the altar, once a Scorpio is in, he wants total "one-ness," to merge with you down to your very last pore. Talk about a 180! Now, he doesn't mind being with you 'round the clock, cooking and cleaning, letting you run the show. It's getting here that's the hard part. So, what's the shortest road to his undying love?

**Share his primary intellectual or creative passions.** If you're obsessed with the same thing as Scorpio, it's a good place to start. Are you both into animation and graphic novels? Offer to drive cross-country with him to a comic book convention (Note: You'll have to pay for half the gas). Start a band or a business together. Be the cocreator of a life-altering project where he channels all his passions. If you're always around when he's "in the zone," he could look up one day and realize he can't live without you.

**Have an empire of greater or equal proportion.** If you don't share Scorpio's passions, that's okay. Just have the same level of zeal and dedication for your own life path. He will only commit to a woman who has her s**t together. Be a success story.

**Make his home a better place than it already is.** Scorpio men are incredibly territorial about their turf. Still, his home can feel a bit austere. He likes if you add a subtle, softening touch, provided it matches his tastes. He needs to pick out the paint colors and artwork. Note to the domestic: He's a pack rat, so don't be too quick to open up a can of Feng Shui on his ass, and never throw out his "clutter." Two words: storage locker.

**Significantly increase his position on the food chain.** Marriage for love? Maybe. Marriage for status, street cred, and social dominance? Definitely. Until the twentieth century, that's how it was done. Until the end of civilization, that's how it will be done for Scorpio.

**Want the same future.** There's no faking it with Scorpio—you're either his soul mate or you're not. Don't bother pursuing him if you don't want the same things in life. He'll string you along until he finds the person who does.

# Prep Yourself For...
## Your First Date

Pass the Valium! A first date with Scorpio can be a nerve-wracking affair, and you won't know what to expect until you get there. Get enough sleep the night before, because you'll need to be on your toes. Trying to stay calm is futile. Enjoy those junior high jitters for what they're worth. Isn't that what makes romance so exciting, after all?

**The Basic Vibe:** Are you on a date, or just hanging out with an extremely talkative (or uncomfortably silent) new friend? It might be hard to tell. Secretive Scorpios like to keep things a little mysterious at first. Rather than let his aloofness rattle you, it's important to remember that his sign is insecure and terrified of rejection. So whether he's playing it cool or coming on stronger than a smarmy salesman, it's all a ploy to protect himself from getting attached.

The Scorpio man needs to admire and be admired. Your first date is equal parts audition and performance. He's testing to see whether you could be soul mate material. He'll try to impress you with well-chosen details, so if nothing else, you should have a fun—albeit energetically charged—evening. Put your best face forward, and don't forget to applaud his efforts. Compliment his choices, but don't go over the top. He needs to see that you're sophisticated, and if you're too easily impressed, he'll think you're not worldly enough for him.

If he name-drops obscure bands, books, or artists, don't pretend you know them. Stay composed. Scorpio men love to introduce you to new things, so ask interested questions instead. He's used to intimidating people, so he wants to see how well you can hold your own.

After a reading, concert, or gallery opening, he'll want to talk for hours. Chances are, he'll take you to his favorite restaurant or bar, and will procure his usual table. Food is erotic for Scorpio, but be warned: this man eats sloooowly. You could polish off your entree and his before he's done pontificating about his favorite film noir period. Eat before you go out—you'll need the energy and patience for this intense evening!

**What to Wear:** Scorpios like natural beauty and style, so aim to look effortlessly chic. When it comes to sexy, use the power of suggestion instead of anything obvious. "I like when a woman wears a skirt—it can be short but never trashy—and then later on I discover that she doesn't have any underwear on," says Pierre, a Scorpio. "It's about the discovery for me. I want to be the only one who finds out her little secret." Scorpios like elements that show originality and personality, like rock 'n' roll or vintage touches. Your outfit should be simple, sexy, and polished with an edge. Add a few sexy details in unexpected places.

**What Not to Wear:** Scorpio is the sex sign, but that doesn't mean he wants you to dress like a ten-dollar hooker. Although one Scorpio tells us he likes "a woman with the confidence of a stripper," this guy is possessive. Don't make him think the whole town has seen the waistband of your thong. He's not going to take a Vegas stripper to meet his friends and family, so skip the perfume, heavy makeup, and inappropriately low-cut shirts. A hint of burlesque, like a lacy bra strap peeking out of your blouse, is enough to stoke his imagination. At the same time, don't be overly modest or stuffy. He needs to see your shape, so skip the high-rise jeans and business suits.

**To Pay or Not to Pay?** Bring money. The Scorpio man is tight with his resources, and thinks nothing of going Dutch. He's hypersensitive to being used, and is always either recovering from some large purchase or saving for his next one. Show that you give back, too. If he pays for dinner and show tickets, pick up a round of drinks.

**Saying Good night.** Want to see him again? Don't give him the whole enchilada tonight. Use the power of suggestion: a lingering look or touch, an "accidental" brush of your breasts or crotch against him, then adios. Leave him wanting and wondering. He's an obsessor, most likely to fantasize about what could be. A kiss will stoke his fantasies, but it's hard to stop once you start making out with a Scorpio. Limit yourself to one passionate liplock, max.

## His First Home Visit

The Scorpio man is very home-oriented, so he's actually more interested in his own digs than yours. Restless though his soul may be, he's a nester who needs a comfortable, stylish home filled with books, musical instruments, artwork, and objects he's collected on his worldly travels. His home is his private sanctuary, the one place he feels safe and in control. He's rarely comfortable going to other people's houses, so if he comes to yours, don't expect him to stay long. Pack an overnight bag, because after a couple hours, he may just suggest that you both go back to his place. If you have a great book collection, he may borrow a title or two on the way out.

**Don't act like the president's coming.** Remember rule number one: never, ever kiss his ass. Just make sure there's a comfy place for your Scorpio to sit or sleep, some herbal tea, and room in your closet for his guitar amp or giant backpack. He'll probably just plop down on your couch and talk, or zone out with a book. And that's a good thing. If he can just "be," the same way as he is at his house, he'll stay a lot longer than if he has to play the gracious guest.

**Save the family album for another time.** Scorpios are hypersensitive to manipulation, and they can smell an agenda a mile away. Don't pull out the family scrapbook and show him your six nieces and nephews, or your maid-of-honor photos from your sister's wedding. He'll think you're going way too fast—and he's probably right.

**De-cheese your house.** The Scorpio man is a snob in his tastes. If he thinks you're corny, that can be your death knell. Take down the Ikea art posters and hide your Celine Dion albums. He will occasionally rifle through whatever's on your living room shelves, commenting snidely about anything he deems unsophisticated. You'll want to kill him, but later, some truth in his observation will resonate, and possibly even inspire you to evolve your tastes.

**Put your passions on display.** To the Scorpio man, hobbies speak louder than words. What does your soul respond to? He wants to know about your tastes and passions. Display your collections, artifacts, art, and favorite things so he can quietly study your character.

**Don't look too settled in.** The Scorpio man likes to leave his mark, so the less "done" your place looks, the better. Should you someday move in together, he needs to know that your styles will blend—or rather, that your décor won't overpower his. Use his visit as an excuse to de-clutter your house and toss out some junk.

**Hide all evidence of other men.** Is your home a shrine to your wild and crazy sexcapades, or your jet-setting lifestyle? He's a jealous guy who wants you all for himself. Tuck those booze cruise photos in a drawer, hide your journal, and don't leave your Match.com profile open on the computer screen. Sounds obvious, but we've heard tales!

## Meeting His Family

Scorpios have complicated relationships with their families, often best left to a trained psychiatrist. On the one hand, he wants to prove something by bringing home a "catch" that his family will love. Yet, the more he plays the dutiful son, the more he seethes with resentment. He desperately wants to be his own man, and hates feeling dependent on anyone's approval.

The Scorpio man goes into "intimacy overload" around his family, and the addition of you can make his entire system shut down. He escapes all the closeness by blanking out, drinking too much, or zoning out with a home improvement project (he's such a mama's boy that she'll probably have a few waiting for him). Pressure? You bet. The stakes are raised higher the farther you go from his home base, because he feels less in control with every mile. And you thought you were just going for a nice Thanksgiving dinner. Ha!

If you meet his family, don't expect him to hold your hand. In fact, you could find yourself standing uncomfortably in the kitchen with his mom, forced to make conversation. Just be yourself and wing it. Unlike a Taurus, he's not the guy that falls in love with you because you get along perfectly with his family. It doesn't hurt, but he's more interested in how the two of you connect than whether you leave with his mom's giblet gravy recipe. (Frankly, we think his priorities are straight on this one.) Besides, *he's* Mommy's favorite. He doesn't need you competing for that role.

One cardinal rule: If his family criticizes him, always take his side. Remember, you're the Bonnie to his Clyde, and your loyalty is essential. Eventually, he'll adjust to you being part of his family, but after the first visit, he may pull away for a few days. It could be confusing—after all, you expect to feel so much closer now that you've had this inside look. Remember, closeness frightens him when it comes in such large doses. Give him his space and he'll come back around.

# Saying Good-bye
## Breaking Up with a Scorpio

So you want to end things. Best of luck, because it won't be pretty. He will obsess over you for years on end. Scorpio men bond at a soul level, so when you leave him, it will feel like you've ripped out a piece of his insides. Even if you break up because he won't commit, or you're sick of waiting, it doesn't matter. He will still blame and resent you in some way.

He's the king of the "curtain call," so don't be surprised if he makes a comeback a few months later, attempting to charm you back. Do not, we repeat, do not have sex with him. If you sleep with him, you're done. This guy uses sex as a weapon. He'll make sure he gives you the lay of a lifetime, at once punishing you for leaving him and making it impossible to get him out of your system. The powerful oxytocin "bonding hormone" will add another five years to your relationship.

# Getting over Him: When a Scorpio Dumps You

Trying to get over a Scorpio? Approach it like detoxing from a drug. Your body will ache for everything you loved and hated about the guy. Even if he grossed you out with his piercing gaze, clammy hands, or the smell of patchouli seeping through his pores, these will be what you long for, inexplicably. If you can't pack up and move to another continent, take a long no-contact break. He will probably stalk you on the Internet, even though you may never know.

**Have yourself one good last cry over...**

- His gaze
- His touch
- The sex
- Feeling like a goddess
- Feeling like the only thing that mattered to him
- His creativity
- The new experiences he constantly introduced you to
- How hot you felt when he looked at you
- The vulnerable little boy within him
- His tenderness with animals and kids
- The naughty thrill of surrendering to his dark side

**Praise the universe that you never have to deal with...**

- His endless angst and soul-searching
- His self-absorbed banter
- Paying for half (or more) of everything
- Feeling jealous of his female friends
- Being studied like a bug under a microscope
- Constantly wondering if you're "too much"
- His passive-aggressive tantrums
- All that goddamn intensity

## Love Matcher:

### Can you find a common language?

| You are a(n)... | He thinks you're... | You think he's... | Common Language |
|---|---|---|---|
| Aries | A loose cannon who could dominate him for at least one night. | The sexiest man you've met in your life. | Sex, sex, sex... and power |
| Taurus | A real catch, but a little formal and hard to read. | A little bit too intense. | Film, art, travel, music... especially obscure bands |
| Gemini | His spiritual soul twin. | Your tantric love god. | Everything |
| Cancer | The sweet girl next door. | Your sexy hero. | Fairy-tale romance, domestic bliss |
| Leo | An impressive powerhouse who makes him feel a little insecure. | Sexy, but almost more like your girlfriend than your boyfriend. | Deep, heady, 12-hour conversations about everything under the sun |

| You are a(n)... | He thinks you're... | You think he's... | Common Language |
|---|---|---|---|
| Virgo | Caring and smart enough to be trusted. | A sweet and tortured soul who needs you to mother him. | Abiding friendship. Crunchy pursuits ranging from organic food to yogic meditation |
| Libra | The essence of feminine grace. | Possessive, pushy, and a tad suffocating, but potentially worth the hassle. | Drama and escaping into fantasy romance |
| Scorpio | Him in female form—he'll either be lovestruck or repulsed. | Arrogant and needs your help bringing him back down to reality. | Power, control, spirituality, forming an "us against the world" vibe |
| Sagittarius | Admires your luck and ambition but thinks you're a jack of all trades, master of none. | A creative genius who is too intense and hypersensitive. Needs to get out of his head. | Dreaming, spirituality, creativity, discovering new things |

| You are a(n)... | He thinks you're... | You think he's... | Common Language |
|---|---|---|---|
| Capricorn | A sexy socialite, but a little too popular to pin down. | Sexy but needy...plus he calls a little too often for your liking. | Name-dropping, cool-hunting, clinging to the past, striving to make others jealous |
| Aquarius | A ballsy babe who can hold her own. | Too needy and a bit of a downer. | Logic, creativity, a fascination with life's mysteries and hidden truths |
| Pisces | The only person who can truly understand him. | As sensitive and emotionally scarred as you are...a dream come true. | Shared values and priorities—living a creative, artistic, passionate life |

# The Sagittarius Man

Dates: November 22–December 21
Symbol: The Archer
Ruling Planet: Jupiter, the planet of luck
and expansion
Element: Fire—passionate, dynamic, active
Quality: Mutable
Mission: Lust for Life

**Natural Habitat—Where You'll Find Him:** Backpacking through Central America with a single change of clothes, growing his hair long, lecturing or doing postgraduate work at a university, outdoors, planting a garden, cracking jokes, publishing a tell-all magazine, writing a novel at a coffee shop, strumming an acoustic guitar, preparing a feast for twenty of his closest friends, meditating in a fruitless attempt to get Zen, at a network marketing convention, waxing philosophical about his favorite political cause, devouring books and newspapers, sitting in front of his computer until 4 A.M. working on his latest mega-project, taking a spontaneous road trip, at the airport catching an international flight, leading a march for farm workers' rights or environmental policy reform, producing and directing a documentary about an oppressed social group in a foreign country

**What He Does for a Living:** Entrepreneur, professor, publisher, adventure travel guide, naturalist, geologist, landscaper, philosopher, web developer, motivational speaker, career coach, salesperson, politician, preacher, comedian, television or movie producer, writer, lounge singer, Internet evangelist, sportscaster, broadcast journalist, game show host

**Noteworthy & Notorious Sagittarius Men:** Ozzy Osbourne, Jamie Foxx, Mos Def, Jake Gyllenhaal, Jay-Z, Winston Churchill, Mark Twain, Jimi Hendrix, Jim Morrison, Clay Aiken, Brad Pitt, Bo

Jackson, Ben Stiller, Samuel L. Jackson, Shel Silverstein, Bruce Lee, Ed Harris, Woody Allen, Jon Stewart, Gary Shandling, Tom Waits, Donny Osmond, Walt Disney, Kiefer Sutherland, Ray Romano, Don Johnson, Adam Brody, Steven Spielberg, Keith Richards

# Sagittarius: How to Spot Him

- Dressed like a dirty hippie (shirtless in overalls, threadbare camping or hunting clothes)
- Rocking the "nerdy schoolboy" look, complete with worn backpack or messenger bag filled with books and projects
- Always looks like he's smiling or deep in thought
- May have long hair, even a ponytail or dreadlocks
- High forehead, laughing wide-set eyes

- Powerful legs, strong thighs and a firm booty that sticks out
- Dressed in his idea of "formal wear": sporty-casual and comfortable, like a Banana Republic button-down shirt, khakis, and Timberlands. Would rather hang himself than wear a necktie—he doesn't see much difference between the two anyway

- Holding court and spouting his philosophies to anyone who will listen
- Walks faster than any other human you'll meet

- Cracking up the room with outrageous jokes and stories
- Fearlessly talking politics with anyone who will listen
- Clowning around with wild gestures and physical comedy
- Talking animatedly with his hands

- Tripping over his own feet, bumping into people, knocking stuff over by accident

# Sagittarius: How He Deals With...

## Money

Total entrepreneur. Needs to make it doing something he loves, and would rather squat in a gutter than sell his soul. Must always make enough money to feel like the master of his own destiny. Nobody controls a Sagittarius!

## Family

"Who? You mean those people who look like me? Oh THAT'S right—we spent the holidays together last year. I mean, for the last forty years. Sorry, I've been busy!"

## Love

Wants a best friend, soul mate and playmate in one. Rolls his eyes at the sappy s**t and mocks it mercilessly. Inside he's incredibly sensitive, just so not the hearts and teddy bears guy. Expresses his sentiment in an original, creative way that shows he really sees you.

## Sex

The most uptight horndog you'll ever meet.

## Children

Just tie the noose around his neck a little tighter, why don'tcha? If he has them, loves to teach and guide them. Would gladly skip their entire infancy and just get to the part where they can hold a damn conversation—in other words, listen to him impart his glorious worldviews and wisdom. Can make an incredibly devoted dad, much to his own surprise.

### Pets

Sure, why not? As long as they don't tie him down. Actually, he needs something to tie him down, and pets can be the perfect gateway.

### Your Meltdowns

Tells you to get over it, and if you don't, goes into hyper-problem-solving mode. Attempts to fix, coach, and rescue you as fast as possible, so he can get back to what's really important: his own life.

### His Meltdowns

Nothing could possibly be more important, serious, and urgent. Close the banks, alert the Feds, and declare an international disaster!

### Breakups

Freaks out at first, but eventually takes a philosophical approach and becomes great lifelong friends with his exes. May even introduce you to your next true love.

# Sagittarius: What He's All About

So you don't like your men easy, except in the sack. Welcome to Sagittarius. He's cocky, outrageous, and brashly outspoken. He can be a total sweetheart one minute, a pigheaded jerk the next, volleying between breathtaking arrogance and paranoid insecurity. His jokes are hilarious, always teetering on the edge of offensive—if not completely over that cliff. For some reason, he always gets away with it.

Sagittarius rules the higher mind, and this guy knows that he's smarter than most of the planet's population. He may seem to be smirking at the world, as though he's above all the tiresome "little people" with whom he must wearily share this mortal coil. His know-it-all nature makes him a natural director—and a control freak. He usually wears many hats at once, and can be a jack of all trades, collecting one new hobby or career path after the next.

Like a plaid vest paired with a polka dot tie, the Sagittarius man is bound to clash with everyone at some point. He may charm the pants off your parents and friends, but he'll never shy away from discussing politics, religion, or other explosive taboos with them. In fact, he may even bring up those topics, usually at the worst possible times. Like Pinocchio, he can't tell a lie. Honesty and authenticity are his virtues. Alas, they're not always appreciated, especially since he doesn't bother dressing up his brutal version of the truth with a tactful delivery. Like the Archer that rules his sign, his arrow flies straight at the mark.

The Sagittarius man needs the "Three P's" to be happy: productivity, purpose, and pursuit. This guy absolutely hates to stand still. Settling down is not in his vocabulary; he'll sleep when he's dead. He thinks he's wasting space on the planet unless he's working, producing, and making moves. Our father, a Sagittarius, dreams out loud about winning the lottery. What would he do with his millions? Instead of working seven days a week, he plans only to work three.

We love this *People* magazine story that epitomized the Sagittarius man's need to exercise his elbow grease. Like so many celebs, Sagittarius Kiefer Sutherland served jail time for DUI. Rather than hole up in his cell, Kiefer cheerfully folded laundry and served meals to his fellow convicts. After finishing, he reportedly asked the guards if they had anything else for him to do, inspiring them to call him a "model prisoner."

When life hands a Sagittarius man lemons, he opens an international lemonade franchise. He's a true visionary, and nothing short of an empire can satisfy his hungry soul. He loves to dream big, and he needs to be surrounded by limitless possibility. If he can't get his hands on something to mold, he'll dig up the dirt himself and start from scratch. In fact, "start-up" could be his middle name.

The Sagittarius man prefers having total control over his destiny, and is usually at least six months ahead of the curve. He has vision, an ability to see through the veil of reality far into the future. This is the guy who's dismissed as "crazy," only to resurface years later as a multinational sensation, heralded as a genius. Nostradamus, the famous medieval prophet who supposedly predicted Hitler and 9/11, was a Sagittarius.

Like the Archer that symbolizes him, Sagittarius must always have a distant target, something huge to pursue where he can leave his indelible footprint. When a Sagittarius man believes in something, nothing can stop him. Some of the grandest visionaries are Sagittarians: Steven Spielberg, Walt Disney, Jay-Z, Mark Twain, Shintaro Tsuji (the creator of the "Hello Kitty" brand). He's always restlessly seeking his Next Big Thing. Without it, the zodiac's alleged optimist can become a total drag. He'll complain to anyone in earshot about how horrible his life is, obsessing until things go his way again. Everything the Sagittarius man does, he does on a giant scale. When he gets in a funk, he thinks it should be declared a national crisis. He's absolutely unreachable during these times, and the best of your advice will fall on deaf ears. He stubbornly insists on finding the solution himself, even if it takes twice as long.

Meanwhile, you want to kick his ass and scream, "Do you have any idea how privileged you are?" He doesn't. The Sagittarius man is one of the zodiac's luckiest sign, and he's accustomed to getting second, third, twentieth chances. That doesn't mean he doesn't fail; in fact, he falls flat on his face many times. Lucky for him, he's ruled by Jupiter, the planet of fortune and opportunity. Just as he's about to drown, the universe magically throws him a lifeline. It happens time and again.

Nor does he remember how unsympathetic he was when you were in the same boat and he just barked, "Get over it already." He has little tolerance for other people's drama, and zero recognition of his own. Thank God he rarely stays down forever, even if his sulking seems to last an eternity. When he snaps out of it, the "disaster" suddenly strikes him as hilarious. He laughs at himself for being so heavy-hearted, and gives a colorful recap of his foibles to anyone who will listen. The national crisis has now become standup comedy material.

If he can't laugh at himself (which is rare), Sagittarius waxes philosophical, turning each negative experience into wisdom once it's solidly behind him. Once he's "been there, done that," his tough-love stance softens. The Sagittarius man makes an excellent coach and motivator. He'll encourage you to pull through with his infectious, can-do attitude.

It's that very attitude that keeps the frazzled, frustrated friends of Sagittarius coming back for more, even when he's pushed them over the edge. His indomitable spirit, fearless irreverence, and honesty make a rare and refreshing cocktail. Thus, Cirque du Sag is usually worth the price of admission.

Our wise Libra uncle asked us, "Do you know the difference between being a friend versus being friendly?" As Sagittarians ourselves, we love a good riddle.

"A friendly person," explained Uncle David, "tells you what you want to hear. A friend tells you the truth."

Amen, brother. And that is where the magic happens with a Sagittarius man. Even though he's spilled coffee on your laptop, told your staunchly Democratic boss that he thinks George Bush was a godsend to the United States (at the company Christmas party, loudly, just before bonus season), and shafted you with the bill at your own birthday dinner, it was all somehow done with good intentions. In his own special way, he could be the best friend you'll ever have. If you want a man who respects your mind and individuality, and can crack you up like nobody else, Sagittarius is your guy.

# What He Wants in a Woman

So you want to settle down and live the traditional life. Maybe pick up a Costco membership, a house in the suburbs and some rocking chairs? You don't really need to see the world or further your education. Why would you? You realized your ultimate mission at the altar, and you've earned your "MRS" degree. You're already saving keepsakes for your future grandchildren... and you're only twenty-two.

Newsflash: You're with the wrong guy. The Sagittarius man doesn't want to grow old together. He needs someone to stay young with him. The only thing he'll do with a white picket fence is impale himself on it—because in his mind, life is officially over once he "settles down."

This man needs a soul mate and a playmate in one. Like Sagittarius Brad Pitt, he thrives with an Angelina Jolie-type—an adventuress for whom there are no rules, limits, or boundaries, except the ones you invent together. He doesn't want to follow a script; he wants to write his own. The Sag man needs a woman who will never suffocate him or tell him what to do, but will entertain, inspire, and challenge him.

Sagittarius Frank Sinatra sang, "I did it my way." If you want to be with a Sagittarius man, you're gonna have to do things his way, too. Not everything. But he is a true leader, and he trusts his own instincts above all else. He needs a mate who has her own leadership qualities, but still goes along with his agenda, and lets him live on his own terms.

Above all, the quirky Sagittarius man needs a woman who accepts and adores him exactly the way he is. Have we mentioned he's a handful? Ask him, of course, and he'll tell you he's the most easygoing dude on the planet. But if you've ever been with a Sagittarius man, you know the paradox that he is. He's the most sensitive insensitive person you'll meet. He's a freedom-loving control freak, an open-minded conservative, a stick-in-the-mud who's the life of the party, a tragically insecure egomaniac, a really responsible flake. Make sense? Only if you truly, madly, deeply understand your Sag.

The Sagittarius man needs a smart woman. His sign rules higher education, and he loves an intellectual whiz (as long as your theories and ideals don't clash with his strong opinions). It doesn't matter if the deepest questions he asks are "Paper or plastic?" or "You want ketchup with that?" He needs a brainy lass with personality and a mind of her own.

Sporty and active are good, too. The Sagittarius man usually has an outdoorsy side, and he can walk faster than anyone you'll ever meet. If you have a two-hour primping routine, forget it. He'll have climbed Mt. Everest and started his fifth company by the time you put down your Shu Uemura eyelash curler. If you're a "dry clean only" type, you might fare better with a Pisces or Taurus. He prefers his woman wash-and-wear, and he's far more interested in the person behind the war paint, anyhow.

That's the upside of the Sagittarius man's skittishness about commitment and tradition. He is able to see you as an autonomous human being. When you get married, he doesn't want to meld into a two-headed monster, peppering every sentence with "we" and "us." You each had a mind and life of your own before you met, and he continues to honor that.

For that reason, Sagittarius men usually click best with a bold, self-determined woman who likes her space, but can still happily share her crayons. So if you approach life as a blank canvas, like he does, imagine the picture you can leave behind when you put your minds and hearts together.

# What He Wants from a Relationship

The Sagittarius man's vision of love is an interesting paradox: He wants a devoted mate who gives him his freedom. Mmm-kay. Talk about doing things the hard way. If you want to be free, stay single, right?

Well, that's what most people would do, but he's not most people. Sagittarius is the sign of the gambler. The odds (and the gods) tend to favor him. He knows that if anyone's gonna find that needle in the haystack, it's him. Besides, he'll enjoy the whole adventure of searching for what he wants—it's an excuse to see the world!

Like a knight, the Sagittarius man loves to charge off on his worldly quests, then return to share his delightful tales with anyone who will listen. A jack-of-all-trades (and a master of one or two), he's ravenous for knowledge and experiences. Sagittarius rules travel and the higher mind, and he's always expanding his repertoire with books, classes, hobbies, friends, and globe-trotting. This man must sow his oats before settling into a relationship. Otherwise, he'll always have one foot out the door, wondering "what if?"

Once he's satisfied his adventure quota, the Sag man suddenly grows lonely exploring the world by himself. Out of nowhere, he begins to crave a companion to join his eternal seeking. Our Sagittarius friend Dan, a television producer, describes his own maturity as sudden and fast. "I just woke up and started going back over everything in my life, all my relationships and everything I'd done," says Dan. "It happened in an instant." At that point, his bachelorhood no longer becomes quite the prize it once was, and he yearns to share his life.

The mature Sagittarius can make an excellent, though intense, partner. Only a well-ripened Sagittarius should be plucked off the vine, and he's pretty much useless as a mate until then. Once he "grows up," he's like a kid with severe ADHD whose Ritalin suddenly kicks in. After tearing through life like a crazed bull in a china shop (or occasionally, moping along like Eeyore), he morphs into a serene Buddha figure, floating above the chaos.

At this point, the Sagittarius man's best qualities come out—like wisdom, empathy, and generosity. He's able to put his full focus on a partner and champion your visions. Your relationship and shared life become his new adventure, his mega-sized project. He loves to coach, mold, and direct, and as long as you absorb his teachings, he'll gladly be your guru.

Be sure to keep him a little in check, though. Sagittarius is the know-it-all sign, and he can be quite a bulldozer. Partnership skills like compromise, negotiation, and delayed gratification don't come naturally to him. It's healthy for him to learn that the word "no" actually can apply to him. Left to his own devices, he'll do whatever he wants, and just assume you'll come around eventually.

# Sex with a Sagittarius

Sagittarius is symbolized by the Centaur, which is half human and half animal. The Sagittarius man has an idealized vision of sex, along with a very base and primal hunger for it. He wants a best friend, sexual goddess, and soul mate in one—a John Lennon and Yoko Ono love story. Below the belt, however, he's all animal. He can be a little schizophrenic. You never know which head he'll be thinking with from moment to moment.

While he holds fast to his vision, Sagittarius also knows that finding a soul mate can take a decade or six. In the meantime, he's got to get laid—and so he does. Impulsive Sagittarius is famous for screwing first and asking questions later. With his rose-colored glasses and huge appetite, he becomes enchanted a little too quickly. Swept up in the moment, he leaps into bed, only to regret it in the morning. Still, he's impossible to reform. Rash, brash, and headstrong are his undying traits.

Sagittarius rules morals and religion, and he has a surprising prudish side. He's not big on kink, especially if he feels it degrades women. Save your whips, chains, and bondage for a Capricorn. He might open his mind if there's an academic reason behind your fetishes and elaborate sexuality. For example, if you teach women to masturbate because you believe it's a form of feminist empowerment—or you moonlight as a stripper while working on a master's degree and a memoir on sex, power, and gender—he can intellectualize it enough to explore.

There's a dirty hippie in every Sagittarius, and he's a no-muss/no-fuss guy in the sack. Skip the perfumes, soft lighting, and elaborate lingerie. It's all about immediate gratification for Sag. He doesn't want to wait all night for you to unhook a corset or tease him for hours with a riding crop. As one Sagittarius man puts it, "I just want someone to get hot and sloppy with." The sooner you're naked and rolling around on the floor, the better.

Sagittarius loves to learn, and he may go through a phase where he studies sexual subjects like tantra, G-spots, or female ejaculation. Eventually, though, he gets bored with all the details and returns to basics. In other words: strip naked and screw like rabbits in your favorite positions. It worked for thousands of years, after all. Why stray?

The best way to mix things up with Sagittarius? Vary your location rather than your technique. Sagittarius is the travel sign, so a little vacation nookie goes far. Pull him away from his laptop and projects. Take him out into an open field, pull over on a deserted highway during a road trip, or camp out in the wild. Only in the expansive outdoors does he reconnect with his wild, untamed spirit. You're more likely to have great sex by the light of a campfire than a candle. So fetch yourself some firewood and grab your sleeping bag. Instead of a five-star hotel, you could hook up under a sky filled with brilliant stars. Come on—where's your sense of adventure?

# Sagittarius: Turn-Ons & Turn-Offs

## Turn Him On

- Joie de vivre: be spontaneous, free-spirited, and in love with life
- Look on the bright side of every situation
- Make him laugh when he gets down on himself or lost in his head
- Share books, ideas, and knowledge
- Keep him laughing; have a killer sense of humor
- Bring new, exciting adventure and growth to his world
- Hail from another country or culture, especially a "warm" one (Latin, Caribbean, or Mediterranean)
- Be a foodie or adventurous eater
- Proposition him
- Wear a super-short skirt that shows off your legs
- Have well-established hobbies, career, and interests that you love at least as much as you love him
- Engage in ongoing personal development, education, and self-awareness
- Be a self-sufficient: own a power drill and a vibrator
- Keep it natural—light makeup, short fingernails, wash-and-wear wardrobe
- Don't give a rat's ass whether his clothes are rumpled or his chest is waxed (it won't be)

## Turn Him Off

- Be overly practical or schedule-obsessed
- Be predictable (eat, do, wear the same thing again and again)

- Take too long getting ready or fussing with your appearance
- Overspend (by his standards) on your clothes, shoes, haircuts, or appearance
- Show no interest in reading
- Be a "neat Nazi" or hygiene obsessed
- Lack warmth, depth, or passion
- Pick fights or criticize him—there are so many other things you should be talking about. Why drama?
- Be a Daddy's girl or overly dependent on your parents; he needs you to think for yourself
- Need too much attention—he can't stand to be distracted from his big-picture projects and plans
- Be thin-skinned and easily offended by his crude or tactless remarks
- Insist he dress up in a suit, tux, or tie more than once a decade
- Prefer trendy "scene" hangouts to low-key lounges or restaurants
- Waste his money or time
- Take him for granted
- Be a diva in any way

# His Moves

## First Moves: How He Courts You

Sagittarius is the sign of the hunter, and he stalks his game like a cheetah prowling for a gazelle. "We want to know what that animal is doing, where it's going," says one Sagittarian.

Feel like a piece of meat yet? Just wait. When a Sagittarius man has his eye on you, he plays to win. Although his attention span is shorter than a celebutante's miniskirt, when he wants you, you'll get his full focus. The only courting he does is a full-court press, moving in a little too close for comfort to stake his claim. You'll rarely have to wonder whether he likes you or not.

Here's how a Sagittarius man signals his animal attraction:

- He tells you point-blank he wants you
- He gets really loud and showy around you, pulling out all the stops
- He starts cracking jokes to get your attention
- He showers (make that tsunamis) you with his attention
- He hits on you shamelessly, without an ounce of subtlety
- He tracks your movements and follows you around
- He gets all up in your personal space
- He engages you in a flirty but intellectual conversation
- He starts trying to coach you or give you advice
- He scares off 95 percent of the women in the room by acting totally over the top, and takes home the girl who doesn't run away terrified

## He's In: How You Know He's Committed

As the zodiac's Archer, the Sagittarius knows how to pursue, hunt, and aim for a target. He loves a woman who keeps him chasing her just a little. However, he doesn't want to play that game forever. Once he hits his bulls-eye and gets the girl, he moves on to his next mission—usually a career coup, or realizing a personal dream. If he feels even remotely limited by your relationship, or that it distracts him from his other pursuits, he'll break free. If you share his dreams, then come on along for the journey! With the right chemistry, he makes a fun lifelong mate who may infuriate you, but will never bore you. Here are some signs that your globe-trotting Sag is ready to hang up his saddle at your inn:

**You've become his "pet project."** The Sagittarius man is a teacher. There's nothing he loves more than a keenly listening ear, someone to take his (usually unsolicited) advice. If he showers you with his guidance and you sprout like a Chia Pet, he'll be thrilled to watch you grow and grow. One disclaimer: You need massive amounts of potential and to quickly show progress for him to stay interested. He only bets on a winning horse.

**He shows you his sensitive side.** He's always clowning and entertaining, putting on a show. But you know underneath the tap dancing and war paint, there's a little boy in there… with feelings. Deep, deep feelings. He's a friend of many, but known by few. Does he allow you to see his tears and insecurities when the house lights dim? You've become part of the Sagittarius man's small inner circle.

**He tells you.** This is the zodiac's bluntest sign, the truth-teller who calls it like he sees it. Don't expect any romantic dressing up with him. Our father, a Sagittarius, told our mom when they were dating: "Listen, if you want to keep dating me, you can't be with anyone else." Boom. (Note: Don't ever try giving him an ultimatum; it will only backfire.)

**He sees you as his muse.** You can't even tie your shoes without him whipping out his camcorder or digital camera. He wants to sketch you nude, and he jots down your witticisms or quotes you in his pocket journal. You're shooting his favorite drug into his veins: inspiration. If you make him see rainbows and possibilities, he'll treat you like a pot of gold.

**He's still got a gleam in his eye.** When a Sagittarius man is inspired, his eyes light up like a Christmas tree. If he seems dull, dead, and despondent around you, he's either lost his life direction or he's over you. If he's excited, lively, cracking jokes, and beaming at you, he'll stick around.

**You're the only one who will put up with him—and he knows that.** Listen, we don't need to tell you that the Sagittarius man isn't easy. He can be more high maintenance than a teenage girl getting ready for a prom. Once that actually dawns on him, he may stop believing the grass is always greener somewhere else.

## Unfaithful Sagittarius: Why He Cheats

Now, we need to sit you down for an honest talk here. The Sagittarius man, though he can be faithful and morally righteous, has an appetite as wide as the sky. He's symbolized by the Centaur—a mythical half human, half horse. In spite of his hardcore ethics, his animalistic bottom half may trump his lofty, philosophical mind. As Ophira's husband likes to say: "Why have a handful when you can have a land full?"

When a Sagittarius man cheats, it's never personal, and it's rarely malicious. He follows his impulses until he ends up in over his head. If he's caught cheating, he takes a philosophical approach, which can be summed up by this great quote: It's better to beg for forgiveness than ask for permission. The Sagittarius man could have that engraved on his tombstone. So, here are a few reasons your Sag might wander:

**Opportunity knocked.** The Sagittarius man hates to waste good fortune, especially when it falls right into his lap. And gives him a lap dance. I mean c'mon, wouldn't you?

**He needed some variety.** The Sagittarius man loves a challenge, and he hates stagnation. Even if he likes what you're serving, he might want Stove Top instead of potatoes every now and then. If you've been having sex in the same location, position, or routine—or you've fallen into some other rut—he may renew his zest with a Thanksgiving feast in another pilgrim's camp.

**He felt boxed in and needed some freedom.** The Sagittarius man hates rules, and only follows the ones he makes up himself.

Commitment goes against his animal nature, no matter how much he loves you. Unless he has enough freedom in other parts of his life, he may give into his roaming instinct. As one Sagittarius man says, "When I'm comfortable in a relationship, I just need to know I can be a little outside the boundaries—that I have some breathing room."

**He's over you.** He's done, finished, told you and you didn't listen. Now, you're just bringing him drama. If his direct dumping didn't work, he'll have to make it easier for you to catch him in the act of betrayal. Ouch.

## Dig the Grave: It's Over

Once he's fed up, the Sagittarius man can't hide his honest feelings. His face and body language give it away, for one. While he may not leave you physically (yet), he'll check out of your relationship mentally, emotionally, sexually, and spiritually. When he grows distant and refuses to discuss a solution, it's not because he can't think of one. He just doesn't want to. Here are a few clues that your Centaur's hooves are heading for the stable doors:

**He tunes you out.** You were his pet project, the apple of his eye. Now, he barely hears a word you're saying. He's lost interest, and without that, there's no relationship with Sagittarius.

**He calls his travel agent.** Not because he's sleeping with her (though anything's possible). By traveling, Sagittarius is symbolically announcing, "I'm getting back out in the world again." When he packs his suitcase, it may be for a permanent vacation.

**He turns into a passive-aggressive jerk.** He no longer gives a crap, so why should he pretend to care? Little barbs and insensitive actions fly. He leaves the top off the peanut butter (your pet peeve), the toilet seat stays up, and he shows more affection to the dog than to you. Suddenly, he forgets all the manners he pretended to learn when you were together.

**He withholds.** That means everything: sex, conversation, fun, jokes. He starts keeping the best parts of himself from you, and saving them up for somebody else.

**He pulls a few too many all-nighters.** He comes home from work at 10:00 P.M. (instead of 10:00 A.M., like when you first started dating), laptop in tow. He immediately hunkers down on the sofa until 4:00 A.M., working on a "big project" until he falls asleep on the cushions. Yeah, he's got a big project: lining up the next chapter of his life so he can smoothly exit the one he's in with you.

# Interpreting His Signals:

## *What does he mean by that?*

| When he | It means... | So you should... |
| --- | --- | --- |
| Gets quiet | He's obsessing about work, bills, or a project. | Remove yourself from the gathering storm cloud, go do your thing, and catch up with him when he's done with his work. Or, listen to him talk it out; sometimes it helps Sagittarius to vocalize his thoughts. Encourage him to write it down on paper. |
| Doesn't call | He's either busy with his many projects, or he's not into you and is hoping you'll figure it out on your own so he doesn't have to deal with the drama. | Drop him a line. If he answers or calls back, you're still in the running (though maybe just barely, and maybe just because he hasn't gotten laid in a while). If he doesn't return the call within a couple of days, move on. |
| Calls a lot | He likes talking to you, and probably wants to lock you in as a girlfriend. | Talk to him. A great conversation is one of his favorite aphrodisiacs, and the path to his heart. |

| When he | It means... | So you should... |
| --- | --- | --- |
| Doesn't make a move after a couple of dates | He's on the fence about you, or still not sure what he wants in a woman, which has nothing to do with you. | Downshift to friendship level if you genuinely like him as a person. Getting to know you over time could open his mind. He may need a few more dates or experiences. |
| Doesn't make a move after a few weeks | He either doesn't see you as girlfriend material yet, or he's still sowing his oats (e.g., still trying to date that supermodel, leaving on a six-month backpacking trip through Southeast Asia next semester) and he's not ready to be locked into something serious. | Start dating other guys. You can't make a Sagittarius grow up any faster than he's ready. But if he realizes he's about to miss out on a great catch, he'll either s**t or get off the pot. |
| Moves fast | He's horny and wants to sleep with you, or he thinks you fit his dream profile and he wants to lock it in. | Pace him a little, at least until you're sure of his motivations. Or, have a wild, steamy hookup if you don't want more than a fling. |

| When he | It means... | So you should... |
|---|---|---|
| Picks up the tab, gives flowers and gifts | Aliens have abducted him and sent him back to Earth as a gentleman. Only kidding (sort of). He's trying hard to win you over, and showing you with his effort that he really, really likes you. | Be grateful and receptive, especially since the gifts will probably have thoughtful touches that show he understands your personality. |
| Introduces you to his family and/or closest friends | He's seriously considering you as a mate, and he wants to see how well you fit into his life. He's also testing to make sure you won't be jealous of his many acquaintances and friends. | Be yourself, and be genuine, open, and friendly with all. Don't pout, brood, or demand his attention. Let him hold court and mingle freely. |

# Your Moves: Tips for Flirting and Everlasting Love

## Flirting with a Sagittarius

To flirt with a Sagittarius man, you need only one thing: a sense of humor. He's at his best when he's being funny and clever, loudly entertaining a roomful of friends. If you appreciate his raunchy jokes and hilarious turns of phrase, you're off to a rolling start.

Even though he may be the hottest guy in the room, there's a geek inside every Sagittarius man. He's always a little surprised to find himself being hit on. When you're flirting with him, he's often the last to realize it. Besides, he's so used to doing the chasing that he's not sure how to be pursued. Don't worry, though—he's always willing to play once he figures out what's happening. Here's how to get the flirting started:

**Laugh.** There's nothing a Sagittarius loves more than cracking up together. Laugh at his jokes, at yourself, at your own jokes. He wants to be where the party is. Show him it's right where you're standing.

**Be lewd, crude, and really direct.** Match his boldness with a shot of your own. Be as straight-up as he is, if not more. Grab him like a cavewoman and don't even flinch at his offensive jokes— just laugh and tell an even raunchier one. He doesn't want to live out his remaining days with a delicate, thin-skinned flower.

**Make him chase you a little.** Sagittarius is the hunter of the zodiac. If getting your number is as easy as "shooting elephants in a zoo" (as one Sagittarius puts it), he'll bore quickly. At the same time, you need to be available and approachable—and never phony. Abandon your copy of *The Rules*. He's too full of himself to work that hard.

**Stand out from the crowd.** Smart and original women are a turn-on for Sag. There's nothing a Sagittarius man hates more than being bored by a generic, cookie-cutter, conventional mate. He doesn't want the cheerleader or the Prom Queen. He wants the chick wearing neon orange hot pants and a sequined top who's debating seventeenth-century French literature with the Rhodes Scholar and handing him his ass on a platter.

**Be a captive audience.** When a Sagittarius man lifts the curtain, he plans on giving you the Greatest Show on Earth. Truly listen to what he's saying and show deep interest in what he has to say. He loves to pontificate to an attractive admirer. He loves the sound of his own voice, and you'd better, too.

## Everlasting Love with a Sagittarius

Sagittarius is the big-picture sign, the ruler of long-term vision. He wants an equally curious mate who will remain interesting for years to come, sharing his thirst for knowledge. Lifelong learning must be a shared priority—Sagittarius wants to do, see, discover. He also needs plenty of time for his other projects and goals. Yes, those will always be the "other women" in your relationship. He may avoid committing because he fears the obligation will distract him from his ambitious undertakings. Sagittarius is a hunter, and he always needs a target or conquest. The woman who keeps him is secure enough to either join him on the hunt or send him off with good wishes.

Although part of him may doubt such a woman exists, Sagittarius is still the zodiac's optimist. In every Sag, there's a romantic idealist holding a torch for his soul mate. He's a late bloomer, so it could take him a long time to be ready for her. Once he finds her, though, the Sagittarius man moves quickly to seal the deal. Here's how he knows you're it:

**Fascinate and inspire him.** The Sagittarius man is impatient, and he prefers the sound of his own voice to yours. He thinks he's smarter than most, and he's prone to finishing people's sentences, or just interrupting them. In his mind, he's already heard 99 percent of what most people are going to say before they even say it, anyway. Borrrrring. Are you the woman who brings fresh conversation, new material, and exciting ideas to his jaded world? Oh my God, I think he actually just shut up.

**Be fascinated and inspired by him.** He needs to see your eyes light up at his shiny pearls of wisdom, too. While you're at it, take some of his advice.

**Be completely devoted to adventure.** If your priorities align with his—in other words, if you see the world as your oyster and you just want someone to help you shuck it—he'll sign on to your cruise forever.

**Give him space to be himself.** This guy is gonna make some messes in your lifetime. "We're gonna say stupid things, come up with bizarre ideas," says one Sagittarius. True, but if you love him through those little "foot-in-the-mouth" moments, his tactless ass will be on the rocking chair next to yours when you're ninety.

**Never tell him "no."** That two-letter word is like nails on a chalkboard to a Sagittarius man. If you're an automatic "yes" to even his wildest stunts and ideas, he'll always want you along for the ride.

**Travel the world together.** He's a restless globe-trotter who loves to pack his bags and go. If your connection can survive more than two continents, or if you travel well as a team, you could soon be sporting his-and-hers luggage.

**Believe in him when nobody else does.** The Sagittarius man is often six months ahead of the curve, if not more. He's the guy who voices the unpopular vote and gets shot down, only to end up having been right all along. If you believe in his foresight and make him feel sane and smart, he'll see you as his indispensable sounding board.

# Prep Yourself For...

## Your First Date

It's a casual hangout and a date in one! The Sagittarius man doesn't roll out the red carpet on a first date (though he may on the second or third). He's terrified of being trapped, so he doesn't want to give you the wrong idea by romancing you full on. Once he makes up his mind that you're the One, though, he moves at warp speed. More than what you wear or where you go, he needs an intellectual connection. Your ability to hold an inspiring conversation is all-important to Sagittarius. Rest your vocal cords, read the newspaper, and prepare for an engaging chat at the very least.

**The Basic Vibe:** As our Sagittarius friend Seddu always lectures us: "Meet for coffee on the first date! That way, if you don't like the person, you can leave after half an hour." The Sagittarius man is looking for his best friend first, and a mate second. Of course, if you do click, you could end up closing down the café after talking for seven hours straight. Or, he'll want to wander and explore together: used bookstores, a friend's party, the video arcade, the mall, a walk to the other side of town. You never know where you'll end up once you connect with Sagittarius.

**What to Wear:** Sagittarius is the half-horse sign, so concentrate on your "mane and tail." In other words, leave your hair loose and wild, and show off that booty—and any other curves you may have. He's not afraid of skin. Other than that, dress in simple, sporty, and funky clothes. Sagittarius is an explorer and he loves to play tour guide. You might end up wandering around for hours. Most importantly, your outfit has to be an expression of your personality. It doesn't matter if it's a preppy blue blazer or a hot-pink tube top that squeezes your love handles—as long as he can sense that it's totally you.

**What Not to Wear:** Forget about anything too matchy-matchy or put together when you date a Sagittarius. He's into natural women with personalities who are comfortable being themselves. The Sagittarius man can smell a poseur a mile away—literally. Go easy on the product and perfume. If you have "the hip, cool artist" look or the "ultra preppy" look, or you're too much of a label snob, he'll write you off as a phony. Err on the side of casual, rather than wear a too pulled-together outfit that's devoid of any personal touch.

**To Pay, or Not to Pay?** Prepare for anything. The Sagittarius man is relaxed and spontaneous about money. If he asks you out, he'll probably pay for the main event, but he won't mind if you pick up a round of drinks, buy the condoms, or fund any additional activities. He's a modern man.

**Saying Good night:** He'd rather say "good morning." This man has no impulse control and his appetite is huge. If he's enjoying the evening, he'll want it to keep going… and going. You might need to kick him out or drop a serious hint for him to leave. One Sagittarius man we know nearly scared his Aries girlfriend away on their second date when he pulled up in front of her apartment and announced, "I've got pajamas in my trunk if you want me to stay." If he likes you, don't expect him to be the one setting limits. You'll have to be firm about your boundaries—or not! He won't necessarily respect you any more if you make him wait. As our Sagittarius father told us when we were fourteen years old, "Sex is a natural, wonderful thing; it's nothing to be ashamed about." Um… thanks, Dad. Save your old-fashioned values for a Virgo or a Libra.

## His First Home Visit

The Sagittarius man moves quickly when he likes you, so he could end up in your house on your first date! Fortunately, as long as you have food and comfortable seating, he's not too demanding. Curious Sag is a nosey houseguest—not to mention blunt. He'll offer his unsolicited commentary on your décor and possessions, so try not to take offense. If he's interested in you, he wants to know your true personality—the real, un-vacuumed, dust-bunny you, that is.

**Make dinner together.** The Sagittarius man can be an amazing cook, and he often arrives with a bottle of wine or a cool, edible treat (not including himself, that is). Head to the gourmet market together and pick up ingredients. Then laugh, talk about everything under the sun, and sip wine as you prepare dinner. He'll gladly look up a recipe online, or bring one of his own.

**Watch a really good (or really bad) movie.** The Sagittarius man is great for deep conversations or total silliness. He loves to laugh. If you've recorded a few bad reality shows (*The Littlest Groom*, anyone?), you can bond through making fun of them together. Or, if you've got the latest foreign documentary, lauded by the *New Yorker*, pop it in the DVD player and discuss.

**Stoke his curiosity.** He loves dusty used bookstores, open-air farmers' markets, and international bazaars. The more your place resembles an outdoor souk in Marrakesh, the better. Show off your books and magazines (Sagittarius rules publishing) and all your worldly objects. Put collectibles from trips on display, along with academic awards so he can admire your intellect and international savvy.

**Hide your delicate objects.** The Sagittarius man is clumsy and sloppy. He could absentmindedly rest his coffee mug on your family album, or send your grandmother's heirloom china crashing to the floor with an animated gesture.

**Keep it real.** The Sagittarius man doesn't need things to be spic and span. He prefers lived-in and authentic to anything too polished. Leave a few piles around, and don't worry about the dishes in the sink. If you have a kid, he'd rather see Cheerios on the ceiling and crayon on the walls than a perfectly appointed nursery and a "Baby Einstein" robo-child. After all, how can he be his quirky self if your whole world is so… contrived?

## Meeting His Family

Are you eager to meet the parents? Relax. When it comes to family, the Sagittarius man could win an Independent Spirit award. His relationship with his clan stems from duty more than desire. He's likelier to head home for the holidays than eat mama's home cooking every night. That's rarely an option, since his parents' address is usually hundreds of miles from his own.

Visionary Sagittarius is more interested in the relationship between you two, and he'd rather create his own family than follow his parents' mold. He hates dependency, and strives to be a self-made man. Parents are an unsavory reminder that somebody else had a hand in his creation. If he's close with his mom and dad, it's usually because they give him plenty of breathing room.

If he drags his feet before taking you home, be glad. Family visits make everything too real for Sagittarius, and can temporarily kill his mojo. He may imagine the deadly picket fence closing in on him, especially if you get along too well with his family. If you stay at his parents' house, he may not want sex for a week. To Sagittarius, family is better in theory than in practice. He favors relationships based on chemistry, not biology.

Sagittarius is a "live and let live" guy, and he believes his life is his business. Although you may meet his siblings right away, if you meet mom and dad, he's usually serious. Be yourself, and don't try to become their best friends. Freedom is everything to Sagittarius, and he doesn't want family interfering in his life. God forbid his parents start campaigning for grandchildren or getting him to "settle down." Keep your womb at a safe distance from their breeding fantasies. Be cordial, warm, and open around them, but maintain a healthy distance.

That said, he's always happy to meet your family—as long as you have a healthy separation and act like a grown-up. If you're a daddy's girl or mother's helper, he wants no part of it. He doesn't do well with humorless or narrow-minded parents, but if yours are fascinating and worldly, he'll talk to them for hours. He's genuine and warm, and can usually win over your whole family in a single sitting (entertaining them as well). Nieces, nephews, and cousins will adore him; his childlike spirit endears the whole family.

Eventually, the newness fades, and he'll be less enthused about kissing up to your relatives. By your third year together, he'll probably just want to skip off to Bali over Christmas, or rent a ski lodge for the whole family (combining duty with entertainment). If you're a "home for the holidays" type, don't expect him to swoon over your traditions and family customs. But if you're the type who likes to create her own traditions, he'll gladly write that book together with you.

# Saying Good-bye
## Breaking Up with a Sagittarius

The Sagittarius man might be completely oblivious to your feelings, but he takes breakups incredibly hard. His insecure, hypersensitive side comes flying out if you dare to dump him. He gets moody, emotional, depressed—and shocked. The arrogant part of his nature believes you're lucky to be with him. A part of him will be outraged: Don't you know who I am?

He's the sign of the optimist, so if you're serious about ending things, you'll need to be clear and firm. For Sagittarius, hope springs eternal. If you base the breakup on one of his shortcomings, he'll derail your argument by promising to work on himself. It's far better and smoother to dump him with a variation on the old "It's not you; it's me."

Besides, if he feels you strung him along, he can get nasty when he realizes you mean business. All of his unkind opinions about you rush out in a regrettable tirade. "Who's gonna love you with that fat ass?" or "You were never smart enough for me anyhow." God help you if you cheat on him or betray him in any way.

However, if you've simply outgrown each other, he probably knows it. Once he moves on, Sagittarius usually comes back around as a lifelong friend. In fact, you may like him even more as your buddy.

## Getting over Him: When a Sagittarius Dumps You

He's done, it's over, and he thinks there's no spark. When an impatient Sagittarius is through, he wants to make a swift, painless exit. He hopes you'll just get over it with as little grief as possible. As one Sagittarius man says, "I want a no-fault divorce—no shame, no blame, just move on."

Emotional suffocation is a big impetus for a Sagittarius man to bolt. Have you become too needy and dependent? Too straight-laced and unadventurous? If he can't grow boundlessly inside your relationship, he'll look for one in which he can. He needs passion and possibility.

If you've temporarily lost that edge, you may be able to win him back. But you'd better move fast. When a Sagittarius man dares to leave you cold, he's probably met someone else, or at least has a transitional booty call lined up.

You won't want to know the details of his life and rebounds, so spare yourself by cutting off contact for a while. He has a way of justifying his insensitive actions, and probably won't consider your feelings before moving on to the next conquest. Better to move on and be friends again later in life.

### Have yourself one good last cry over...

- His adventurous spirit
- His hilarious jokes and sense of humor
- Having someone to champion your dreams
- Losing your companion and best friend
- Being introduced to so many new experiences
- The way he could entertain the crowds at dinner parties
- His passion, spirit, and excitement
- Losing the most interesting person you ever met

### Praise the universe that you never have to deal with...

- His selfish impulses
- The lack of tact and grace
- His dominating moods
- The random smells that floated around him (grease, dirt, sweat, farts)

- His endless "what am I doing with my life?" spells
- Those periods of financial ruin when his latest project crashed and burned
- The blunt, opinionated remarks he made, embarrassing you to high heaven

- His completely unrealistic fantasies that never panned out or paid the bills

# Love Matcher:

## Can you find a common language?

| You are a(n)... | He thinks you're... | You think he's... | Common Language |
|---|---|---|---|
| Aries | Sexy and powerful, but a little high-maintenance and diva-ish. | Funny and warm, but could use a few hygiene and grooming upgrades. | Entrepreneurship, travel, adventure, education, fun, laughter |
| Taurus | Boring and predictable. | Hairy and delusional. | Food, wine, art, literature |
| Gemini | An androgynous love goddess, endlessly fascinating, but a little bit cold. | A perfect playmate and travel companion, but a potential heartbreaker. | Travel, global issues, humanity, books, education |
| Cancer | The reason "mother" rhymes with "smother." | Infuriating, crude, and callous—a total fair-weather friend. | Hypersensitivity |
| Leo | The perfect blend of nurturing, passionate, adventurous, and adoring—but a bit of a drain. | Dynamic, intelligent, exciting, and sexy. Someone to make love and war with. But could the bastard at least bring you long-stemmed roses on your birthday? | Talking about yourselves endlessly, singing show tunes, going back to college for yet another degree |

| You are a(n)... | He thinks you're... | You think he's... | Common Language |
|---|---|---|---|
| Virgo | Incredibly intelligent and disciplined, but way too anal. | The One who's really neurotic, even though he keeps accusing you of that. | Conversation, politics, nature, the outdoors, education, judging and analyzing people |
| Libra | Pretty, charming, but way too concerned with your looks. | Badly in need of an extra-strength Prozac and Ritalin cocktail | Lighthearted fun and activity (bowling, karaoke, movie rentals) |
| Scorpio | Scary-sexy and way too intense—but potentially an exciting sexual challenge. | Gross. Just gross. | Dirty, sweaty, nasty, drunken, regrettable, unforgettable sex |
| Sagittarius | Hilarious fun, admirably ambitious, but maybe a little too similar to keep things exciting. | Really hot at first, but his constant angst and over-thinking gets on your last damn nerve. You might need a little more stability than he can provide. | Cracking each other up for hours, laughing so hard your stomachs hurt, building your empires, inspirational books and quotes, pop culture, karaoke and silly fun, travel |

| You are a(n)... | He thinks you're... | You think he's... | Common Language |
|---|---|---|---|
| Capricorn | Composed and goal-oriented in a way he wishes he could be. May dismiss you as cold, controlling, and too traditional for his tastes. | Passionate and inspiring, but too much of a dreamer to provide the material security you need. | Entrepreneurship, wacky jokes, sports |
| Aquarius | A kindred free spirit, adorable and fun. | The perfect playmate—a free thinker with a nomadic spirit who also wants to change the world. | Clever jokes, social causes, being secretly neurotic, a love of freedom, unconventional ideas, world travel |
| Pisces | Feminine in a way he finds far too unsettling. Estrogen overdose! | Completely devoid of the subtlety and tenderness you need from a romantic partner. | Self-absorption, a knack for disappearing from people's lives for weeks, months, even years, then resurfacing out of the blue |

# The Capricorn Man

Dates: December 22–January 19
Symbol: The Mountain Goat
Ruling Planet: Saturn, the planet of discipline and restriction
Element: Earth
Quality: Cardinal
Mission: The Ultimate Trophy

**Natural Habitat—Where You'll Find Him:** Commanding a board meeting like a five-star general, rock climbing, winning a long-distance relay, starting a successful business, studying a complex form of martial arts, in the V.I.P. lounge of a club or sports event, practicing his hobby/craft/obsession to absolute perfection, at the gym for an early morning workout, photographing beautiful women with a top-of-the-line camera (professionally or as a hobby), sleeping until 4 P.M. on the weekend, trying a little too hard to hit on a model or younger woman, brooding at home in a private melancholy funk, at a burlesque show or strip club quietly dominating the room, shopping for, entertaining, and taking care of his family, surrounded by grade school chums who knew him when, serving his nation in the military, racing around in a sports car, playing poker with his buddies, traveling alone through South America or Southeast Asia

**What He Does for a Living:** Businessman, CEO, doctor, director, political leader or pundit, media personality, photographer, musician (usually the lead singer), graphic designer, actor (leading man or brooding bad boy), screenwriter, novelist, military officer, professional athlete

**Noteworthy & Notorious Capricorn Men:** Jude Law, David Bowie, Marilyn Manson, Dave Grohl, Tiger Woods, Howard Hughes, Mel Gibson, Rod Stewart, Ryan Seacrest, Sacha Baron

Cohen, Martin Luther King Jr., Al Capone, Howard Stern, Aristotle Onassis, Kevin Costner, Rush Limbaugh, Muhammed Ali, Michael Stipe, Cuba Gooding Jr., Elvis Presley, Patrick Dempsey, Denzel Washington, John Singleton, Orlando Bloom, Jim Carrey, Benedict Arnold, Isaac Asimov, Nicolas Cage, Jimmy Buffet, Ralph Fiennes, George Foreman, Barry Goldwater, Robert E. Lee, Cary Grant, Ricky Martin, Edgar Allan Poe, J.D. Salinger, J.R.R. Tolkien, Sean Paul, LL Cool J

# Capricorn: How to Spot Him

- Long face with striking bone structure
- Stoic expression that is nearly impossible to read or interpret
- Handsome, manly jaw, like a cartoon superhero
- Eyes that constantly gaze out into the distance (goal-oriented Caps are always thinking, "What's next?")
- Flat, expressionless voice that belies a hilariously deadpan sense of humor
- Athletic build—even wiry or chubby Capricorns have decent muscle definition
- Sexily disheveled hair rifled with "product"
- Expensive jeans and designer sneakers—this guy pays good money to look like a rock star
- Small tattoo peeking out under his shirtsleeve, revealing a private freaky side
- The hulking stance of Lurch, the Franken-servant on *The Addams Family*
- The good-looking prepster hanging with the geeks and freaks—loyal Capricorns never dis their childhood friends
- "Come to Daddy" stance that draws you to him inexplicably
- Somewhat shy, but obviously confident energy

- Tracking gaze—if he wants you, he'll quietly stake out your every move
- Thoughtful listener... he'll ponder what you have to say, then offer wise feedback
- Helpful hero vibe; the first guy to reach the damsel in distress
- Quiet restlessness... if he's not drumming his fingers or shaking his knees, there's always a kinetic energy brewing below the surface when he's awake

# Capricorn: How He Deals With...

## Money

Obsessed with gaining financial security and playing "provider." A good budgeter and planner, but can blow his whole nest egg on a bad business deal. Always looking for something to invest in and is apt to own real estate.

## Family

Duty-bound to his clan, often plays the "rock" for everyone, even if he's the youngest child.

## Love

Yeah, yeah, whatever. It's great, but it doesn't conquer all.

## Sex

Always ready, willing, and able. May have strange or secret fetishes.

## Children

Those aren't kids, they're his legacy. Paternal and protective, expects them to live up to his high standards. Struggles to see them as separate entities from himself. This is one area where he could stand to be more realistic.

### Pets

Often the only creatures to witness his most tender feelings. Ah, the tear-stained fur of a rottweiler.

### Your Meltdowns

If he thinks you have a legitimate right to be upset (and it's not about something he did), he'll be a wise sounding board. Or, he'll point out something so absurd, you laugh and forget the whole thing.

If you're upset about him or acting "irrational": total hardass, and can even be cruel. Your ranting or tears are observed with stony silence, or he just takes off until you cool down. Call your mom if you need comfort.

### His Meltdowns

Completely internal—system shut-down! He either implodes and beats himself up obsessively, or sinks into a depression that lasts for months. Too proud to ask for support, and may lash out if you try to help.

### Breakups

A "soft close"—he lets things go gray, hoping they fade to black on their own. Expedites process by getting really busy with work or saying something mean, hoping to scare you away. If you don't get the hint, he'll sit you down for a brief, emotionless "this isn't working" talk. Stubborn once his mind is made up.

# Capricorn: What He's All About

It's 9:00 p.m. Do you know where your Capricorn is?

Before you file a Missing Persons report, call the office. Chances are he's hunched over his desk, engaged in his number-one priority: work. Capricorn rules the zodiac's tenth house of career, success, and structure, and he can be quite the Company Man. Armed with a ten-year plan, he's always doggedly pursuing his goals—or at least, trying to figure out where he's headed. Without direction and a dream, he's lost.

It's said that life doesn't really start for this "old-soul" sign until he turns forty. Until then, he's often elbows-deep in projects and ventures, or good old-fashioned preparation. He's painfully aware of hierarchies, and needs to be high on the totem pole. If he can't be in the top percentiles, he'd rather not play. Capricorn is a born manager. He takes pride in playing the gatekeeper, being "the guy who doesn't need anyone, but who everyone needs," as one Capricorn frames it. This man needs to set regular goals, break everything into measured steps, then cross them off his to-do list, item by item. One Capricorn we know plans to retire early and tour the world by yacht. A couple of others bought their fantasy cars (a Porsche, in both instances) after turning thirty-five. There's an ascetic quality to this guy; he'll nobly "go without," then reward himself for reaching a big goal.

If he's not at the office, chances are he's in some solitary state, absorbed in thoughts of "Where am I going? What should I do next?" A master strategist, life is his chessboard, and he makes slow, careful moves. In fact, the Capricorn man usually loves chess, baseball, or war stories—anything that requires strategy and calculation. The Capricorn man is a back-to-basics guy who can be a bit of a loner. He'll happily ride off into the sunset on his motorcycle, pausing for brief comfort, then venturing down the endless road again. There's a Marlboro Man or Lone Ranger quality to this sign.

Capricorn rules the teeth, jaw, and bone structure, and his are often prominent, giving him a striking face and dazzling smile (think of Caps like Kevin Costner, Mel Gibson, Denzel Washington, and Elvis Presley). His ability to stand still and let you come to him lends him a charisma that drives women crazy. At times, his lankiness can make him gawky and socially awkward. Vegetarianism is not advised for this sign. He needs to keep meat on his bones!

Fortunately, he has a great appetite for life's pleasures, especially food. Will he let himself indulge? Depends. Capricorn is ruled by Saturn, the sign of discipline, restriction, and repression, and he can be as restrained as he is greedy. We know a Capricorn man who took a vow of celibacy. Another has kept a twenty-year pledge not to drink liquor—and he's not even an alcoholic! As he explains, it gives him a sense of honor and dignity to keep his word. Capricorns love that patriotic stuff.

And yet, how Capricorn can be a slave to his senses! In some cases, Capricorn men develop obsessive-compulsive disorders as a result of this inner conflict. He's like the metaphorical fox jumping for the grapes, but never reaching them. Oddly, it's his own hand that keeps snatching the grapes away. Much as the Capricorn man yearns to reach his goals, he struggles with deep self-doubt, which is only worsened by his massive pride. Inches before the finish line, he may hesitate and sabotage his victory. Capricorn is the sign of public image, status, and glory. He'd rather quietly fail than be seen as a fool.

The Capricorn man is the most complicated simple person you'll ever meet. Buttoned up as he appears, there's a pent-up wild man in there. Hang out with him for a while, and you'll feel his restless intensity. He bottles up everything, and his repressed emotions can manifest as an alter ego (picture Capricorns like Marilyn Manson or David Bowie's "Ziggy Stardust" persona)—as if emancipating himself from his self-created prison. Out of nowhere, he might even break into insane physical comedy, leaping over couches. Like Capricorn Jim Carrey, this guy can contort his face, voice, and body into unbelievable forms.

As an Earth sign, he's a dyed-in-the-wool realist, and at times, a skeptic. Like a cantankerous Doubting Thomas, he scoffs at serendipity and demands hard evidence of every miracle. It's hard for him to trust anything he didn't fashion by the sweat of his own brow. Yet, he of little faith desperately needs something to believe in, and later in life, he can become quite spiritual. Until then, his God is in the rules, order, and laws of life. He likes to clearly learn the playbook before he even considers improvising.

His earthbound existence seems dour, but it also helps him view life as a divine comedy. When he's not worrying (or perhaps because he worries so much), he has a surprisingly silly sense of humor. His rich, booming laugh is infectious. He can be an amazing storyteller, and is way more observant than he appears. Although he takes himself far too seriously, this is the guy who will help you lighten up and laugh at yourself. One friend, a singer-songwriter married to a Capricorn, was pulling her hair out over how to finish a set of lyrics. As she launched into a tirade, her Cap husband looked her squarely in the eye and said, "Wanna f**k?" After singing a different kind of chorus with him, she was able to return to her studio and complete the song.

That's the magic of a Capricorn. What he lacks in speed, he makes up for in wisdom and patience. If you let him be your rock, he'll gladly provide you with a safe, happy landing on his shores.

# What He Wants in a Woman

Are you a smart, worldly woman who oozes feminine grace? A PhDiva who's still spacey enough to forget where she left her keys? A pedigreed show pony decked out in Prada? You'll be irresistible to the Capricorn man. His existence can be a harsh one, filled with sharp angles and vertical lines. He needs you to soften those rough edges. Want to steal his heart? Throw him a curve. Make him laugh. Add some fuchsia to his taupe-colored world.

The woman who wins him over is bubbly, confident, and outgoing enough to charge over his stony walls. At first impression, reserved Capricorn can seem stoic and uninterested, which discourages women from getting to know him. Getting a strong reaction from him is "like trying to get blood from a stone," as one Capricorn's former girlfriend describes it. When he tells you he hasn't had a girlfriend in five years (in spite of being a hottie), this is usually why.

The Capricorn man cherishes the days of old, and he can be annoyingly close to his family and childhood friends. He's a "bros before hos" type who romanticizes his boyhood and can be infuriatingly old-school about gender roles. The woman who integrates herself into his everyday world will have the easiest go with him. Otherwise, you may have to compete with his parents, siblings, and band of brothers for his attention—and it won't be pretty. With Capricorn, you've gotta come to daddy. He's not one to change his lifestyle or make a huge effort to be part of your world. He'd rather you just show up on his doorstep unannounced than coyly ask, "Soooo, what are you doing tonight?" and hope he invites you over.

Of course, once you're there, he'll expect you to fade into the background or make yourself at home until he's finished with whatever he's already doing. He's not a multitasker. When you show up in the middle of his band practice, you'll need to entertain yourself until the boys have finished their last set, patted themselves on the back, and passed a bong. He needs a thick-skinned, supportive woman who either patiently waits in the wings, or happily does her own thing in the meantime. If you're the type who feels easily taken for granted, this is not your guy.

Status-conscious Capricorn will carefully consider your credentials, history, and position on the food chain before he links up with you. Whatever his version of a "trophy" is, that's what he wants. If he prizes intellect, he'll marry a Rhodes Scholar with five degrees from Oxford. If he's a family guy (and Capricorn usually is), then you'll need to come from good stock. If he's a man about town, he'll lust after a socialite or a supermodel with velvet-rope access. The question "So...what do you do for a living?" might be as close to a pickup line as he ever gets.

Capricorn is the father sign, and he loves to provide for his woman. Could you use a helping hand, a hero, even a sugar daddy? Step right up. He'll greet you like a wise king, parceling out his riches to a pauper. Playing papa is his winning strategy. In insecure times, he may seduce women much younger than he is, banking on their "daddy issues" to feel like a man again. It's not uncommon for a Capricorn to date someone ten, twenty, even thirty years younger than he is. Of course, he will eventually tire of his young plaything once he's back on his feet.

Ultimately, Capricorn wants a mature woman, not a little girl. As Mike, a Capricorn in his mid-thirties says, "It's nice physically to be with a younger woman, but for the emotional and mental investment, you don't get the returns." Whatever their age, Capricorn can't stand overly simple women who lack ambition. He'll be glad to support you while you pursue your dream of becoming a writer, painter, or French literature scholar. Just remember that Capricorn is the sign of masculinity, and he wants to protect you. He doesn't need you to be Xena the Warrior Princess. That chick can slay her own dragons. On the other hand, neediness is a turnoff—especially if it interferes with his work schedule and productivity. This is not the dude you want to call at the office five times a day "just to say hi." When he's working, he's working.

Capricorn likes a little bit of crazy in his girlfriends. If you laugh too loud, wear your shirts cut too low, or trip on every sidewalk crack, he'll adore you. He's happiest being the stabilizing force in your relationship, which is why your colorful lifestyle can excite him. He may even tease you in an infuriatingly sexist way. One friend's Capricorn boyfriend told her, "You just like those 'ladies can do things' movies." She was watching a documentary.

Remember when Nicolas Cage, a Capricorn, married Lisa Marie Presley? On paper, she was a Capricorn man's trifecta: a trophy wife, connected to a historical legend, and a little nuts (c'mon, she married Michael Jackson). Who else could say they got hitched to Elvis's daughter right at the 25th anniversary of his death? To a Capricorn man, that's a coup.

Of course, their marriage only lasted four months. And herein lies the lesson many Capricorn men learn on their rocky, altar-bound trail: trophies eventually gather dust and lose their luster. Once the leggy supermodels have been sampled, the Capricorn man often marries the girl next door, a simple sweetheart who just lets him be himself. As one Capricorn friend says, "I just want someone I can decompress with." Nicolas Cage is now married to a cocktail waitress twenty years younger than he is. (Interestingly, Cage named their son Kal-el—the birth name given to Superman in the legendary comic book series.)

Fortunately, the Capricorn man matures over time, and so does his taste in women. "When I was younger, I used to like my girlfriends hot and damaged," says Will, a thirty-four-year-old Capricorn restaurateur. "I'm not really turned off by baggage; it makes it interesting. Still, as time has gone on, my girlfriends have been less and less tweaked."

If you imagine your relationship as a coloring book, the Capricorn man is the black-and-white outlines, and you're the crayons. He's glad to provide the template, while you add the sparkle and pizzazz. Of course, if you color too far outside the lines, he'll get a little nervous. Still, Mr. Vanilla needs some sprinkles and hot fudge in his life. If you make him laugh and help him unwind, that makes you the perfect cherry on top.

# What He Wants from a Relationship

When you link up with a Capricorn for the long haul, it's not just to live happily ever after. It's to raise a family, make his ancestors proud, create a legacy, and pass on wisdom to the next generation. No pressure or anything.

The Capricorn man wants a relationship that's built to last. He'll take pains to make sure you're a solid bet, and the evaluation process could be lengthy. He prefers to meet people through trusted sources like family or friends, or at a comfortable hangout where he doesn't feel awkward and out of place. To Capricorn, relationships are obligations he takes very seriously. He doesn't commit to anyone unless he knows he can give it his all. Sure, he may go through the boyfriend motions, but he'll usually back out before it goes too far.

What's the big deal, you may wonder. Don't those vows include "for better and for worse"? Besides, you're a modern woman who doesn't care if she out-earns her man. It's all about love. Superwoman doesn't need Superman. It's okay if he's Clark Kent—or even a male Lois Lane.

Not gonna happen. The Capricorn man's worst nightmare goes something like this: You arrive at a party with your Capricorn hubby Rob, and the hostess steers you into the living room for introductions. "Everyone, this is Amy. She's an amazing trial lawyer who's just made partner at her firm, and she's running for city council! Oh, and this is her husband Rob. He's been working odd jobs for the last ten years, while dreaming up how to make his millions. Amy pays the mortgage in the meanwhile, but we know that's just a short-term thing—right? Everyone, say hello to Amy and Rob!"

The Goat is stubborn. Many Capricorn men wait until well into their forties to settle down. He won't marry (or at least, won't marry permanently) until he's reached a few of his major milestones: traveling Latin America, becoming a board-certified surgeon, selling his first business. A firm footing on his chosen life path gives him the confidence to commit.

Capricorn is the zodiac's patriarch, and he's a proud papa to his brood. The Capricorn man is a bit like a soldier: dutiful, hardworking, and best when he has a country or family to serve. Becoming a father is like being elevated from private to four-star general. He now has troops to direct, missions to launch, and something bigger than himself to build. Family is the ultimate undertaking for him, and he's a consummate project manager, and may even rule his with an iron fist if necessary.

Of course, should he become a father before he's ready, this could be a different story. The unestablished Capricorn can be a total deadbeat dad. His sign can only focus on one thing at a time, and he doesn't do well when life happens out of sequence. In his mind, the path goes: love, financial security, marriage, kids. When an unscheduled pregnancy messes with the master plan, he's forced to juggle his duties, something he's not very good at. To Capricorn, not being able to provide for his kids is the ultimate shame. This is the father who may be estranged from his children until much later in life, when he's found the wisdom and direction to face them with dignity.

Okay, now for the warning label. This is sticky territory that we hate to cover, but feel we must. If you want a working relationship with Capricorn, ask yourself: How willing am I to be submissive? There will be compromises and power dynamics to navigate. If you're a go-getter who accomplishes goals at the speed of sound, take extra care that he doesn't feel left behind. Should you be more established than your Cap, you'll need to bolster his ego (without being obvious) and let him build his own empire, at his own ambling pace. Excruciating patience is a must.

Hard as this is to swallow, you'll need to carve out areas where he gets to be dominant. It may be the bedroom, or choosing where you live, or tolerating his boys' nights out without interrogating him for details. Can you live with that? Our feminist principles recoil at the notion, but we also know that love comes with its own set of rules. Sometimes, a powerhouse diva just craves the arms of a big, strong man. Early childhood patterns figure in, too. As the zodiac's father sign, the Capricorn man appeals to an only child, a daddy's girl, or the daughter of an absentee/difficult father. You could either work out those issues with a therapist, or with him.

Should you find yourself on such Freudian turf, be careful. The allure of this daddy-daughter dynamic can find you willingly handing over your power, making too many compromises to keep him. He can become a real tyrant if you open that door. Take care not to muffle your voice or strength with Capricorn. Pave the road for equality early with this guy unless you want to create your own personal Mussolini. Decide where you're okay letting him rule the roost, and stand firm in your boundaries everywhere else. Guard your "sacred space." Try this visualization: imagine drawing a line of demarcation, and planting your body firmly on that border like an impervious iron wall that nobody—not even your Cap—can penetrate. He may not like it, but you'll win his respect, which is ultimately one of the most important cornerstones for long-term love with a Capricorn.

## Sex with a Capricorn

So you think he's a straight-laced workaholic whose fantasy involves an executive title and a corner office? Well, only if you're dressed up like a French maid and splayed across his mahogany desk. The Capricorn man is a lusty creature whose stoic exterior hides a deep kinky streak. Don't judge this book by its cover—at least not sexually. As one Capricorn explains, it takes him a long time to open up and feel comfortable, and sex helps. "Sometimes it's easier to express my feelings physically than verbally," he says.

Once the ice is broken, the Capricorn man is pretty much an anytime, anyplace kind of guy. Alright, he's a total horndog. When he's in the mood, he's got to have you. Spend a little time with him and you'll sense his sexual charisma. Nobody can undress you with his eyes quite like this man. Sex with a Capricorn can be a little unemotional, even rough at times. He is the Mountain Goat, after all. He may just ram right into you like his symbolic animal.

Got a fetish? He's your man. Because Capricorn is ruled by Saturn, the planet of repression, his bottled-up issues come out behind closed doors. Chips, dips, chains, or whips, he's got no sexual taboos. Some Capricorn men even veer into more "gourmet" territory with their treasure trove of fetishes. You might come home after five years of marriage to find your "by the book" investment banker wearing your fishnets and heels (and looking better than you in them—bastard!).

Even S&M isn't off-limits to this connoisseur of kink. Of course, you may have to initiate the first round of master-and-servant games. Once he crosses the threshold, he could make a dominatrix blush. As one Capricorn man put it, "I'm not gonna be like, 'This is my dungeon.' But if you have a dungeon, I'd be happy to play in it."

For career-oriented Capricorn, the boardroom and the bedroom can become one and the same. The man of this sign often ends up marrying his secretary, just so she's available for a quickie between conference calls or high-powered meetings. A little noonday nookie is about the only thing that can distract him from his work (his other true love). Hard as he works, sex is his favorite way to blow off steam. So catch him as he's snapping his briefcase shut and remind him that all work and no play makes Cap a very, very dull boy.

# Capricorn: Turn-Ons & Turn-Offs

## Turn Him On

- Be a little ditzy—the Lois Lane to his Superman
- Share your vulnerability and solicit his wisdom
- Make him feel like a king or hero
- Be quirky and full of contradictions; he'll get off on teasing and correcting you
- Admire him, honestly… this guy can sniff out a fake compliment and hates them
- Be neat as a pin and a borderline clean freak

- Dress in classy and sophisticated clothes, splurge on that La Perla lingerie!
- Balance your need for him with an independent spirit
- Be a success in your own field… a different field than his
- Show this family guy that you'll be a good wife and mother

- Have a current or past career as a model (and let him photograph you in panties and his undershirt)
- Sleep in with him on Saturday and wake him up with a gentle, morning blow
- Fit in neatly with his friends and surroundings—this guy wants a no-fuss, natural fit

- Work at his office so he can conveniently shag you between meetings

- Be well read and well traveled, a trophy he can bring to those company functions
- Have a slightly edgy, somewhat dicey past—he'll be intrigued… if you're discreet
- Cook for him; he's probably too busy to do it for himself
- Be ready to travel on a moment's notice when his spontaneous wanderlust strikes and he wants someone to share it with

## Turn Him Off

- Refuse to lean on him or let him be your rock
- Call him in the middle of work and expect him to drop everything and talk to you
- Be too pulled-together or dressed-down: Capricorn wants a girl with style
- Get caught up in gossip or catty chatter—he'll consider you "beneath him"
- Compete with him, especially at work!
- Be too busy to accompany him on spontaneous dates and vacations—he'll invite another pretty lady along if you say no too many times
- Act like a "needy little girl" or have no ambition of your own
- Interrupt him while he's practicing or rehearsing, even if it's "just a hobby"—this guy takes everything he does seriously
- Criticize his family or childhood friends; question him when he gives money to his relatives
- Be an impediment to his daily routines, or worse yet, try to change them!

- Invite yourself along for his Boys Night Out or try to stop him from having one

# His Moves

## First Moves: How He Courts You

You know the guy slouching against the wall with his hands jammed in his pockets, or standing stiffly around the punchbowl? The one who can't quite relax (unless the punch is spiked), and seems a little aloof—yet, you get the feeling that he's watching you? If he's not a Scorpio, he's probably a Capricorn.

Capricorn is the zodiac's father sign, and he's a "come to daddy" type. Don't expect him to get off his butt to hit on you. He might send you a drink from the other end of the bar, or grab your arm as you walk by. As one Capricorn half-jokingly puts it, "I track her like a gazelle, waiting until she falls into my range." Just don't expect this coolheaded sign to leap over the buffet table to get your phone number (again, unless the punch is spiked). Here are some of the subtle ways he might signal his interest:

- He tries to impress you with his refined taste or knowledge
- He gradually gets to know you through mutual friends or hangouts
- He arranges to be formally set up with you on a blind date
- He engages you in an opinionated or spirited conversation to test how interesting you are
- He watches you from the sidelines and waits for you to notice him
- He conveniently shows up where you are or "runs into you" (he planned it)
- He teases you like you're his little sister
- He frowns like he's concentrating really hard when you talk (he's nervous)

- He gets flushed, flustered, and tongue-tied around you
- You fall in love while he's your boss, manager, coach, trainer, mentor…
- He meets you online through the "safety" of a chat room

## He's In: How You Know He's Committed

The Capricorn man may have many sex partners (or not), but his serious relationships are few and far between. This is not a man of many words. He prefers to show how he feels, rather than tell you straight out. You may have to be a bit of a mind reader to realize that you're dating exclusively, so pay attention to cues like these:

**He wants to be with you as often as possible.** Don't you get it? He's spending his free time with you (well, after he fulfills his duties to his family, best friends, pets, and career). That makes you his girlfriend. Do you need him to spell it out for you? Well, of course you do. Alas, it ain't gonna happen. His actions speak louder than his words, so he'd rather you just put the clues together. As one Capricorn says, "Time is so important; I really want to share it with the people I care about."

**He gets nostalgic about you.** Is he reminiscing over your early years together, or gazing at photos with an unusually soft look in his eyes? You've now become a cherished part of his sacred personal history.

**He formally proposes, or takes you ring shopping.** It may take another decade before the actual wedding, since he'll want to have his money and life in perfect order first. But if you've known each other a while and it feels solid, it is. (Sidenote: Like Elvis Presley, Caps can also initiate impulsive shotgun weddings. If you've known each other a week and he drops to one knee, just say no—or make sure you get half in the inevitable divorce.)

**He starts making more money or advancing in his career.** Rather than distract him from his goals, you've motivated him to achieve. Capricorn loves a woman who "makes me a better man," as one Goat says. Keep him from stagnating and he'll keep you around like a lucky charm.

**He takes care of you financially.** If he's providing for you, that means he feels like "the man" around you. Nothing's more seductive to Mr. Cap than feeling duty-bound to a woman he also finds incredibly hot.

## Unfaithful Capricorn: Why He Cheats

Capricorn is a sign that values loyalty and honor, so it's rare to find too many cheaters among this sign's ranks. Still, until this guy is ready to settle down—in other words, he's well on his way to achieving the ambitious goals he's set for himself—he will waver in his loyalty from time to time. In his mind, until he knows where he's going in life, he can't possibly choose the right criteria for a suitable mate. So, like a mountain goat tripping on the rocky trail, he may stumble for these reasons:

**You play too many games.** This dude can be infuriatingly unexpressive, so you'll be tempted to test his love by pushing his buttons. Don't sit on his best friend's lap to make him jealous. He likes a little mystery, but if you mess with his head, he'll assume you're not serious about the relationship—thus, why should he be?

**A breakup is imminent, so he figured he might as well get a head start on single life.** As the saying goes, "luck is where preparation meets opportunity." Once he plans his exit, he has a knack for finding a quick rebound (he usually has an ex or two in the wings, standing by for his booty call).

**He's horny and you're never around.** The Capricorn man is a realist to a fault. Cheating can be a practical matter. In his mind, sex is a basic human need, like eating or going to the bathroom. You wouldn't ask him to starve or hold it in, would you? If you're off on a six-month European tour, he may snack while you're away.

**Sabotage!** He knows he's not ready for something this serious, and he needs a way out. Behold: a sexy young thing that he could never take seriously—flirting with him!

**He never really ended it with his last girlfriend (or three).** Maybe he's still paying child support for the kid he helped raise. Maybe she was his high school sweetheart, and he still feels obligated to take care of her. Nostalgic Capricorn feels most comfortable living in the past. His sign rules history, and if he has too much of it with somebody, beware.

**He thinks he's entitled to it.** Some Capricorns have a very old-school, "men will be men" idea of masculinity, and can separate sex from love. Make sure his ego and maturity are solid before getting involved.

## Dig the Grave: It's Over

A relationship with a Capricorn is like a chapter in an epic novel. Even if he leaves, he could return a year later to pen the sequel. To quote the famous line from *Brokeback Mountain*, the Capricorn man "can't quit ya." To Capricorn, everything in life is a deal, including your relationship. Here are a few of his deal-breakers:

**You're too dramatic.** Are you lively, outgoing, even a little messed up? He can handle it. Do you hyperventilate, hurl accusations, and interfere with his productivity? Not worth the hassle. Adios, diva!

**You're not dramatic enough.** If anyone's going to be the "boring one" in the relationship, it will be him. Fail to keep him entertained, and he'll find a new showgirl to amuse him.

**You're farther ahead than he is in life, and he can't catch up.** His worst nightmare is to have people observe your relationship and wonder, "What's she doing with him?" If you've got a multi-platinum album and he's just starting a band, he'll never feel like a rock star. Being compared unfavorably to you is excruciating to Capricorn.

**He's "not ready."** Translation: He hasn't achieved 95 percent of the life goals he planned to reach by age twenty-two—and he's about to turn thirty. He needs to focus on catching up, and he sees your relationship as a distraction.

**You tried to control him.** The stubborn Mountain Goat is a creature of the wild. He doesn't take kindly to anyone trying to fence him in. If you turn the relationship into your personal petting zoo, he'll break for the hills.

**He senses disloyalty or betrayal.** Capricorn cleaves to old-fashioned values, like honor and fidelity. If he smells *Eau de Rat* on you, he'll drop you back into the woodpile.

# Interpreting His Signals:

## *What does he mean by that?*

| When he | It means... | So you should... |
| --- | --- | --- |
| Gets quiet | He's thinking about work or his personal goals. | Just chill and enjoy the silence, or ask him what's on his mind. He may appreciate a chance to talk it through with a trusted companion. |
| Doesn't call | He's working or hanging out with family or friends. | Wait until after work hours, or send a casual text message (limit yourself to one). Don't be offended if he doesn't respond for a few hours. He can only focus on one priority at a time. |
| Calls a lot | He likes you. | Pick up. Soon enough, he'll be working like a fiend, so enjoy the attention while it lasts. |
| Doesn't make a move after a couple of dates | Nothing. He doesn't like to be rushed. | Make a move yourself, or just be patient. He wouldn't waste his time if he weren't interested. |
| Doesn't make a move after a few weeks | He's either scared you don't like him, he's involved with someone else, or he's just taking it slow. | Make a move or ask him honestly if he sees it going anywhere beyond a friendship level. |

| When he | It means... | So you should... |
| --- | --- | --- |
| Moves fast | He's drunk, or he doesn't see you as a serious prospect, so he has nothing to lose. | Have a no-strings fling if you're in the mood. If you want a boyfriend, start shopping around—it ain't him. |
| Picks up the tab, gives flowers and gifts | He likes you and wants to impress you with his provider abilities. He's definitely wooing you. | Be gracious, receptive, and feminine. If you don't like him "like that," let him know now before he invests further. |
| Introduces you to his family and/or closest friends | You're in the running for long-term mate status. These are his most cherished companions, and he'll want to know what they think of you. | Be warm and friendly without trying too hard. Put your best foot forward. |

# Your Moves: Tips for Flirting and Everlasting Love

## Flirting with a Capricorn

The Capricorn man loves to flirt, but he's rarely comfortable enough to start the proceedings. For him, setting is everything. If he's somewhere comfortable—at home, among friends, slightly buzzed at his favorite lounge—he may work up the nerve to approach you. In most cases, you'll have to be confident enough to hit on him first. If he likes you, he's probably checking you out from a distance, doing a cost-benefit analysis of whether you're worth the risk of rejection. Here's how to make it easier for both of you:

**Walk past him slowly... and linger.** Make it convenient, safe, and easy for him to start a conversation. Set the stage for a "natural" interaction. You may literally have to fall into his lap for him to talk to you.

**Pierce the veil.** With the Capricorn man, it takes work to get past his initial reserve. Boldly go where few other women have gone, and tough out the initial awkwardness. Summon the courage to be yourself and share your passions, even if he's quiet. Turn up the volume to 10 and keep it there. If he likes you, he'll slowly crank up his own volume to an enthusiastic (for a Capricorn) 4. Before you know it, he'll be asking for your digits.

**Ask him a slightly racy question.** He might look like the guy who'd blush at the word "breast," but you'd be surprised. He'll shock you with a raunchy, direct, and funny answer, and the ice will thaw from there.

**Flirt with him at work.** Capricorn is in his element at the office, so if you connect through your job, all the better. Start by going to lunch together. Keep him excited with suggestive, sidelong glances in the hallway and "accidental" contact in the copy room. Soon, your lunch breaks could get veeeery interesting.

**Tease him.** He has a boyish, pigtail-pulling streak so take it back to first grade. Try some childish tactics to loosen him up.

**Intrigue him.** Capricorn loves a good project. If you seem complex or mysterious, he may want to solve the puzzle.

## Everlasting Love with a Capricorn

It's a long, looong road to eternity with Capricorn. Can you tough it out? You may even part ways and reunite before making it to the altar. Fortunately, the Capricorn man only trusts things that stand the test of time. If your connection can endure a few cycles, he knows you're a solid bet. How can you make sure to end up in his lovin' arms forever?

**Let him be king of something.** The Capricorn man needs his turf, and if you grant him rulership of that territory, he'll build you an adjacent throne. Bonus points if you come with a "dowry" from your own queendom (trust fund, VIP access to high society, other credentials that boost his status by association).

**Be his ultimate playmate and companion.** Capricorn men love to dig into life, and they want someone to experience that with them. Are you curious about art, design, travel, new restaurants, wine? He'll be glad to introduce you to what he knows and explore new venues together. One Capricorn friend is teaching his girlfriend how to play baseball (his passion), and she's showing him how to cook (they're both foodies). If you're receptive and open, he'll love to be around you.

**He can be himself around you.** After a long day wearing his game face at work, the Capricorn man needs to rip off his mask and be real. If you can "talk him out of the tree," as one Cap puts it, he'll want you there as the perfect end to a long day.

**Be worldly.** Self-absorbed? Forget about it. Capricorn men love a woman who's interested in the bigger view of life. Says Capricorn Will, "If you can only talk about your new Gucci bag or the micro-drama at your workplace, that's a turn-off."

**Challenge him to grow.** For Capricorn, stagnation equals death. He needs you to push him out of his comfort zone, where he easily gets stuck. The world can be daunting to this guy, though he'll rarely admit it. Remind him of his big-picture goals and champion his efforts to reach them.

**Be a seamless fit with his friends, family, and lifestyle.** This guy is set in his ways. He has his few close friends, his family, and his routine. He's not very adaptable, and prefers if you make yourself at home in his world. Even if you have a tricked-out apartment and he sleeps on a curb-salvaged twin bed with a makeshift nightstand, he'd rather hang at his place. Pull up a fruit crate and have a seat.

# Prep Yourself For...

## Your First Date

If a Capricorn man has actually made the effort to ask you out, the largest hurdle has been crossed. It means he's forged past the pessimistic voices in his head berating, "Dude, do you really want to date right now? Shouldn't you be focusing on what you're doing with your life? Is it worth the trouble?"

Although Capricorns are good planners, he may take a more spontaneous approach to your first date. "I plan so much during the day," says one Capricorn, "a date is a nice escape from that." He'll choose a cool restaurant or activity, but he may not tell you where you're going until the last minute. Wondering could keep you on edge (what should you wear?), but it will also infuse the date with a sexy charge. Go with the flow and enjoy the adrenaline rush.

**The Basic Vibe:** Time is precious to the Capricorn man. To him, the perfect first date is a "twofer"—the chance to hang out with an attractive woman and go somewhere he's wanted to check out. One Capricorn, a DJ, takes his dates to clubs "so I can also keep an eye on my industry." Selfish? Yeah. It's also his practical nature. He doesn't expend energy on something that may not have the ROI. Combining business and pleasure is a form of dating insurance to him.

Don't expect a red carpet and limo—at least, not until later on in the relationship. The first date may be extremely casual. He may invite you to hang out with a group of friends, or to show up somewhere he already plans to be. After all, he needs to see how well you fit into his world—and above all, how comfortable he feels around you.

Although conversation is important to him, Capricorn can be a little bottled-up at first. Activity dates are advised, so feel free to suggest a movie, museum, or sports event. "That helps me loosen up, and relax my inhibitions," agrees one Capricorn. "It's easier to warm up through common interests." Ultimately, he loves having a partner in crime to try all the new places he wants to go.

The Capricorn man may approach your first date like a job interview, taking one step at a time. Take the classic case of our Capricorn friend Mike, who was fixed up with his cousin's co-worker. Before going on an official first date, they had what he calls a "semi-interview." He invited the woman to his company cafeteria for lunch hour, so he could assess whether it was "worth it" to make a real effort. "We met, talked a little bit to see if there was some compatibility," Mike explains with businesslike logic.

After discovering they were both into art and restaurants, Mike took the next logical step on his Capricorn checklist: a low-risk activity date. "We went to the museum," Mike recalls. "There was a French Impressionism exhibit I wanted to see." The Capricorn man will hedge his bets—if he doesn't like you, at least he'll get some value for himself. Things progressed steadily for Mike. After four months, their parents met, and now their families spend the holidays together. He proposed at a baseball game on their one-year anniversary.

In other cases, you may not know that you're on a date until halfway through the evening. One woman, a high-powered art dealer, was invited for after-work drinks by her cute Capricorn male assistant. "I thought it was a welcome wagon kind of thing," she laughs. "Imagine my surprise when he put his hand on my thigh and tried to kiss me!" Of course, the Happy Hour indulgences had loosened his inhibitions. Still, you never know what kind of surprise a Capricorn can pull out once he relaxes.

**What to Wear:** Dress to impress. The Capricorn man loves a woman who's polished, sophisticated, and has a natural sense of style. Elegance goes far. He wants to feel like he could walk into the most exclusive establishment with you, and the velvet ropes will part. Put some real effort into your look, and add some glamour. He loves you to be femme and sexy—break out the red lipstick and heels. Don't worry about outdressing him. He wants to be blown away by your great taste, even if he wears hiking boots and a sweater (he just might).

**What Not to Wear:** Playing it safe? Nuh-uh. If your outfit is forgettable, chances are, you will be, too. The Capricorn man is an Earth sign, and as such, he will judge you by your surface appearances first. Skip anything generic, tasteless, or overly simple. "It looks like you think you're not special—like you didn't put any thought into it, or even like you have no class," explains one Capricorn.

**To Pay or Not to Pay?** Capricorn is a provider sign, and if he can't pay for the whole date, he'd rather not go out at all. If you want to toss a few bills down, cool, but he won't expect it of you.

As one Capricorn said, "I want to try new restaurants, order an expensive bottle of wine, or go somewhere nice. I don't want her to feel obligated to pay for that."

**Saying Good night:** Most of the time, Capricorn will act like a proper gentleman, safely shuttling you to your doorstep and leaving with a squeeze. Want to make out? You have to initiate the action. It won't take much for him to oblige.

## His First Home Visit

If a Capricorn man goes out of his way to enter your world, he either feels really comfortable with you, or he thinks you're worth getting to know. Otherwise, he'd keep sitting on his own damn recliner with his feet up, letting you come to him. As with your outfits and makeup, he wants to be impressed by your decorating style. He'll observe and comment, whether you ask him to or not. To his minimalist sign, that means having enough taste to edit your possessions down to the most interesting and well-appointed basics. It's quality over quantity for Capricorn.

**Have a comfortable couch and bed.** Being with you is part of his great escape from work, so feather the nest. The comfier the cushion, the better the pushin'.

**Keep it neat, clean, and simple.** The Capricorn man is a minimalist and he can't stand a pack rat. Haul some boxes to storage or the Goodwill. Consider his visit a great excuse to clear out some clutter.

**Make it easy for him to observe your personality.** Perceptive Capricorn assesses your character through clues in your material world. He wants to see your authentic nature, and he finds that by considering your color schemes, or by browsing your books, CDs, and collections. It's easier for him to get to know you this way than by making uncomfortably intimate conversation. Hint:

Place some conversation pieces around so he'll have something to talk about.

**Put your trophies on display.** Status is important to Capricorn. He wants to see your awards, credentials, and claims to fame. And yes, he will judge you based on these.

**Don't look too settled in.** The Capricorn man likes to leave his mark, so the less "done" your place looks, the better. Should you someday move in together, he needs to know that your styles will blend—or rather, that your décor won't overpower his. Use his visit as an excuse to de-clutter your house and toss out some junk.

## Meeting His Family

The Capricorn man has an intense, dutiful relationship with his family. Their opinion matters to him, and he wants to marry well enough to make his ancestors proud. If you're not bring-home-to-mama material, you may never darken the doorstep of his childhood home. It's nearly impossible for this guy to dishonor his parents. One Capricorn man we know postponed his wedding date because his mom insisted she needed "at least a year to find a dress."

Thankfully, Capricorn is not a whiny infant who blames his failures on his upbringing. You won't hear excuses like, "Well, I never became a doctor because my father didn't love me unconditionally." If anything, he views his childhood through rose-colored glasses—or at worst, with a shrug of practical acceptance. "What can you do?" says one Cap of his nutty parents. "They are who they are. Why dwell on it? Move on."

Still, everything's a tradeoff. This man could stand to dig up a childhood issue or two, if only for closure's sake. Instead, he remains the loyal, tight-lipped son, repressing any anger or rebellion. He may even suffer from depression or addiction if he holds in too much. In severe cases, he channels his emotions into a private, subversive "hobby" like cross-dressing, gambling, or visiting fetish websites. We've seen it all. For the most part, he doggedly plays the golden boy, often even financially supporting his parents.

It's a big deal for Capricorn to introduce you as his "official girlfriend" to his family. He may even present you with a solemn, formal air. If you're invited home for the holidays, you're definitely being sized up as a future family member. Whether he likes his family or not is irrelevant. Duty-bound and loyal, he's usually the "rock" of his clan, even if he's the youngest child. In his mind, it's a basic obligation to stand by them—if not live within a five-mile radius.

Whether or not they like you is crucial to your relationship's future. Our friend Jessica dated a sexy Italian Capricorn (let's call him Giorgio) while he lived in the United States for a year. Giorgio returned to Italy and broke up with Jessica, but a couple years later, he contacted her again. "I never forgot about you," were his seductive words. Jessica decided to fly to Italy and see if they could make a second go of their relationship.

Right after Jessica stepped off a six-hour flight, Giorgio shuttled her to his grandparents' house (surprise!), where his entire brood of aunts, uncles, and cousins were waiting around a long table loaded with his grandma's cooking. Fighting jet lag, Jessica managed to win everyone over with broken Italian, and by heaping her plate with home-cooked food. Halfway through Jessica's third helping, Giorgio's grandma raised a glass and shouted in Italian, "To your wedding!" The rest of the family heartily echoed the toast.

In the end, Giorgio "wasn't ready" for marriage. Later, he told Jessica that the hardest part of the breakup was facing his family (how, um… noble). In fact, he hid it from his parents for weeks before he finally confessed that he had passed on marriage with a woman they (that's right, *they*) adored. So if you want a shot at the altar with a Capricorn, make sure his family falls in love with you, too. It won't guarantee anything, but it can certainly help your cause.

# Saying Good-bye
## Breaking Up with a Capricorn

Capricorn is a practical sign, and he faces breakups with cool-headed logic—at least, on the surface. Crying and public scenes aren't his style. His ruling planet, Saturn, lends him wisdom and perseverance through difficult times. Though he may sink into a depression for a while, he knows instinctively that time heals all wounds. He prefers a clean break with no contact to keep it neat and practical.

He's a man of his word, and he expects you to be a woman of yours. If you tell him it's over, he takes it at face value. The Capricorn man will never beg. He may ask, "Are you sure?" This will be your only window to take it back. Woe betide the drama queen who stages a pseudo-breakup to test how much her Capricorn loves her. Threats and crying wolf will completely destroy his trust.

Dignity is everything to this man. Even if you've shattered his hopes and dreams, don't treat him like a hurt little boy. He doesn't want you to mother his hurt feelings. To him, a relationship is like a business deal. Once the contract's broken, he believes you should both move on—at least in theory. Keep your own dignity intact as much as you can, too.

## Getting over Him: When a Capricorn Dumps You

The Capricorn man is a practical heartbreaker. Lack of love is rarely his motivation for calling it quits. It's usually simple: He's reached the point where he has to ask himself, "Could I be a good husband and father right now?" If the answer is no, he doesn't care if you've already picked the wedding china and subscribed to *Modern Bride*. He'll officiously tell you it's not working, let you cry a little, then leave. Usually, he'll do it in person "for basic respect," as one Cap puts it.

Still, it's never really over. As one Capricorn friend of ours says, "I tend to keep my exes around." Months, even years, after you've burned his photographs, you could receive a text message or an email: He's thinking of you. Perhaps he's now in a place where he can handle a relationship, and you may reunite. If his life is status quo, beware. It's a seductive ego trip to believe he can't get over you, but reality check: He might be hiding behind the safety of nostalgia, instead of risking a real relationship. The Capricorn man bathes in melancholy and often dwells in the past. Unless you want your life to resemble a bad country music song, proceed with caution.

## Have yourself one good last cry over...

- His lusty, earthy attractiveness
- That chiseled jaw and sexy smile
- The comfort of having a big, strong man to lean on
- Feeling incredibly feminine around him
- Your now-empty wallet: Sugar Daddy's left the building
- His wise, practical insights
- Losing a good social companion for lounges, concerts, and restaurants
- His discerning taste in food, wine, scents, clothing, and just about everything
- Breaking up with his family (parents, siblings, uncles, cousins...)
- Sex, sex, sex

**Praise the universe that you never have to deal with…**

- That melancholy cloud that follows him
- His slooooooow pace: make a move, man!
- Pretending to like his annoying, immature childhood friends
- Pretending to like his annoying, crazy family members
- His skepticism and pessimism shooting down your dreams
- Moodiness, even manic mood swings
- That reserved, stoic façade you always had to break through
- Being awake for hours on the weekend while he stays in bed until dinnertime
- Feeling like you're "too much" around him
- Being a "work widow"—does he have to stay at the office 'til 10 P.M. every night?
- Those strange perversions, addictions, and habits
- Lonely days waiting for him to call or email
- Wondering what other skeletons are in his closet

# Love Matcher:

## Can you find a common language?

| You are a(n)... | He thinks you're... | You think he's... | Common Language |
|---|---|---|---|
| Aries | Excitingly ambitious, but ultimately, his competitor. | Too rigid and not enough of a free thinker, but also a nice grounding force. | Ambition, goals, a desire for world domination |
| Taurus | Elegant, sophisticated, and just his speed. | A good long-term investment. | Money, status, tradition, and long-term stability. Both big on "taking it slow" |
| Gemini | A total head case, but the most exciting person he's ever met. | The daddy you've always wanted. | Kinky sex 40 times a day, supporting each other's career goals |
| Cancer | His wife. | Too aloof, but a potential husband/security blanket. | A cliqueish approach to family and friends, the desire for status and security |

| You are a(n)... | He thinks you're... | You think he's... | Common Language |
|---|---|---|---|
| Leo | A trophy and his personal show pony, but way too dramatic. | The infuriating case you need to crack. | Bossing each other around, domination and power struggles that end in the bedroom (whips and corsets optional) |
| Virgo | A safe bet, but a touch neurotic. | The ultimate provider and sounding board. | Travel, outdoor activity, hobbies, sharing daily routines, friends, and family |
| Libra | The ultimate trophy chick, but too hard to tame. | The sugar daddy who gets a little too "daddy" for you. | Wining, dining, 69ing |
| Scorpio | Hot. | The kinky playmate you could marry. | Control, one-upping, competition, a touch of S&M |

| You are a(n)... | He thinks you're... | You think he's... | Common Language |
|---|---|---|---|
| Sagittarius | An impressive go-getter, but too hotheaded and unfocused. | Impressive, sexy, but impossible to connect with. | A quest for spiritual truth and wisdom. Ambition: when life gives you lemons, you make lemonade |
| Capricorn | Not quite crazy enough for his taste. | A status symbol and a practical pick. | Work, goals, tradition, the desire for a picture-perfect life |
| Aquarius | Endlessly fascinating. | A grounding force. | Travel, philosophy, broad-minded worldviews |
| Pisces | Creative but crunchy. | Straight and narrow. | The arts, photography, mutual friends |

# The Aquarius Man

Dates: January 20–February 18
Symbol: The Water Bearer
Ruling Planet: Uranus, the planet of originality, surprises, and rebellion
Element: Air—intellectual, changeable, social
Quality: Fixed
Mission: Romantic Revolution

**Natural Habitat—Where You'll Find Him:** Auditioning for a TV pilot, working the special effects on a movie set, playing basketball, lifting weights, screaming at the umpire at a baseball game, coding a website at 4 A.M., hamming it up at karaoke, drinking beer (at a sports bar or strip club) with the boys, on a selling spree at a trade show, on a spiritual pilgrimage in South America, studying quantum physics at a retreat, inventing a new school of thought, dancing naked at Burning Man, studying with a guru, taking his family on an adventure vacation, performing improv at a comedy club, coaching a high school sports team, playing chess, running for political office, winning a sales award

**What He Does for a Living:** Internet guru, sales (he can sell anything!), computer programmer, advertising exec, high school teacher, TV actor, chef, restaurant owner or manager, Wall Street banker, mathematician, scientist, defense attorney, movie producer, politician, futurist, pop star

**Noteworthy & Notorious Aquarius Men:** Justin Timberlake, Abraham Lincoln, Franklin Delano Roosevelt, Ashton Kutcher, Chris Rock, John Travolta, Axl Rose, Oscar de la Hoya, Bobby Brown, Michael Jordan, Jerry O'Connell, Tom Selleck, Ed Burns, Joey Fatone, Alice Cooper, Bob Marley, Garth Brooks, Henry Rollins, Chris Farley, Peter Gabriel, Matt Dillon, Dr. Dre, Ronald Reagan, Elijah Wood

## Aquarius: How to Spot Him

- The life of the party, he's on a first name basis with everyone at the bar
- Sporty style—he's usually wearing jeans and sneakers (though they may be bright orange)
- Can't sit still, drumming his fingers, pacing around, and making other nervous gestures
- Pentagonal jaw
- Boyish grin and a mischievous twinkle in his eyes
- Warm energy—he's the cool, popular guy who's nice to everyone
- Clowning around, making faces, cracking up everyone around
- Talking fast with his hands
- Schmoozing in a "let's make a deal" kind of way
- Edgy jock—he may be wearing a baseball cap, but he's probably got a few tattoos and earrings, too
- Strong hands, nicely shaped fingers
- Leaning forward, engaged in conversations
- Loud, contagious laugh

# Aquarius: How He Deals With...

### Money

Doesn't stress it. He likes nice things but knows they aren't the be-all and end-all. Knows he can rely on his natural sales abilities to drum up more cash when he needs it. Will always find money for travel and adventure.

## Family

Protective, dutiful, but needs a healthy separation.

## Love

Needs a powerhouse partner who can hold her own. Likes to brag about his girlfriend's accomplishments. His love life must have an unconventional twist to keep him interested. Has "friendship love" with many and "true love" with only a few.

## Sex

A freak in the sheets *and* on the streets.

## Children

May not be part of his Grand Plan. If he does have kids, he'll enjoy teaching them and taking them on field trips.

## Pets

Gotta have 'em. Turns into total mush around animals. May adopt a shelter dog or stray cat.

## Your Meltdowns

Detaches and shuts down until the storm has passed. May make a joke out of the situation to deal with the discomfort.

## His Meltdowns

Shocking, rage-filled, scary, and can come out of left field—all his repressed emotions make a messy explosion.

## Breakups

Slowly transitions you into best friend status over the course of three to six months. Stalks you if you dump him out of the blue.

# Aquarius: What He's All About

Okay, here's a riddle: What do you get when you mix the boy next door with a mad scientist, a jock, and an alien? Answer (drumroll): an Aquarius man!

On the outside, he looks like your perfect pop star or boy band frontman: dimples, cute face, angular jaw, perhaps a tattoo to flaunt his rebel edge or his allegiance to a particular philosophy. The original Mr. Popularity, he's funny, flirty, successful, and well liked without even trying. This is the dude most likely to end up in a *Teen Beat* centerfold (think of Aquarians like Justin Timberlake and Backstreet Boys' Nick Carter). He could sell ice to Eskimos. In fact, there have been more U.S. presidents born under the sign of Aquarius than any other, including memorable leaders like Abraham Lincoln, FDR, and Ronald Reagan.

Inside, this dude is anything but vanilla. Just observe him for a while. He crackles with kinetic energy. He's twitchy and nervous, and can't sit still. His eyes dart around, taking everything in. He might even move in robotic, jerky ways—or like a futuristic wind-up toy. He knows he's a little offbeat (or extremely so), and he usually embraces it with good cheer. As a boy, he might have been a prodigy, at sports, performing, computers, or something else inventive. Either that, or he just lived on his own special planet, the family's adorable extraterrestrial.

Aquarius is governed by Uranus, the planet of originality, revolution, and sudden events. Like his celestial ruler, the unpredictable Aquarius man never truly follows convention. Rules were made to be broken—or at the very least, given a modern makeover. Like Aquarius comic Chris Rock, he's known to blurt out a shocking comment that either cracks you up or stuns the room into silence. Still, even his rudest and most outrageous stunts are for a higher purpose. Ashton Kutcher, an Aquarius, brought celebrities down a well-deserved peg with his MTV show *Punk'd*. This equality-minded sign turns sacred cows into steak dinner.

While you might find some Aquarius men in fringe lifestyles, like spiritual communes or polyamorous clans, for the most part this sign changes the system from within. He participates in conventions like marriage, or he'll hack it at a corporate job, bringing his own vision and radical approach. Nothing can be done by the book with this guy. To Aquarius, history is meant to be made, not repeated. As one Aquarius man puts it, "I want to take a quantum leap from my parents' generation."

Aquarius is also the sign of friendship, groups, and casual connections. He has a million friends and makes them easily wherever he goes. Everyone is his "buddy" or "brother." Our Aquarius friend Chris is aptly nicknamed The Mayor. Even while running his own technology company, Chris took a job at Starbucks, partly for health benefits, but largely because he needed doses of human contact. While cheerfully handing out lattes, shoveling snow, and wiping tables, Chris developed a warm bond with all his customers, who found his genuine smile as addictive as their Venti Frappucinos. The Aquarius man has a way of making everyone feel like his best friend.

One-on-one is where the Aquarius man struggles to find his beat. Although the "enlightened" Aquarius makes an excellent partner, not all of them make peace with those strange sensations known as feelings. The notion of intimacy and connection freaks him out at first, and it can turn him into a neurotic, hypersensitive mess. Derek, an Aquarius actor and comedian, jokes, "When do I talk about feelings with a woman? Uh, when I'm unconscious?" He's only half-kidding.

The Aquarius man's ability to detach from his emotions is also his gift. It allows him to stay focused on his vision of a better tomorrow, rather than get discouraged or distracted. Thomas

Edison, an iconic Aquarius, had 10,000 failed experiments before he invented the lightbulb. (Lucky for Edison, Aquarius rules science and electricity.) In one of his most famous quotes, Edison said, "I haven't failed. I've just found 10,000 ways that won't work."

That inspiring, can-do attitude is incredibly exciting to be around, though you may never feel fully secure. Thomas Edison also said, "Show me a thoroughly satisfied man, and I will show you a failure." Settling down is not in the Aquarius man's lexicon. He needs to continuously evolve and expand, and he's on a lifelong quest to do that. This astrological nomad is a collector of experiences and a wise teacher of what he's learned. As the sign of humanity and society, his soul is charged with an obligation to give back what he's learned, leaving the world better than he entered it.

If you want a guy who will nurse your emotional wounds, hire a male psychiatrist or date a Water sign. And if you don't make your Aquarius man talk about his feelings (unless he wants to—then it will be a very long night), his feminine side will slowly emerge. Before you know it, the class clown will become quite a sap. He'll cook you amazing dinners with exotic ingredients, serenade you at rush hour in the middle of a commuter-packed business district, or set up an elaborate night of sexy surprises.

If you crave a life of adventure and discovery, Aquarius will gladly take you on his vision quest—as long as you let him steer the spacecraft. You never know which galaxy you'll end up in, and he may not either—but getting there will be half the fun. So if you're a student of life, why not develop a crush on the cute boy making paper UFOs and redefining the string theory while break dancing or standing on his head?

# What He Wants in a Woman

Wanted: sexy SF, fellow "seeker," race/culture/religion not important (we are all one), to share uncharted adventures on the physical and spiritual planes. Join me for fun and laughs, dancing, dinner parties for 1,467 of our closest friends. After I wash the dishes and you dry them, we'll explore life's mysteries as alien copilots. I can't resist an incredibly open-minded, active woman who's willing to try anything once (or twice, or ten different ways). Me: Cute, charming, eccentric and out-there—nuttier than a bag of Chex Party Mix, and the most fun you'll ever have. Please come with accessories such as: your own life, your own friends, a thriving career you love, costumes. Needy, jealous, and clingy types need not apply. Must love animals.

As one of the zodiac's ultimate free spirits, the Aquarius man wants a high-minded fellow nomad and idealist—someone who could aptly be described as "her own woman." In other words, you love men, but you don't need a guy to be happy. Your biological clock should not be waking him up every hour with loud ticking and alarms, either. Kids may not be part of the picture for this guy.

The Aquarius man loves a woman with a cool head and a warm heart. "Even in tough times, she's still strong enough to carry herself through a situation," describes Hal, who in true Aquarius form has created an alter ego for himself called Dr. Lobster. "And she carries herself with calm and poise." Nothing piques his interest like a smart, self-possessed woman with a well-defined life and identity. He craves strong opinions and lots of character. He doesn't care if you're a pink-haired punk or a supermodel (he'll date either), a dominatrix or a devout Catholic, as long as you know yourself inside out. The more blocks you've been around, the better. Nothing surprises the Aquarius man, and if it does, it will only excite him. He'll gladly go places with you that no man has gone before.

Could that be why Aquarius Ashton Kutcher fell for his Scorpio wife Demi Moore, fourteen years his senior? Yes, Aquarians also love to shock people, but Demi had a life history that included two marriages, three daughters, her mother's death, and a serious acting career before they met. All that was left was to have fun and explore life together.

Neediness is like Kryptonite to this guy. Above all, he does not want to take care of a dependent little girl. If you call out "who's your daddy?" the room will empty of Aquarius men. He's a modern, equality-minded man who doesn't play into gender stereotypes. He expects you to be an adult—to know what foods you like, to have well-defined tastes, to embrace adventure. He loves to introduce you to new experiences, to teach and guide— but only as playmates on an equal plane, rather than some kind of weird Svengali dynamic.

Jaded, picky, or cynical women make a horrible match, but the Aquarius man will date many in his early years. "I seem to keep attracting somebody aloof, even though I say I want somebody available, vulnerable," admits Gary, a forty-year-old financial advisor.

The Aquarius man's discomfort with his own emotions, along with his fear of being trapped or limited, narrows his options. The unavailable mates are only reflecting back what he puts out. The coldness of his Air sign nature needs warmth, which comes from an open heart and an available partner. He must overcome a lot of fear to get there.

As much as clinginess turns him off, the Aquarius man finds a little feminine vulnerability extremely attractive. Underneath his smooth exterior, the Aquarius man can be shy and awkward initially. He's hypersensitive about not being liked, or worse, being taken for granted. "I like a girl to need me a little bit at first, just until I feel secure," says Chris. "Then it's like, you go do your thing, I'll do mine, and we'll come back together and just have a blast."

Love can bring out a shockingly corny side of Aquarius. Ashton Kutcher was quoted as saying, "I hope the love [Demi and I] share can resonate around the world so someday I can hear its echo." Anyone else gagging yet? Mercifully, these cheeseball moments are rare. The Aquarius man prefers to show love by sharing his opinions, his life, and his discoveries—and by including you in some of them. He's the sign of the teacher. If you're going to be needy, then need his advice. Let him be your coach or personal trainer, for example.

Although Aquarius hates neediness, he wants to be needed for what he genuinely has to offer. Be an apt pupil, but leave the nest and fly once you catch on. Show that you can run with his teachings, while always giving him due credit for helping you sprout wings. He needs you to have ambition and drive.

If you're the unruffled girl next door with thick skin, a soft heart, and a sharp mind, the Aquarius man will fall hard. He loves a trendy, modern pop-ette, a sweet and sappy girlie-girl who's also a tough, take-charge broad. If you can read between the lines and recognize love when it's wrapped in an unconventional package, the people-pleaser that lives in every Aquarius will emerge. He'll work overtime to make you happy. Life will never be dull again.

# What He Wants from a Relationship

When it comes to relationships, the Aquarius man will settle for nothing short of a sexual and romantic revolution. Like a bedside Che Guevera, he wants to shake up love as we know it and bring romance solidly into the 21st century—or perhaps even the 22nd.

The aforementioned Aquarius Dr. Lobster has established a movement called Modern Romantic Completionism. Another Aquarius man we know founded Cuddle Parties, a national series of sex- and substance-free workshops where people get together in their pajamas and just… cuddle. His website describes the event as a "playful, fun workshop… for people to rediscover nonsexual touch and affection, a space to reframe assumptions about men and women, and a great networking event to meet new friends, roommates, business partners, and significant others." Classic Aquarius.

Interdependence is the name of his game. In fact, it was our Aquarius friend Miguel who first introduced us to this term when describing his perfect relationship. You both have full lives, then come together voluntarily, to unwind, grow, and have fun. He longs to coexist, rather than merge. Of course, this can only happen once the free-spirited Aquarius man actually decides he's ready for a relationship. When you're from another dimension, bonding with humans can be hard, after all. He can be aloof and awkward, hesitant to commit. The Aquarius man doesn't want to be tied to one woman until he's sampled the whole panorama.

However, in his mid- to late thirties, the Aquarius man may finally decide to reckon with those demons known as feelings. He might plunge into a philosophical movement or a spiritual modality to explore his emotions safely, in an almost scientific way. (Either that, or he smokes a lot of weed and feels those funny sensations—love! anger! sadness!—that are so foreign to him otherwise.)

Once he learns how to process his emotions, this humanitarian sign wants to share what he's learned on his quest. Like a butterfly emerging from its cocoon, the prank-pulling eternal jokester emerges as the ultimate Sensitive New Age Guy. Formerly squeamish about anything more touchy-feely than a backslapping hug or a high five, he suddenly starts training for his massage license, or becomes an eager volunteer to give out shoulder rubs and meaningful embraces.

Aquarius is the sign of the future, and this can prevent him from living in the moment. One Aquarian, laughing at his own quandary, admits, "I just need to know how everything will turn out before I can relax." (Speaking in riddles can be an Aquarius habit.) Another Aquarius describes relationships where, out of nervousness, he locked himself into a commitment before really being sure about the person, then felt trapped. His anxiety and nerves often get the best of him, preventing him from forging deeper bonds because of this knee-jerk response. Tranquilizer, dude?

If an Aquarius does sign on for the long haul, he needs to be handled with care. Once his heart is invested, the Aquarius man can be hypersensitive and overly intense—no longer the cool, devil-may-care dude holding court at the party. As Gary says, "My problem is I think too much, break down and analyze everything. If a woman is late, I think it means she doesn't care."

It's an interesting paradox: Commitment can either tie you down or set you free. Being an Air sign, the Aquarius man needs a relationship that gives him wings and a purpose. "I like to feel useful," says Gary. Aquarius wants a partner to be his pupil, travel mate, and sounding board. Above all, he needs to be trusted. "Anytime the words 'you should' come out of my mouth, he shuts off," says one woman of her Aquarius boyfriend. "So now I say things like 'have you considered...'" She learned to be nurturing, but to never mother or smother him. It's a fine balance.

The Aquarius man will never be in a relationship for relationship's sake. But to fulfill a vision, or live out a future that inspires and excites him with endless possibility? He's in. "It's all about having the whole future mapped," says Gary. If you fit with his master plan, pack your sleeping bag and hiking shoes. You never know where you'll end up—but he will remain by your side, no matter where that is.

# Sex with an Aquarius

As with everything, sex is an otherwordly adventure to Aquarius, limited only by your own imaginations. He regards sex as a natural part of the human experience, and can easily separate sex from love. Although he may seem uptight, this guy has almost no hang-ups. He's like a sexual Dr. Seuss, dreaming up the most outrageous games.

Futuristic Aquarius likes to experiment with gender roles, power, and the darker side of human desire. Because he can detach from the touchy-feely, "lovemaking" side of sex, he can be a little rough or sadistic (who wants a spanking?) in the sack. This is the guy who might secretly visit a dominatrix to unleash some of his control issues. "We make appointments for sex because he has these elaborate scenarios he likes to act out, complete with props," says one woman of her Aquarius boyfriend. "He's very kinky in bed; he likes to tie me up."

As the sign that rules technology, he loves a good sex toy, and may even whip out a battery-powered gadget from his own arsenal. "One of my favorite things," says one Aquarius man, "is to visit an adult store with a woman. I like to talk to people about what's new, hear their recommendations. I once took a girlfriend out for a great birthday dinner, then ended the night at a sex toy shop. She picked out a vibrator and that was her present."

Not exactly romantic in the paperback novel sense, but that's Aquarius—champion of sexual liberation. He wants you to be an independent woman, and the idea of you satisfying yourself without him will only turn him on, not to mention stoke his competitive nature. He loves it if you want him, but don't need him. Neediness is a drag in his world. As much of a human Pocket Rocket as he can be, the Aquarius man may go through unavailable spells—he's juice fasting, solving the mystery of

Atlantis, obsessing over his career—when he has little interest in sex. During those times, he expects you to know how to get off without him.

Aquarius is the sign of groups, so he may dabble in orgies, partner swapping, and (his favorite) threesomes—or at least, he'll fantasize about it. "My Aquarius likes me to pick up other women for threesomes," confesses one woman. "He also once had a limo waiting with lingerie in the backseat. He told me to put it on, then have the driver come to his office. He had ordered sushi from my favorite restaurant. He got in the limo and ate the sushi off of my body, piece by piece. He didn't even care that the driver was watching; it turned him on."

Sex is always casual for Aquarius, even when he's deeply in love. And yet, it never is, either. He wants to experience spiritual elevation, and since he spends so much time lost in his head, he needs to connect to his body first. Sex is the quickest path. Still, experimenting and learning are always part of the package for Aquarius. Once he's in love, he may dabble in tantric sex, or find ways to keep things interesting and off the beaten path. Keep an open mind. He will!

# Aquarius: Turn-Ons & Turn-Offs
## Turn Him On

- Be an independent go-getter who can hold her own
- Have an accomplished career—success is an aphrodisiac for him
- Think outside the box
- Have a few scandals under your belt that you've lived through and learned from
- Let him teach you something

- Pursue separate interests, then bring them back to the relationship
- Be spiritually evolved
- Prioritize fun and adventure
- Exude confidence: he loves a ballsy babe
- Take care of your body—you don't need to be skinny, but be fit and sporty
- Travel, often
- Join him on spontaneous adventures—always be ready to go
- Admire his offbeat lifestyle and don't give him grief about his random work hours
- Be warm and nurturing, but never smothering
- Tell him your kinkiest fantasies and let him help you realize them

## Turn Him Off

- Be cynical, skeptical, or too much of a realist
- Give him unsolicited advice or tell him how to run his life
- Pressure him to marry you, have kids, or follow your time line
- Be a lost soul with no path, vision, or life direction
- Be materialistic, fussy, or high-maintenance
- Have no interest in spiritual or metaphysical issues
- Criticize or laugh at him
- Scoff at his passion and roll your eyes at his jokes
- Be too free-spirited or tomboyish, with no maternal instinct at all

# His Moves

## First Moves: How He Courts You

Subtlety goes out the window when an Aquarius sets his sights on you. He shines in casual first interactions, and will fearlessly approach you. Like a peacock, he preens and shows off to get your attention. He loves a good game, and the playful art of seduction is as good a sport as any. Although he may just walk up to you and kiss you, he can also coolly hold himself back, leaving you tortured and guessing: *Does he like me?* He also goes over the top at first. Miguel, an Aquarius chef, says he gets a woman's attention by "preparing her a seven-course tasting menu with paired wines." Where do we sign up?

Before he's really opened his heart, the Aquarius man is damn near impervious to rejection. It's only after he's invested hopes and feelings that things get tricky. At first, he can just make a joke out of the whole thing if you blow him off. (Don't be surprised if you end up as comic material for his next improv sketch.)

Here's how an Aquarius signals his initial interest:

- Walks up and makes an outrageous "joke" or remark— you'll either slap him or go home with him
- Asks a lot of questions about you, and acts really fascinated with your answers
- Twitches or darts around nervously
- Teases you like a second grader on the schoolyard
- Starts giving you advice—teaching and preaching
- Asks you a shockingly bold question about your personal life
- Shows off like a little boy
- Asks you to go hang out
- Becomes your best friend

- Traps you into an intense, unblinking, lock-gazed conversation—then snatches his attention away

## He's In: How You Know He's Committed

The Aquarius man's path to commitment is a delicate dance. Getting there is hell, but once you're in, it's great. He's petrified about losing his freedom, and he may regard relationships as potential threats to his autonomy. You'll need to endure a long exploratory phase, as he evaluates, like a diligent research scientist, whether a relationship will compromise his independence.

Aquarius is a people pleaser, and he's been known to sacrifice his needs to make others happy, only to later escape through the back door. The more aloof and self-contained you are, the more he's likely to chase you. Prepare to hit "snooze" on your biological clock again and again. Don't corner him with ultimatums. Even if he plays the devoted beau, make no assumptions. Out of the blue he may make his decision that you're the One. Here's why:

**He's found his path and you fit in smoothly.** As Gary, a forty-year-old Aquarius financial planner says, "I don't want to settle down until I've found my purpose." Aquarius is a "fixed" sign, and he's actually really set in his ways. Unlike other signs, he's not able to just orbit around your life. He needs his own solar system, but you can be a shining celestial body rotating happily on your own axis.

**He gets uncomfortably sappy around you.** Once, he was pushing your buttons and teasing you for being the slightest bit sentimental. Now, he's staring at you with soulful, bassett hound eyes and musing about how you "complete" him. (Warning: You'll feel equal parts flattered and nauseous.)

**He declares his love.** These are actual words used by an Aquarius friend of ours. Words are important to the Aquarius man, and when he's finally chosen you as the One, he may announce it with a bit of fanfare.

**He makes an elaborate meal.** Says Hal, "I'll cook her dinner. Definitely. I'll demonstrate some other skill that I have. I'm going to give you a really good, intense one-on-one evening in my house. Let's lie down in the parlor like kittens. We're going to eat well, have significant conversation, chat and get to know each other in a completely safe environment... like come on in, let's have a nice time. A couple weeks ago, I made a soya ginger chili-marinated ostrich for a girl."

**He launches a series of conversations about the "potential relationship."** Although he may be sampling your wares every day, Aquarius likes to try before he buys. He wants to be sure you're not expecting some conventional, picket-fence relationship, so he'll discuss it in theory before he puts it into practice.

**He becomes protective.** Even though he favors egalitarian relationships, suddenly he's cooking and opening every door, treating you like a goddess. Enjoy it! He likes to play the knight in shining armor—but only if milady can take care of herself. Warning: If you start acting like a full-on damsel in distress, he'll flee. He may be playing the chivalrous gent, but it's more like he's acting out a Dungeons & Dragons, Renaissance Fair role-playing fantasy. He doesn't really want to have to rescue you. He just wants to storm the castle and sweep you off your feet.

**He tests you by suddenly "needing space."** Uh-oh, it's another Aquarian romantic science experiment! He's testing you to see how you react. The less you freak out, the more likely he is to respect, admire, and desire you. In *Men Are from Mars, Women Are from Venus*, John Gray asserts that men are like rubber bands— they need to stretch and pull away in order to spring back to their desire for intimacy. Anyone dating an Aquarius man should read up on Gray's theory!

**He treats your friends and family like gold.** The Aquarius man largely defines himself by the groups with which he's affiliated. If he pursues membership in these "clubs," he wants to be part of your life for the long haul.

## Unfaithful Aquarius: Why He Cheats

Because he knows so many people and is naturally flirty, the Aquarius man is often branded a cheater—even when he's not one. The prankster in him may delight in keeping people guessing. He loves to mess with small-minded types who don't grasp that men and women can actually just be friends.

Although some Aquarius men remain immature longer than most signs, he tends to be a hardcore bachelor or a serial monogamist. And since he lives by his own rules, he'd rather establish an open relationship than have you sleep around behind each other's backs. That said, here are some reasons that he might cheat:

**He couldn't resist having the experience.** Somehow, he felt that he would miss out on a life-altering, mind-expanding moment by not doing it. The Aquarius man is eternally curious, and "It was too good an opportunity to pass up," explains one Aquarian of why he cheated.

**Angry revenge.** The Aquarius man is hypersensitive to being done wrong and treated unfairly, and may resort to "an eye for an eye" revenge tactics. Anyone seen Aquarius Justin Timberlake's "What Goes Around" video? Or "Cry Me a River"? He's far too proud to be played and will go to extremes, even cruel ones, to have the last laugh.

**He hasn't asserted his independence or masculinity enough.** He might be the king of compromise, ever accommodating, but watch out. This testosterone-laden jock, poker champion, or pot-smoking philosopher needs his boys-only outlets. One Aquarius man says he'd cheat "to have a deep dark secret." Why would he need one? Well, the Aquarius man lives in his head, and he needs physical outlets, like sports and sex, to unwind his nervous mind. If he's overdosed on book clubs and emotional work and can't say "enough," he might passive-aggressively cheat.

**You're not really friends.** He may selectively forget the Golden Rule with some people, but when it comes to friends, the Aquarius man rarely breaks the honor code. If friendship isn't the foundation of your relationship, he may not value you enough to spare your feelings. Indeed you may catch him "doing unto others"—in a scandalous way, that is.

**Or, you're not really more than friends.** Because he values the unique bonding and connection of friendship, the Aquarius man may fool himself into thinking that's all he needs from a partner. That is, until he stirs up some sizzling mind-body-soul chemistry with that hot girl in his Sci-Fi reading group or in the box seat next to him at a basketball game. Oops.

**He wants an open relationship (or other sexual adventures) and you don't.** Not every Aquarius man is into kink, but he may be curious about going places that frighten you. Best to find out early how wide his sexual proclivities range.

# Dig the Grave: It's Over

Sensitive as an Aquarius man can be, when he's done, he feels no need to stick around. Once his bruised ego recovers from any slights, he can step back and evaluate your relationship with cool, emotionless logic. His first love will always be life—and what woman can compete with the juicy promise of a new day or discovery? Second in line are the fellow pioneers with whom he shares his time in this brief mortal coil. Here's how you'll know that you're not part of his permanent history after all:

**He made too many compromises.** The Aquarius man can be a people-pleaser, but if he compromises his ideals or life vision to please you, the resentment will stew until it boils over. He needs to become more of himself, not less, in the relationship. If he feels his world shrinking, he'll fade away, or notch the romance down to buddy status until you're forced to part as friends.

**You stepped all over his dignity.** The Aquarius man is a competitive Alpha dog who needs to stay ahead of the pack. Did you make him look stupid in front of his friends? As one Aquarius man says, "I believe you should honor your partner and never put him in a bad light." He's big on humanity and if he feels you've treated him with disrespect or cruelty, buh-bye.

**He fades away or disappears.** There's no greater anathema to Aquarius than a heavy, tearful, emotional good-bye. It will send his system into total shutdown. If he thinks you won't go along with the whole "let's just be friends" idea, he'd rather just vanish and let you figure it out. Ouch.

**You were the pursuer.** He's a competitive conquistador who needs to hunt his trophy and score the grand prize. He needs to seek you out. If you had to talk him into the relationship or beg for his attention, forget it. There's a better match out there for you anyhow.

**He suggests an open relationship so he can explore other partners.** If it includes a threesome for you and him, that's one thing. But if he wants to tryst the night away without you, forget it. If he can stomach the idea of you sleeping around, he's just not that into you. Aquarius is far too possessive to imagine another dude scoring some action with his lady-love.

**You've made him responsible for your self-esteem.** Be honest: Do you often find yourself depressed and dramatic—yet refusing to do any inner work to heal your situation? "People like that live a negative existence," says Derek, "they're like negative Kryptonite in your life when you hang out." The future-focused Aquarius man is proactive, and he expects you to be, too. As Hal puts it, "You can't hunt with a puppy in your pack."

# Interpreting His Signals:

## *What does he mean by that?*

| When he | It means... | So you should... |
| --- | --- | --- |
| Gets quiet | He's planning the new world order or lost in his quirky daydreams. | Give him space and don't disturb his groove. It's not personal. |
| Doesn't call | He's feeling insecure and worried that he called too much or "bugged you." | Call him. He's an equality-minded sign who doesn't play into gender stereotypes. He turns into a girl when he likes you. |
| Calls a lot | He wants to have sex with you. | Pace it if you want more than just a friendly fling. |
| Doesn't make a move after a couple of dates | You're drifting toward "let's just be friends" status. | Show him another side of yourself—preferably the strong, sexy but receptive one. Throw him a curveball and you could get him interested all over again. |
| Doesn't make a move after a few weeks | Meet your new BFF. | Abandon hope and move on. |
| Moves fast | He likes you, he really likes you. But that doesn't mean he's in love. Sometimes he rushes into the sack just to ease his nervousness. | Pace it, unless you just want a fling. But openly communicate that you're interested so he doesn't get discouraged. |

| When he | It means... | So you should... |
| --- | --- | --- |
| Picks up the tab, gives flowers and gifts | He's actually considering a relationship. He doesn't do this with just anyone. | Warmly receive his generosity and tell him how happy he made you feel. |
| Introduces you to his family and/ or closest friends | You're in. | Be warm and friendly, but don't try to outshine him. Make him look like he brought home a prize. |

# Your Moves: Tips for Flirting and Everlasting Love

## Flirting with an Aquarius

It's not hard to flirt with an Aquarius man. You only need two things: a pulse and a voice. Since the Aquarius man is always playful and jokey, he flirts with everyone. Of course, this gets him into trouble, but heck, he loves trouble anyway. The key is to know the difference between friend flirting (in other words, playful banter), and seduction flirting, which looks more like this:

**Laugh at his jokes and throw one back.** Be playful and receptive, but show you've got bite. He admires a clever, dexterous mind.

**Listen to his theories about the origin of the universe.** The Aquarius man loves to talk about life, people, and ideas. This is the guy who keeps *Conversations with God* on his nightstand. Have one of those deep, mind-melding exchanges where you pontificate on everything from conspiracy theories to quantum physics.

**Play-fight with him.** There's a little boy in every Aquarius, so set your maturity meter at second-grade level. Let him pull your pigtails and steal your math homework. Play-fight with him. Get immature and silly and sporty. A game of touch football, or any opportunity to tackle you? Even better.

**Be impressed, but not too impressed.** The Aquarius man is an "up-dater," and if you're too starry-eyed about him, he'll bore quickly. Be equal parts available and aloof; challenge him if you disagree. He loves a puzzle, so be your multidimensional self.

**Flaunt your quirks and uniqueness.** Toot your own kazoo and be a fearless individual. If you're world-traveled or have a special talent (circus performer, literature expert, neuroscientist), talk about it. Never dumb yourself down, or he'll move right on to the next person.

# Everlasting Love with an Aquarius

When he makes a woman his lifemate, the Aquarius man will be sweetly devoted to her greatness. He will call you forth to be the best version of yourself. He gets inspired watching you grow, like his own personal Chia Pet. Being ambitious, he doesn't really need much more from you than that. Just allow him to contribute and leave his mark.

**Be a Saccharine Superwoman.** He likes his women sweet and tough, confidently capable but still exuding feminine grace.

**Be an explorer, journeyer, or seeker.** Blaze your own trail and bring back your discoveries to share. "I need her out there gathering raw material for the nest," says Hal. "I expect she's going to gain experience separately from me that she can come back and teach me."

**Be the "Grand Prize" that he can brag about to his friends.** Aquarius is competitive, and he needs to subtly one-up them on a regular basis. Be a little bit ahead of him in the looks or career department. He needs to be totally in awe of you, to feel like you're just out of his league.

**Share his spiritual or ideological quest.** He's got a utopian life vision; are you the woman who shares it? "What I'm looking for is a woman whose life path coincidentally is going along with mine," says Hal. "There's no need for sacrifices." He wants to become more of who he is with you, not less. Our Aquarius friend Chris dreams of buying a VW bus, then taking his kids out of school and driving through the States, educating them about history and life.

**Have a generous heart.** The Aquarius man admires genuine acts that come from the heart. Our friend bought her Aquarius boyfriend an autographed guitar he'd been ogling for months but couldn't afford. When she handed it to him, he cried—shocking her, since she didn't realize how sentimental he really was until that moment.

# Prep Yourself For...
## Your First Date

Aquarius is the sign of the future, so as spontaneous as he can be, he still likes to have a solid plan. "I want to know where I'm going, what to expect, so I can relax," says one Aquarian. Mostly, this is because he wants to outdo every other guy you've been with—it's this weird, competitive side he has. He can become utterly consumed with winning you over and impressing you, forgetting to live in the moment. A gentle reassuring gesture like a laugh or a touch can snap him out of his head.

At the same time that he's trying too hard, the Aquarius man will also be a little distant, which can be confusing. He doesn't want to give you the "wrong idea" or create expectations. Derek, an Aquarius actor and comic, likes the casual, no-pressure strategy of lunch dates for a first-time hangout. "It's all about being low-key and letting things take their course," says Derek. "With lunch, she's not wondering, Is this dude gonna try to kiss me? Where does it go from here? Besides, I prefer to know a person before I'm stuck with some crazy beeyotch for the next five hours."

**The Basic Vibe:** One word: casual. The Aquarius man needs to survey the landscape and gain his foothold to ensure that you will never take away his freedom or try to fence him in. It will be a slow, elaborate process for him to determine that. Rather than try to show him what a perfect future wife you'll be, just keep it friendly, flirty, and build up the sexual tension. "I like dinner at a great restaurant, followed by karaoke," says Miguel. Fun and *joie de vivre* are essential elements of his dream girl. He wants to make sure you know how to keep things light. Be yourself, talk about your passions and interests, and keep the conversation more cerebral than emotional. Then let loose and play!

**What to Wear:** This modern man likes all things contemporary, hip and trendy, with a touch of sexy cyborg. Put time, thought, and sex appeal into your outfit—enough style to make him the envy of other guys, but not so much that he looks like a schlep next to you. His favorite? A really hot pair of jeans that shows off your shape, sexy ankle boots, and a fitted black top. Anything sleek and of-the-minute goes far.

**What Not to Wear:** Anything too high-maintenance or old-fashioned. He might not be into the vintage look or anything too costumey either. In other words, "not a floor model from Betsy Johnson," says Derek. Turn heads, but don't embarrass him. Better to look like you stepped out of a J. Crew or Banana Republic catalog than to resemble an overly done model from a *Vogue* spread.

**To Pay, or Not to Pay?** If he invited you, he'll pay, but as a sign of reciprocity, not for everything. Bring your own cab fare or gas money. He might invite you for dinner, but he'll ask you to proofread his résumé the next day. He's a give and take, 50/50 guy. Bring cash and plastic. If the conversation doesn't stimulate him or he doesn't enjoy himself, he may not spring for the bill.

**Saying Good night:** Prepare for a full-on pounce. If he's feeling the love, he'll lunge for your lips, seemingly out of nowhere. This go-getter guy always aims for exactly what he wants and rarely holds himself back.

## His First Home Visit

The Aquarius man likes to control the pace of intimacy, so you could be dating for quite a while before he comes over. He doesn't want wedding bells going off prematurely in your head, so he'll try to temper your flow of oxytocin (the bonding hormone released in women during sex). Unless you were friends before dating, chances are, you'll go to his house long before he ever sees yours. He likes to host and entertain, and wants to show off his place, even if he sleeps on a bunk bed or lumpy mattress. When he finally feels ready to come over, here are a few tips for entertaining your entertainer:

**Turn your apartment into a conversation piece.** Chatty Aquarius likes to talk about things and ideas more than feelings. Ease his nerves by putting interesting books, travel artifacts, mementos, and other conversation pieces on display. Bonus points if you have anything that he knows a lot about (e.g., he's a paleontologist and you display a rare fossil)—then he can flaunt his expertise and look like the man.

**Make it a teach-in.** Aquarius men love to learn and teach. Host a group meditation, a screenwriters' workshop, a Dance Revolution championship, a massage lesson—whatever fits his current passion or intellectual quest.

**Go light on the romance.** Easy on the roses and candles, Harlequin novel girls. The Aquarius man gets squeamish about the sentimental when he doesn't initiate it, and has a talent for making a joke out of heavy feelings. He doesn't want to walk into an obvious love den, or be blindsided with a "so… where is this going?" talk over a painstakingly prepared meal. Here's a novel idea: just have fun. Plan a few activities and leave the house after a while to mix things up.

**Let him impress you.** This Alpha male in egalitarian's clothing wants to be number-one in his game. Competitive Aquarius needs to piss on his virtual fire hydrant and establish his supremacy—not over you, but over other men. If he's studying shiatsu, let him bring over his massage table and practice on you. If he's got a golden voice, invite him to set up a karaoke machine. If he's a talented chef (and he often is), spring for groceries and let him prepare a feast.

**Invite fifty of your closest friends.** Who said first visits have to be only for two? The Aquarius man thrives in a group, and he will definitely form a better opinion of you based on your friends. Help his research by throwing a casual, buffet-style dinner party—say, for the Oscars or the NBA playoffs. Show off your hosting skills, and ask him to help you with preparations. He loves to play Master of Ceremonies with you.

**Have a bottle of wine and exotic food handy.** The Aquarius man loves an intense, hours-long conversation that spans everything from global politics to stem cell research to sports to metaphysics. You're gonna be sitting around talking for a long time, so why not flaunt how fascinating you are a little more?

## Meeting His Family

Unconditional love is a funny thing for the Aquarius man. While he takes forever to develop it romantically, he's got it in spades for animals, mankind, and his family. The Aquarius man can be downright reverential about his clan. Parents are sacred territory, and not just any woman is good enough to meet his. His mother, especially, sits high on a pedestal and he can be painstakingly protective of her. ("Damn, why can't he treat me that way?" you might wonder.) Maybe that's why Aquarius men often end up with Cancer, Pisces, and other women with a strong maternal nature.

So when it comes time to meet his peeps, he can get very controlling about the impression you'll make. Never mind if you've lashed him to a bedpost, cohosted a Halloween partner swap, and chased each other through a makeshift S&M "dungeon" in leather masks. You'd best know how to turn off your kinky side and play the classy lady. "I've been known to tell a woman, 'We're gonna go in good behavior mode now,'" says Derek, our Aquarius actor friend, adding in his sign's sarcastic style, "You can't take a hooker to the Harvard Club."

He considers his family an exclusive society of sorts, so it's best to know the rules upfront. He can be very uptight about how you act around his parents, which will annoy you, so take preventive measures. Make sure you have a thorough conversation about what his family is like, their expectations, and their no-no's. Are they huggy or standoffish? Will they adopt you like a long-lost child or expect you to earn your way into the club?

Once you're in, his family can provide valuable clues about his true feelings, which his aloof, unexpressive sign may not readily share. "His mother told me he said I keep his head on straight," says Theda, a music executive. "He would never tell me this, but she did. I know he worships his mother, so it was a big deal to me."

Bravo to Theda for bonding with mom, but take note: Don't ever become closer to an Aquarius man's family than he is. As much as he loves them, they're still the people who at some point in his life might have imposed (necessary) rules and limitations on him. Freedom is everything to your Aquarius. He does not want to be reined in by anyone, and must maintain a healthy level of detachment from his parents. Don't rope him into family stuff he doesn't want to do. Let him take the lead.

# Saying Good-bye
## Breaking Up with an Aquarius

As much as he may deserve to be dumped, the Aquarius man doesn't take kindly to breakups. In his world, he's the one who calls the shots. You'll need to recognize that you're breaking up with two people: him and his ego. And the Aquarius man's ego will always respond first. The degree to which you respect him determines how much of your dignity he spares. Woe betide ye if you're leaving him for another guy. He may bitterly dis you to your friends (who will likely be mutual ones), making snarky comments or spilling accidental snippets of personal information.

Being a talented salesman, he may even try to talk you out of it. Like a petulant child he'll whine things like, "It's just not fair" or "I wouldn't do this to you." Recognize one thing, sister: yes, he would. One Aquarius man admits that he doesn't take no for an answer, and once practically camped on his ex-girlfriend's doorsteps in his campaign to win her back. There's a borderline stalker living inside the scorned Aquarius man. If his ego can't recover, you'll need to erect some firm boundaries.

You can avoid some of this by easing your way into a gradual "let's be friends" downgrade. Yes, you'll need to be a little calculating to disentangle yourself, and he may well obsess over you for a while. He can be worse than Scorpio when it comes to holding on.

## Getting over Him: When an Aquarius Dumps You

Okay, get ready for the double standard. When the Aquarius man wants to break up with you, he thinks it's all part of some divine scheme, and he rarely thinks twice. You're expected just to understand and go along with it. "It just wasn't meant to be," he'll tell you. He usually expects to morph from boyfriend into best friend quickly from there. As long as blood wasn't spilled on the emotional battlefield, the Aquarius ex does make a fine BFF.

Aquarius is ruled by unpredictable Uranus, the planet of sudden events, making him famous for abrupt exits and fade-aways. He may even disappear, only to resurface with a new girlfriend on his arm a few weeks later. Oh, the pain. He figures you must have gotten the hint when he didn't return your 337th message of the day. Don't actions speak louder than words? Actually, he's just avoiding having to face your tears, fury, and emotional outbursts, which make him distinctly uncomfortable.

Eventually, the Aquarius man detaches from the drama, becoming philosophical about his breakups. "In a relationship, you're like two planes flying in the air," says Raj, an Aquarius father of two who's separated from his wife. "Sometimes, one plane is taking off and the other is landing. You always have to know which direction your planes are flying." If only he could be such a Breakup Buddha when the lotus blossom is on the other foot.

### Have yourself one good last cry over...

- His utterly unique, eccentric worldview
- Losing your best friend
- The amazing dinners he cooked or treated you to
- The excitement of his unpredictable nature
- Losing some good mutual friends as casualties of your breakup
- The whirlwind of fun and adventure
- Having someone who kept you young and on your toes
- The thrill of unpredictable, imaginative sex
- The great advice and keen listening ear he offered

### Praise the universe that you never have to deal with...

- The flakiness and inconsistency
- The immaturity and Peter Pan syndrome
- His sudden flashes of angry temper
- His talent for turning your most heartfelt sentiments into a joke
- Having to process everything through his "chin-stroking philosopher" filter—sometimes, a cigar is just a f**king cigar
- Waiting forever for him to make up his mind about you
- His nomadic need to be on the move and inability to nest anywhere for long

- The selective memory, and his refusal to learn from his mistakes
- His endless exploring, wondering, and pontificating—does he stand for anything or is he just full of hot air?

# Love Matcher:

## Can you find a common language?

| You are a(n)... | He thinks you're... | You think he's... | Common Language |
|---|---|---|---|
| Aries | You're a fun firecracker who sparks his desire for a challenge. | Funny, sexy, and a little bit of a bad boy—just the way you like 'em. | Friendship, competitive banter, and crude humor |
| Taurus | Pretty, but your old-fashioned values make him gag. | Wildly unsettling and an annoying showoff. Pass the Ritalin. | Ambition and success |
| Gemini | His intellectual equal. | A match for your mind. | Books, music, offbeat ideas, New Age-y adventures |
| Cancer | You're the tough yet tender flower he's been waiting to pick. | A roller-coaster ride of sexy adventure. | Sex and emotional exploration |
| Leo | His competition—he may date you just to figure out how to one-up you. | Addictively attractive. One of the bad boys you have a knack for finding. | Performance, battling for the spotlight, desire to be number one |
| Virgo | Cold, aloof, and addictively unavailable. | An obnoxious jerk who needs you to spank him. | Control and emotional repression |

| You are a(n)... | He thinks you're... | You think he's... | Common Language |
|---|---|---|---|
| Libra | Easy, breezy, and a little bit shallow for his liking. | Too much of a clown, missing the romance gene. | Parties, networking, mingling |
| Scorpio | Darkly sexy and seductive. | A sweet puppy dog. | Sex, mysticism, and intense conversations |
| Sagittarius | Hilarious, sexy, a kindred spirit—possibly more of a buddy. | Sharp, witty, best friend material. Romantic chemistry may run high but burn out quickly. | Entrepreneurship, love of freedom, independence, travel |
| Capricorn | Cool, composed, and good for his image...though a tad uptight for his liking. | A little goofy but might pair well with your repressed wild side. | Family, ambition, philosophy, sports |
| Aquarius | Flighty, ungrounded, good for a night or two. | Interesting, but no one you could take seriously. | Fun and activity |
| Pisces | His soul mate. | An attractive but slightly unsafe bet. | Imagination, spirituality, food, sensuality |

# The Pisces Man

Dates: February 19–March 20
Symbol: The Fish
Ruling Planet: Neptune, the planet of
fantasy and illusion
Element: Water—sensitive, intuitive, receptive
Quality: Mutable
Mission: Drowning in Your Love

**Natural Habitat—Where You'll Find Him:** Downloading music, at an underground bar or concert, watching movies, getting moved (even to tears) by the beauty of art, poetry, music, film, nature; escaping into his own fantasy world, reading, drawing, snuggling on the couch with his pets, on the beach, surfing, swimming, boating, overindulging on food and drink, taking care of someone in need (a sick parent, a homeless runaway teen), at the seediest spot in town, walking the streets after dark courting danger, getting pierced or tattooed, playing "foot" sports like ice hockey, skateboarding, or soccer; at the theater or opera, drowning in emotions and self-pity, hanging out with a bunch of female friends, shoe shopping, cooking, martyring himself for a family member

**What He Does for a Living:** Musician, writer, composer, actor, filmmaker, photographer, web designer, artist, massage therapist, marine biologist, critic, nutritionist, nurse, doctor, hospital or institution worker, coach, teacher, computer programmer, video game designer, stylist, pastry chef, surfer

**Noteworthy & Notorious Pisces Men:** Jon Bon Jovi, Albert Einstein, Bruce Willis, Quincy Jones, Seal, Timbaland, Michael Bolton, Freddie Prinze Jr., D.L. Hughley, Mark Hoppus, Billy Corgan, Taylor Hanson, Brian Littrell, Ja Rule, Johnny Knoxville, Benicio Del Toro, Chris Martin, Chris Klein, Sean Astin, Joe Hahn,

Kurt Cobain, Jay Hernandez, Billy Zane, Tone Loc, Billy Crystal, Rob Lowe, Bow Wow, Mark McGrath, Shaquille O'Neal

# Pisces: How to Spot Him

- Luminous, soulful eyes—almost like a fish
- Preppy Pisces is perfectly put together, dapper in a jacket and/or button-down shirt or fisherman sweater
- West Coast grunge, rocker, skater/surfer-boy look that he secretly spent hours perfecting
- Tattoos, piercing, other torturous rituals that signify his twin devotions to style and suffering
- Making sharp, sarcastic jokes and comments
- Intensely engaged in a provocative conversation
- Wearing a tortured, helpless expression
- Bleary-eyed, sexily disheveled, and drinking coffee at noon
- A bad-boy, devilish look that says, "I'm about to misbehave—big-time"
- Shamelessly hitting on woman after woman
- Trying a new stunt without a helmet
- Directing a video shoot or the setup of an art installation
- Surrounded by a gaggle of women, totally engaged in the girl talk
- Playing with his iPhone while successfully carrying on a conversation
- Wearing his sister's pink argyle socks or other feminine accessory that only he can pull off
- Tending bar amicably or joking with the bartender while giving overly generous tips

# Pisces: How He Deals With...

## Money
Flies right out of his slippery grasp. Would prefer to make enough to be able to avoid dealing with how much he spends. Needs a really good accountant.

## Family
May rebel or run away, but can never truly detach. Can be a major family guy, almost a little too close at times. Guilt is a major theme—he's either dishing it out or taking it.

## Love
Sappy, hopeless romantic who's always chasing a fantasy. Craves the true love depicted in his favorite movies, where the sensitive misfit gets the girl.

## Sex
Harbors a kinky, perverse imagination and a rich fantasy life. In reality, prefers tender, heartfelt emotional bonding.

## Children
May feel like way too much of a reality check or commitment for him, especially if it means he has to work for "the man" to support them. However, makes a nurturing, caring dad—even when he's a crappy husband.

## Pets
A total mush once he actually gets one, but may avoid the responsibility (walks! schedules! routines!). Animals can be a little too needy and blindly devoted—much like him. Does he really need to be reminded of it?

### Your Meltdowns

The perfect fodder for the dramatic, twisting romantic plotlines that are already brewing in his overactive imagination. Without a couple of these, love's just not the same.

### His Meltdowns

Often the result of major pent-up resentment, or a reaction to extreme unfairness. Unleashes a passive-aggressive campaign, stonewalling you and possibly disappearing, leaving you to figure out what's wrong.

### Breakups

Foggy, often with no real closure or explanation. Can obsess about what happened for years, never really letting go.

# Pisces: What He's All About

The magical, mystical Pisces man is a complicated creature—a riddle, a romantic, and a tortured soul in one. It's said that Pisces embodies every single astrological sign. As the zodiac's last sign, he's an old soul with hidden layers of talent and depth that can take years to comprehend. Although his sensitivity torments him (is he too fragile for this world?), he's as serene as a wise, elderly person who's surrendered to fate's master plan—a regular Yoda. Rather than grasp for control, like his opposite sign Virgo, he greets it all with an amused half smile—and occasional daredevil antics—knowing there's only so much he can do. He moves like the ocean's tides, in slow, rhythmic cycles, guided by a divine whisper that only he can hear.

The best way to understand the Pisces man is to study the astrology "glyph" that symbolizes him. Pisces is represented by two fish swimming in opposite directions—one toward security, the other toward freedom. You're never sure if he's coming or going, and neither is he. This man is a walking paradox. He champions women's rights and listens to your traumas with compassionate nonjudgment. Minutes later, he remarks how ugly someone's shoes are—then heads home to read a dirty magazine. Still, the contradiction doesn't occur to him. He's many people in one, a walking kaleidoscope who can fluidly shape shift between patterns and personas. He means all of it—and none of it. (Are you starting to feel a little bit insane? Welcome to the world of Pisces.)

The Pisces man's trademark feature is usually his eyes. Either round and luminous, or small and beady, they have a look of inner knowing, and even a touch of sadness. Whether any of this pain and depth is actually going on in his mind, who knows. But sensitive Pisces is always feeling something. An emotional Water sign, the Pisces man takes everything personally. Even if someone blows up at him for no reason, he'll wonder, "Was it something I did?"

Creative and highly attuned to the arts, the Pisces man's soul responds to music, art, and poetry. Pisces rules the feet, and he may be light on his, a gifted dancer, or excelling in sports like soccer and ice hockey. He can be a divine "channel" for the arts, like Pisces mega-composer Quincy Jones. We know a Pisces man who never took a piano lesson in his life, but could just sit down at the keyboard and play—sonatas, jazz, the most intricate compositions just naturally flowed from his fingertips. He was an incredible, intuitive cook as well, preparing expertly seasoned roasts without ever having cracked a cookbook.

The Pisces man is a true romantic. Still, as sappy as he can be, he has a dark, even violent sense of humor. Even when his jokes are self-deprecating, they're unsettling, because you're always left wondering if he's really kidding. He loves to walk that provocative edge. There's a part of Pisces that seems to enjoy pain and suffering. Daredevil Johnny Knoxville, creator of the MTV stunt show *Jackass*, is a Pisces. He famously did a motorcycle backflip up a dirt hill, only to fly off and have the bike land squarely on his crotch. After recovering from (ugh!) a torn urethra, he proudly continued with more insane self-torture—in that irresistibly cocky Piscean way.

No other sign can embody such saintly highs and gutter-dwelling lows as Pisces. In fact, Pisces is associated with the Christ figure, resurrection and life after death. This generation's iconic Pisces martyr was Nirvana's Kurt Cobain, who once said, "If you die, you're completely happy and your soul somewhere lives on. I'm not afraid of dying. Total peace after death, becoming someone else, is the best hope I've got." Cobain exhibited the dark side of Pisces that can sink to the lowest depths of depression, drug addiction, and despair. After a happy childhood was disrupted by his parents' divorce, Cobain was bounced between relatives, even homeless for a while. He was in and out of rehab, then died from a suspected suicide.

The Pisces man can be so emotionally fragile that he falls into extreme living, both inviting death and defying it. Pisces is the ruler of jails, hospitals, rehab, and mental institutions—any kind of enforced isolation from society. If he's not careful, he may write his name on the walls of these places. Or, he may simply choose to live as an "outsider" to some degree. He always needs to rebel against someone or something, even if he becomes a multimillionaire or a mainstream success doing so. Too much reality clips his angelic wings, and cuts his connection with the divine.

The Pisces man is often accused of being lazy or unmotivated, another misperception. Indeed, he can move sluggishly, or seem to lack any kinetic energy. He may even begin to think of himself as a victim of life—"Why does this always happen to me?" After all, he was sitting in the exact same position, wallowing in self-pity, when that plum job went to his rival, or his wife left him, or the IRS chose him for an audit.

Coincidence? Look closer. In our society, we prize action and movement. We think a body must be in motion, doing things, to produce a result or reach a goal. Not so for Pisces. Ever do a visualization exercise? You imagine what you want, focus your intentions, and will it to happen. With Pisces, this happens all the time, though on a less conscious level. The Law of Attraction asserts that one must only imagine a course of events, and he will draw them to him like a magnet. The more powerful the imagination, the faster these events manifest. Who blurs the lines between his fantasy and reality better than Pisces, ruler of the imagination? Like the powerful ocean tides, or a sweeping undertow, he pulls everything to him, good and bad. Don't be surprised when you find yourself in this force field, inexplicably drawn into his charms, feeling a little unsure whether you'll drown in his depths or be healed by his mystical, comforting embrace. As with all things Pisces, it will probably be both.

# What He Wants in a Woman

It's difficult for the Pisces man to articulate what attracts him, because it's usually a sensory or intuitive thing. A single feature— flowing red hair, gorgeous earlobes, perfectly shaped toenails—can capture his fascination. He may carry a worn checklist of features he likes: good shoes, polished style, feminine, maternal, romantic, soft-spoken, sweet. Judging from the women he ultimately marries, we suspect that list is there just so he has something to rebel against. Otherwise, why does he propose to the Alpha female who maxes out his credit card at Neiman-Marcus (at least she got the shoes right) and orders him around like her personal whipping boy? Stay tuned—we'll get to that in a moment.

First, let's talk about the Pisces man's fantasy girl, the one he chases before settling down with Superwoman. Picture... an enchanting mermaid. The mermaid is a complicated creature, much like him, who's difficult to catch. Already the hook is deliciously baited for Fish-boy. He does have a weakness for long, flowing hair, and a beautiful voice, too. She's alluringly unavailable, a siren and a temptress who views him with unspoiled awe, yet knows the dark depths of the underworld.

Their relationship is doomed to a degree—after all, she's half fish, and will have to somehow live on dry land with him. Yet he'll dive to the ocean's floor to catch her, knowing from his own aquatic nature that she'd prefer the vast sea to his tiny fish bowl. He may spend his life vainly trying to keep his captive mermaid happy—building her bigger tanks, adorning them with real coral reefs, watching to make sure she doesn't escape. Should she swim back to her native habitat, he'll follow her shadow, look for her tail peeking out of a wave, drowning in his own heartbroken regret. Oh, Pisces, she hardly knew ye.

From there, he vows to play it safe. And safe, to Pisces, means Mother. The Pisces man can be a masochist, but he's also a big avoider—and that's how he brings out the "mommy" in you. He'll take any opportunity he can to avoid reality, and often ends up with a very powerful, self-assured mate who runs the show. He'll turn over his whole paycheck if you don't make him talk about how to divvy it up among retirement plans, stocks, and college funds. There's a delicate, almost fragile, side of the Pisces man that brings out a protective, nurturing lioness in women. As a child, he may even have been sick or spent months in the hospital with a mysterious illness or condition. One friend remembers how shyly her Pisces college sweetheart courted her. "He was so anxious, he could barely look me in the eye," she recalls. "But he overheard me saying that I liked Raisinettes. So he started leaving Raisinettes and mixed CDs at the front desk of my dorm." From there, she had to initiate plans for their first date. She remembers choosing a movie because she thought it would feel safer for him. For *him*!

His romance and poetry will be heart-wrenchingly sweet, but he'll soon infuriate the crap out of you by leaving seven dollars in the checking account the day before rent is due, or taking out hefty student loans for a master's degree in poetry while you're eight months pregnant. Quickly, you become the responsible one, shouldering the burdens and bills, tending to his needs and insecurities. You feel so much like his mother, you practically start lactating around him.

If you want to hook a Fish, prepare to give him plenty of line before he takes the bait. The Pisces man needs lots of space before he'll commit. Sure, you can guilt-trip him into it, but it's better to play "tag"—to run in a way that tempts him to pursue and catch you. That's why the mermaid is so appealing. She shares his duality—part human, part magical creature. You'll need to be a box of mysteries that he can't quite solve to keep him transfixed.

How to do that in non-mythological terms? Have a life. Be "the one that got away." Be the person who rejected him, dumped him, broke his heart—and somehow came back. Never be fully in his grasp. Offer equal doses of togetherness and autonomy. Grant him his solitude when he needs it. In other words, combine the magical and the maternal. Be a "Mer-Mom."

Pisces is ruled by Neptune, the watery planet of illusions, and he's a true escape artist. Your Fish-boy can be as flaky as a spotted sea trout, pouring his heart out, then vanishing into the oceanic darkness. Your entire sense of reality may be overturned when he does this. "What the hell just happened here?" you'll wonder. Asking him is futile—that is, if you ever see him again. The Pisces man is capable of crystalline insight, but only years later. Actually, he's more "hindsightful" than insightful. When things become too real too fast, the Pisces man goes into emotional overload. His first impulse, which he often follows, is to flee.

A couple years later, he can brilliantly explain why he did about 85–90 percent of his regrettable actions. The rest is a fog. He may perfectly describe each subconscious urge and motivation ("I was desperately insecure and projecting it onto her" or "I was deeply terrified of rejection, and I emotionally manipulated her"). He'll suddenly stop short, genuinely befuddled about the rest: "Huh. I have no idea why I did *that*." Perhaps he's reserving his right to play the victim. But it's probably all still in his murky unconscious.

For this reason, he's often better on your second or third time go-round. You might even be best off enduring a harsh breakup or two to solidify your bond. What's a good romance without a twist in the plot, after all? No surprise that Fabio, a Pisces, became known as the King of Romance after modeling on nearly 400 romance novel covers. Your life could soon feel like a steamy Harlequin bodice-ripper—euphoric, windswept, and a little surreal.

# What He Wants from a Relationship

Like a slippery fish, the Pisces man is hard to pin down. He needs to protect his freedom before he'll commit to anything. No Fish ever wants to be trapped on the hook, after all! At the same time, when the Pisces man has no structure or boundaries, he flails around like a salmon on the dock, gasping for air. "The more you know me, the less I disclose," says Chris, a Pisces writer.

Negotiating the push-pull dynamic of his dual natures can be a lifelong quest for Pisces. A relationship with him can take a lot of patience and understanding. This is the guy who stays with the same woman for twenty years but never marries her. Or, during a lonely spell, he calls the escort service, then becomes infatuated with his call girl. Her sheer unavailability gives him so much freedom, he freaks out and tries to hold tight. What a mess.

We once counseled a very driven, ambitious Capricorn woman and her Pisces boyfriend of thirteen years. Like many Capricorns, she had mapped out a plan for the rest of her life, and was meeting her goals with the precision of a military general. Except...one. She wanted to be married by thirty-two, and her thirty-fourth birthday was approaching. The Pisces still wasn't "ready." Her biological clock was ticking so loudly, we thought a bomb had been planted.

While she talked and talked, her Pisces gazed at her with an amused half smile—sort of a knowing smirk, though not a rude one. He'd heard this all before. He shrugged and said nothing, just letting her prattle on. He offered no reason for keeping the relationship on cruise control instead of accelerating. "I know he's committed, and he loves me," she sighed, exasperated. "So why don't we just get married? What's it gonna take?"

Although he looked as serene as Gandhi, we were on to him. He was using Gandhi's own favorite tactic: passive resistance. In other words, while smiling like a smug, serene Buddha, he was quietly digging in his heels and refusing to budge. It's the Pisces man's ultimate "f**k you."

"You know what we think?" we asked his distraught girlfriend, while Pisces pretended he was only half-listening. "He feels like you're trying to take away his freedom. Pisces needs space before he'll commit. He's afraid you're going to try to control him. So he's holding back until you chill out."

At last: a slow, definite nod. From the Pisces. Then his smirk broke into a laugh. Busted!

If you're dating a Pisces man, know that if he's playing the "cold fish," you've probably turned up the heat a little too high. Back away a step or two, and he may just swim right back to you—as long as you don't back off too far. We realize this could sound dangerously like *The Rules*, and unfortunately, he does respond to being tortured and teased with mind games. Still, who needs that crap?

Here's a better idea: Get a life, or keep living the one you've got. If you bait your hook with some juicy morsel—in other words, a full, exciting life—he'll nibble and latch right on. The Pisces man is a follower, and he needs a strong leader. Once he's sure you're a queen, he'll court you like a tenderhearted prince.

From there it's all about lavish gifts, flowers delivered to your job, opera tickets, and romantic picnics. Pisces is like a time-release romantic. He becomes more sentimental and tender the longer you're together. It's a trust thing. Make it safer and safer for him to be himself around you—he fears your judgment and craves your admiration more than anyone else's. The "mature love" phase is so much more romantic and rich with Pisces than infatuation. He does everything backward, but that's precisely what's so wonderful about him. If divine timing is on your side, you could be lucky enough to experience it.

# Sex with a Pisces

Ready to make love? Sweet, sensual love? Light the candles, scatter the rose petals, and turn on some Barry White. Ohhhhhhh. Yeahhhhhh. Now baby, put on that sexy little outfit he got you from the lingerie shop. It fits perfectly, of course—he knows your measurements. The Pisces man specializes in the kind of sex that includes tender embraces, gentle caressing, heated massage oil and staring deep into each other's eyes. If you both weep at the point of climax (which will be simultaneous, of course), don't be surprised.

Prince Charming, of course, has another side to him that's not so tenderly devoted. At some point in his life, the Pisces man's curiosity starts to nag at him. "It's great to make love," says the devil on his shoulder. "But what about the kinkier stuff? Don't you want to let loose and get really nasty? Do the things you'd never dream of asking your high school sweetheart to do?"

He'll either repress that urge, or dive down to the murkiest part of his desires. Pisces is drawn to the taboo side of sex that's all about power and control, domination and submission—the themes of his life, basically. Often, sex is an arena where those issues all get worked out. He can fall into the seamy sexual underworld for a spell, though fortunately, he's usually far too sensitive to stay there.

For Pisces, the harder stuff is best left in the fantasy realm. He might daydream about S&M, dressing in leather and being lashed by the whip of Mistress Brigitta. He might watch the most offensive, hardcore, fetish porn. But if he crosses the line into reality with it, it's usually too much for his sensitive nature to handle. One friend recalls a Pisces ex-boyfriend who decided to rebel against his strict, born-again Christian upbringing by visiting a sex club. (As it was, he'd lost his virginity at teen Bible camp.) But the fetish scene was too much for him. "He called me crying from the side of the road, totally freaking out," she says. "He couldn't handle it."

The bait of sexual danger will always be alluring, but knowing it's attached to his ultimate downfall usually prevents Pisces from nibbling again. The Pisces man is actually kind of a prude who just wants to experience his first kiss again and again. Of course, he might need to hit bottom before he swims to clear waters about his sexuality and realizes this. Once his innocence has been tainted, his sex life will become a fight to reclaim it—only to tarnish it again just a little once he does.

# Pisces: Turn-Ons & Turn-Offs

## Turn Him On

- Be a powerhouse who's a little intimidating
- Handle the details he hates (bills, budgets, doctor appointments)
- Give him solitude when he needs it, affection other times

- Indulge in romance with him
- Play come-here-now-go-away mind games—draw him near, then coolly reject him
- Be the envy of his friends (he's easily influenced by their opinions)
- Be neat, organized, and polished
- Nurture and mother him to just the right degree
- Have a brilliant, sharp-shooting and snarky sense of humor
- Be edgy, artistic, or part of an underground scene
- Be somehow out of his league (in his opinion): the "It girl" he pined for but could never get in high school, a model, a superstar
- Have excellent taste in shoes and a beautiful pedicure (he's got a foot fetish!)

## Turn Him Off

- Have no life or pursuits of your own
- Expect him to be the breadwinner if he's an "artiste"
- Have bad taste in art, clothes, shoes, or music
- Put him on a pedestal (he wants to worship you)
- Pressure him to commit to you, or anything, before he's ready
- Be too similar to him (he loves the exotic, mysterious, and things he can't figure out)
- Have an explosive or overwrought temper—shouting, bursting into tears, disturbing his peaceful groove
- Accuse him of something he didn't do
- Play the victim (that's his job, thank you)
- Shoot down his romantic gestures
- Be too emotional and emotionally available
- Bring too much reality into his world (deadlines, debt, etc.)

# His Moves

## First Moves: How He Courts You

Such sweet emotion! Such tender, dopey gazes and doe-eyed worship. The Pisces man turns into a total mush when he's into you. It's the stuff of teen romantic comedies. And oh, how he loves the courtship. There's no commitment, not even the threat of it edging near just yet. There's only the promise of pleasure… and perhaps a light serving of angst to go along with it.

Here's how Prince Pisces pulls you into his sea of love:

- He writes you poetry, makes a mix CD, sends flowers, does all the cheesy romantic stuff
- He buys you extravagant gifts that are almost inappropriately lavish

- He becomes your best friend and confidant, watches reruns of *The O.C.* or rents a romantic comedy with you
- Candles, intimate dinners, movies, concerts
- He sweeps you up in a romantic fairy tale
- You hear through the grapevine from mutual friends that he likes you

- He hovers around, half-flirting and making cute banter
- He drops suggestive comments that leave you wondering "does he like me?"

- He starts talking about other women: what he likes, past relationships
- He gets dopey, spluttery, and tongue-tied around you
- He helps you through a breakup

## He's In: How You Know He's Committed

With the Pisces man, you might exchange tearful vows at the altar, share a pet, and buy a home together. Yet, a part of you may always wonder, "Can this last forever?" And you may not want to ask. The Pisces man always reserves a piece of his soul for himself and himself alone. His lips are saying "I do," yet you may feel him resisting you, a subtle energy like two magnets repelling each other. His actions will speak louder than his words. You have to look at the sum total of his deeds over a length of time. Here are a few ways he shows that he's there to stay:

**He never leaves.** He just doesn't go anywhere. He sleeps over and the next day, he's your roommate. He keeps showing up, and the years keep passing. Sometimes, that's all the evidence you need.

**He gets sappy and romantic.** As indirect as Pisces can be, in other moments, he's solemn and formal when professing his love. There might be candles, massage oil, and rose petals, or a beautifully planned picnic. He gets especially moved out in nature, so if you want to know how he really feels about you, take a walk by the water.

**He wants to be around you constantly.** The Pisces man loves to immerse himself in feminine energy—and if he adores you, he wants to bask in yours. He can also be a little needy, and his insecurities could drive him to maintain a watchful eye on you, keeping you within constant reach.

**He lets you see the "man behind the curtain."** Sharing fantasy is easy for Pisces. Sharing reality is much harder. When he stops playing "man of mystery" and throws his dirty socks in the same hamper as yours, he feels comfortable enough to let down his guard. It could also indicate that you're providing enough fantasy and freedom to make him crave more certainty. Good job. Keep it up.

**He occasionally disappears into his own little world.** The Pisces man will periodically withdraw into a state of solitude. He'll pick up a household project, immerse himself in his computer, read a book, or go for a run. If he comes back happy to see you, all is well.

# Unfaithful Pisces: Why He Cheats

The question might be more like, why doesn't he? Okay, we're being extreme. But the Pisces man does have a secretive side that can emerge, transforming him into the lowest of all life forms. Here's why this sign might slither into sin:

**It's the only way to end the relationship.** In other words, he's too much of a wuss to break up with you directly. So he does it in this sneaky, underhanded way—forcing you to break up with him instead.

**He has absolutely no idea.** The Pisces man is driven by intuition, and he gets easily swept up in a fantasy. The allure of temptation makes him weak. Of course, the guilt might nearly kill him. But he's used to guilt, so it unfortunately won't be toxic enough to stop him.

**He couldn't say no to a damsel in distress.** She needed him. She was really upset about their breakup seventeen years ago—she cried hysterically, fell into his arms, and his pants just kind of melted off from there. She's still not over him. She's not as strong as you are. He isn't either. Why can't you understand that it wasn't personal?

**You've made everything a little too real.** Now, it's time for his emergency exit. Open the escape hatch. Deploy parachute. Out he goes!

**His friends don't like you.** The unevolved Pisces man lacks a strong sense of self, and he's easily influenced. He looks to others for guidance and to "give" him his opinion. Bummer for you if they don't weigh in kindly on you. Our friend Ina recalls her Pisces ex breaking up with her because, as he told her, "my friends don't think you're that attractive." He left her for another woman whom his friends *did* think was hot. Of course, he came back to Ina after she dumped him, crying on her shoulder. As Ina nursed his broken heart, they fell in love and he proposed.

**You're too passive or gullible.** The Pisces man needs a dominant, self-assured Alpha female to set boundaries, deal with reality, and keep him in line. He might open doors and play gentleman, even defend you valiantly. But he'd rather do that for fun, not because you're actually helpless. When he tries to play you for a sucker, he needs you to fight, resist, push back. If he can steamroll or fool you, he might seek a new challenge.

**Angry, bitter revenge.** He pulled out all the stops, gave up everything for you, left his job and apartment behind to be together. You left him for the rich meathead with pecs of steel who hit on you at the gym. Did Mr. Universe ever write you a love poem? Pour out his heart in a self-composed song beneath your balcony? F**k you, Juliet. Parting is such sweet sorrow.

**It was never over between them.** He left the door a tiny bit ajar with his ex-girlfriend. Just the tiniest little crack. A few strong gusts of passion blew the door wide open, and him right through.

## Dig the Grave: It's Over

Boundaries are a foreign concept to the Pisces man. There are never clear beginnings or endings in his life, and thus, no relationship is ever really over. Committing to a breakup is still too firm a commitment for Pisces. Your relationship may have many near-death experiences before he finally just restocks your role with his next serious girlfriend and communication drifts off altogether.

If anything, he starts to flow you out of the girlfriend/wife slot into the realm of fantasy. In his imaginary world (which is vivid and real for him), you're cast into a role: the One That Got Away, the Heartbreaker, perhaps the regrettable victim of his blind stupidity. He loves this drama, so even if he's gone quietly into the night, you will be the subject of his tortured poems, songs, essays, and thoughts for a lifetime. Here are a few signals that he may be slipping away:

**He becomes shut down and suppressed around you.** The Pisces man is the king of the silent treatment. You'll feel him brooding and stewing, bottling himself up. Still, he refuses to discuss anything, insists that everything's just fine. He's lining up his exit strategy (e.g., his next pseudo-relationship) and is just biding his time.

**He stops calling you an hour after breaking up, begging you to take him back.** One Pisces man recalls years spent caught in a "dance" with his ex-girlfriend. "We'd have a two-hour crying, yelling conversation—"We can't do this anymore!" Then, no kidding, a couple minutes later, I'd be like, 'So, want to go see a movie tonight?' Then we'd go out, end up having sex, and the whole cycle would start again." For some Pisces men, that's just business as usual. He craves freedom, but once he has it, he immediately wants security again. When he stages a breakup and doesn't immediately freak out or rush back to you? That's when you can start to worry.

**He takes mean, passive-aggressive shots at you.** The Pisces man hates to deal with conflict, and he can't stand being straightforward about his anger. Instead, he builds up a mother lode of resentment and unleashes it on you indirectly. Oh, he can be a supreme bitch indeed. He might criticize your outfit, dis your friends, slam doors, comment on your poor housekeeping, and throw snide little barbs.

**He starts dating someone else.** Like we said, there are no clear beginnings and endings. He'll stream himself into the next relationship without ever really putting closure on yours. Again, this may not mean it's over. It's just over for now. Don't be surprised if he makes a comeback months or years later.

**He starts speaking about your relationship in the past tense.** Like a novel, a play, or a film script, your plotline has reached a natural conclusion. It's time for the closer. He likes to end with a cliffhanger, just in case he decides to swim back for a sequel (see above). The epic drama is now part of history, a tale he'll love to retell.

**You don't fit his current fantasy.** When you met, you were the queen of whatever scene he was into. If he's an indie film freak, he fancied you his ingénue, his personal Chloë Sevigny. Now he's over that phase, and off to find a new It girl.

# Interpreting His Signals:
## What does he mean by that?

| When he | It means... | So you should... |
|---|---|---|
| Gets quiet | Some passive-aggressive resentment is brewing. He's pissed, but too afraid to say it, or possibly not even sure why. | Confront him directly and make him talk. Don't take what he says personally, because it will come out in a babbling, irrational blurt until he finally tells you what's really going on. |
| | If his eyes are closed and he's smiling, he's probably struck by the beauty of a photograph, a piece of music, or you. | Let him float along on his fantasy trip. |
| Doesn't call | He's seeing (or fantasizing about seeing) other women. He lost track of time. | Move on. He's not ready to commit. |
| Calls a lot | He enjoys making witty, flirty banter with you. Not a sign of commitment, though, because he makes witty, flirty banter with every mildly attractive woman he meets. | Have fun, but keep the calls relatively short. He's a "why buy the cow" kind of guy who likes you to assert boundaries. |
| | You're "safe" (e.g., you're not fully available, live in another state, have a boyfriend) for no-expectations flirtation. | Be cautious. You're playing with fire and could get addicted to his attention. He can be manipulative and seductive. |

| When he | It means... | So you should... |
|---|---|---|
| Doesn't make a move after a couple of dates | He's a little intimidated by you. He sees you more as BFF material. | Make a move on him, or give him a signal that it's safe to take a step. Move on. |
| Doesn't make a move after a few weeks | He may not be able to explain why, but something about your connection just isn't there for him. | Move on. |
| Moves fast | He feels safe around you. | Proceed, but with caution. He can sweep you up, then freak out and disappear. |
| | You fit some fantasy or fetish he's always secretly longed to try (you're from another culture, you're a redhead, lead singer of a band, etc.). | Enjoy a fling, but again: proceed with caution. |
| Picks up the tab, gives flowers and gifts | He's making a romantic gesture. | Soak up the attention and enjoy. Just don't assume he's not doing this for other women, too. |
| Introduces you to his family and/or closest friends | He's gauging their opinion of you. | Hope they either a) tell him how lucky he is and how jealous they are, or b) he's secure enough to know what he wants and stick by you with or without their approval. |

# Your Moves: Tips for Flirting and Everlasting Love

## Flirting with a Pisces

It's not hard to flirt with Pisces. He loves the dance of seduction, and it's where he feels most free. Flirting is his chance to say the most outrageous things and not have to be accountable for them. It's all just a game, with everything in a heightened state, just like he loves it. Here's how to rev his motor:

**Intimidate him.** He loves a woman who's just out of his reach. He needs to be in awe of you, so work that star quality and earn his worship.

**Banter with him.** Meet his sarcastic, cocky remarks with a prizewinning comeback of your own. He adores a sharp mind and cutting humor.

**Fluster him.** Show up with cool self-assurance, unruffled by his charms. Pull the rug out from under him. One Pisces man had an amazing, all-day date with a woman. When he dropped her off at her door he said, "We've got to do this again." She responded with, "We won't be. I'm busy with work." He chased her for weeks and later, even married her.

**Create dynamic tension.** Go ahead, be provocative. Disagree with him and say so openly. "Conflict is the only true creative space," says James, a Pisces who works as a conflict mediation lawyer (and a sculptor—Pisces can't work in the system unless he's an artist on the side). The Pisces man will dive into the most heated conversations headfirst—so much for that laid-back, passive persona. Enjoy it now, before he puts on the mask and stops showing you this fascinating side of himself.

# Everlasting Love with a Pisces

In a way, every woman who ever intertwines her life with a Pisces will be with him forever, either as a friend or someone he reminisces about intensely from time to time. He's indelibly imprinted by every woman he dates. Here's how to remain connected to your Pisces in body and soul:

**Nurture him.** He loves to be pampered, and your sweet little touches will go far. Bring home great wine or his favorite gourmet coffee. Listen to music and cuddle. Watch *Casablanca* while resting your head dreamily on his shoulder. Sing to him. Take time out of your busy schedule to be attentive and receptive.

**Torture him.** If he can't feel the angst, he can't feel the love. After all, if it doesn't hurt, he must not care about you that much.

**Have a near-breakup experience.** The Pisces man needs to stare death in the eye before he finds the courage to commit. If he experiences open conflict (his worst fear), churns up all the buried resentments and hostilities you've both suppressed, and survives—well, there must be a rare quality to your relationship that's worth hanging onto. As one Pisces man said, "Nobody's really afraid of commitment. They're afraid of being honest with each other." After all, the truth hurts—but it also heals. Trial by fire will either destroy your relationship or kindle an eternal flame.

**Be the source of his most blissful moments.** The Pisces man's conceptual thought process doesn't really grasp time. "Happily ever after" is now—not when you're eighty-seven and sitting on matching rocking chairs. To him, eternal love and bliss live in a single, perfect moment. Pisces Bertrand, a symphony percussionist, recalls sweetly kissing his college girlfriend, then looking out her window to notice spring flowers blooming on the hillside. Share enough of these tender instances and he'll fall deeply in love.

**Date him after he's learned it's okay to say "no."** The Pisces man is famous for staying in unhealthy relationships long past their expiration date. Asserting himself is so foreign, he almost doesn't believe it's okay to break up. One Pisces man says that for years after a painful divorce, he had to practice being a heartbreaker. "I would tell women, it's cool if you want to have fun, but I am damaged goods—don't expect a relationship," he admits. "They wouldn't believe me and three weeks later, I'd leave. I'd be like, I told you how it was. Once I realized I could escape again and again, I didn't need to anymore." He's now remarried to a woman he can't imagine leaving, and they have a beautiful son. Which brings us to our next tip…

**Be his second (or third) wife.** He will almost always get it wrong the first time. If he hasn't been married before, at least make sure he's been through a torturous breakup and healed from it. Otherwise, prepare to endure his learning curve.

# Prep Yourself For…

## Your First Date

With Pisces, your first date might be incredibly vague, a sort of semi-date or non-date. It could be quite awkward if you don't know each other well, since he tends to get shy and insecure when he really likes you. A natural evolution from friendship to love is always best for him. You might even be the one to ask him out. A movie, a play, or a concert are his favorite social lubricants (next to alcohol—but don't go there with him unless you want a date with his dark side). Cultural events give you something to talk about and break the ice. He'll read between the lines when you opine on the band, or the film's dramatic turning points—getting cues about your personality, tastes, and intellect.

If he pulls out all the stops—candles, intimate dinners, expensive restaurants—raise a red flag to half-mast. He may just be trying to buy himself a quick booty call. Then again, he might fall madly in love with you over market-price lobster and filet mignon. You just never know… and neither does he.

**The Basic Vibe:** There's always a charge of intensity when you're around a Pisces man. Even if your date begins with him spluttering and stuttering (or covering up his fear by acting overly suave), if you keep an even keel, he'll feel safe enough to relax. Conversation is excellent bait for the Fish. Ideally, he loves dates that are intimate, romantic, and magical. He wants you to get lost in one another, swept away. This could happen over dripping candles, or while ordering pancakes at the local diner at 1:00 A.M. because you can't bear to end the conversation.

**What to Wear:** He knows women's fashion like a gay couture designer—not that he'll admit it just yet. He loves feminine styles with edge, an outfit that shows you're knowledgeable of whatever Italian *Vogue* is hyping on the runway, yet real enough to say "Kiss my ass, Milan!" Go flowy, feminine, and graceful with crisp, tailored accents—or modern mermaid (filmy scarf, lace peasant blouse) meets dominatrix (corset, sexy leather boots). Pisces rules the feet, so it's all about shoes, shoes, shoes. He will probably know a Christian Louboutin from a Manolo Blahnik, so even if you don't own $900 Jimmy Choos, don't make it a Payless night, either. Stop in for a predate pedicure; the night may just end with a foot massage.

**What Not to Wear:** You are not going camping, hiking, or to an executive board meeting. So why would you wear boots and suits to a romantic date with Pisces? Anything too scrappy, utilitarian, or masculine will turn his head… in the other direction. Look polished, tailored, and together, but undeniably feminine and romantic.

**To Pay, or Not to Pay?** The Pisces man loves to woo you with extravagant, romantic gestures. If it's an official date rather than some kind of ill-disguised attempt to spend time with you, he'll pay for dinner, drinks, a play, and a nightcap—even if it means maxing out a credit card or his trust fund.

**Saying Good night:** He's so romantic and sweet, you won't want to leave his tender embrace. He feels so safe and nonthreatening, despite the nipple rings you feel pressing into your eardrum as he pulls you to his chest with tattooed arms, nuzzling you with the barbs of his rough goatee. Before you know it, he'll have wooed a path right to your bed. Good night, sweet prince.

## His First Home Visit

There's a homebody in every Pisces man, and it's important to him that he feel at ease in your sanctuary. You don't need much—an overstuffed couch, a good stereo system and TV. Set up an intimate, sensual, welcoming space that's perfect for cuddling and he'll take it from there.

**Make him comfortable.** The Pisces man loves to lounge. Don't offer him a flimsy wicker chair or a bar stool. Move right into the living room, where he can kick up his feet and get cozy. He'll probably make his way there without prompting.

**Create a romantic ambience.** Turn up the heat with candles, a roaring fire, a wood-burning stove. He's extremely sensual and notices everything in his immediate environment.

**Pay attention to your bathroom.** After all, that's where the tub is—one of his favorite ways to recharge. Take inspiration from a spa: mist a delicate room spray or buy a scented diffuser, roll up your towels instead of folding them, leave little made-for-metrosexual hand soaps out in a woodsy scent. If you make the bathtub look inviting enough, you could end up in there together—or at least, plant that seed in his imagination.

**Play music.** It can be downright mood altering for Pisces. If you're a music aficionado, impress him by spinning the latest underground CD. Better yet, have a speaker where he can plug in his iPod. It will probably be loaded with thousands of great tracks that will transport him into a blissful state.

**Show off your nurturing side.** Pisces does everything upside-down. He prefers you to be a hooker on the streets, a lady in the sheets. He'd rather you flaunt your outrageous persona in public, where everyone else is wearing a social mask anyway. At home, he likes to fling off the façade and express his tender, sensitive side.

**Watch movies.** Pisces rules film, and he loves to escape into a good flick while snuggling on the couch. Anything that transports him to another reality gets him in the mood.

**Change your sheets.** Nine times out of ten, he'll end up in them with you.

## Meeting His Family

The Pisces man has a powerful relationship with his family—either to his greatest benefit or his ultimate downfall. They will be his best friends or distant strangers he doesn't identify with at all. Family is a sacred space for Pisces, and interruptions like divorce, death, and poor parenting aren't easy for him to process. One Pisces man we know cites the date of his father's death as the worst day of his life.

If your Pisces gets along with his family, he worships them—so they'd better adore you, too. He relies heavily on their opinions and approval. Like Cancer, he can be very clannish, and you may need to be jumped into the gang, passing a battery of intimidating tests. It may be quite some time before you meet them—if you ever do. Our friend Amy dated a Pisces for four years and never once met his father. His mother, a snobbish socialite, threatened to cut off his law school tuition if he kept dating Amy. The Pisces man can be weak, and this guy was no exception: He broke up with Amy because he didn't want to lose his parents' financial support.

The Pisces man needs a strong father to admire—not rough or forceful—but a man with great character, who's both loving and firm. Weakness of any sort in his parents can be traumatic for young Pisces. If his father is henpecked or unfaithful, or if his mother is mistreated, Pisces will act out as the "underdog" parent's defender. If his parents divorce, he may even take on the role of an absent parent in the interim. He's deeply protective of his family members, especially if he senses a power imbalance.

His greatest difficulty—even if he may deeply wish to solve it—is figuring out where his family members end and where he begins. Dependent in ways he can't stand to admit, he can be a dutiful martyr, taking care of his relatives or stifling his opinions in exchange for their financial support. Cutting the cord is hard enough for him anyhow. Mark, a Pisces, admits that he never rebelled or fought with his mother until he was twenty-seven. He says he felt too "protective of her." Finally, a critical remark broke the dam, and he unleashed a bitter, bellowing tirade. "We barely talked for a year," he remembers. "It was the only way I could deal with that necessary separation."

Child psychologists suggest that boundaries help kids feel safe, even loved. Since Pisces have almost no sense of boundaries, a negligent, overly liberal or self-involved parent can terrify the Pisces child, scarring him for life. As much as he pushes the envelope, he secretly hopes his mom or dad will say "enough already!" One Pisces man has a mother who cries when he talks back to her. At thirty-seven, he's still grappling with feeling powerlessness and anger toward her.

Feel free to introduce him to your family—he loves it—but move slowly with his. Listen to his tales, but know that they will be laden with mythology. The reality may look quite different, so observe for a while. The first time you meet his mother, you may want to scream "Close the tittie bar—he doesn't need breastfeeding anymore!" or "Stop guilt-tripping him!" Visit a few more times. You'll see all the ways he plays into this dynamic, even fuels it. It will not only give you loads of insight into him, but also it will help you prevent history from repeating itself in your own relationship.

# Saying Good-bye
## Breaking Up with a Pisces

Want to get rid of a Pisces man? Don't leave. Stay and make his life an unbearable hell. You see, breaking up will only make him that much more attracted to you. Rejection is an aphrodisiac to Pisces. But commitment? It's a form of Kryptonite. So cling to him like static to a silk dress. He'll flee to Tibet faster than you can say "Dalai Lama."

We asked one Pisces how he found the guts to break up with a long-term girlfriend who made his life hell. "I married her," he answered simply. Sure, he was being sarcastic, but not completely. Once the unattainable fantasy girl is shifted into the reality plane, there's not much left for Pisces the dreamer to do. His work is done. He got the girl—and it's not supposed to happen that way. He's supposed to be strung along, always a little heartbroken, pining for the woman whom he can never completely reach.

So, easy. Just turn up the reality meter. Pee with the bathroom door open. Give him a copy of your schedule "so he always knows where you are." Skip the local film festival and hold a budget meeting to talk about retirement funds and weekly allowances. He'll be out of there in no time.

If that doesn't work, just be direct. He'll be completely thrown off guard, since he rarely deals with heavy emotional situations in an upfront manner. Tell him it's over. Chances are, he won't really put up a fight—even if he wants to.

## Getting over Him: When a Pisces Dumps You

Breaking up is hard to do, especially if you're a Pisces man. There are no clear beginnings or endings with Pisces. On top of that, he hates conflict, the idea of hurting you, the energy it takes to make such a decisive move. One Pisces man describes a relationship as "I dated her a month, then spent the next five years trying to break up with her." Guilt, codependence, and masochism will often bring him running right back. Time heals all wounds, and you'll definitely need to take a long time-out from him. You'll have to be the one to insist on no communication and enforce it. Change your number and address if you have to—the temptation of his romantic come-arounds can be too hard to refuse.

Because he's so dependent on others, the breakup may be encouraged by his friends or relatives. He needs backup and validation to make such a bold move. This practically guarantees that his timing and delivery will be completely off—not that there's ever a good time to be dumped. One Pisces man asked his wife for a divorce on a ski slope! "I was on the ski lift in a chair with my brother," he explains. "My wife was sitting one chair ahead. My brother said, 'Dude, what's going on with you two?' I looked at him and said, 'I can't stand this marriage anymore. I want out.'"

He pauses for dramatic effect, eyes gleaming. "So my brother says, 'Do it. Do it right now. As soon as you get off this ski lift, just tell her.' So I gathered up the nerve and about 300 feet down the hill I told her, 'It's over.' She fell down and it was this whole dramatic scene. A week later, I packed my stuff and left."

Of course, in typical Pisces style, they talked several years later and he ended up thanking her for the learning experience. "I needed that experience to grow," he reflects. "It brought up all this anger that I needed to get out of my system."

Ah, the Pisces man's great ability to forgive. But wait, wasn't he the one who broke up with you?

## Have yourself one good last cry over...
- The romance and magic
- His tender gaze and touch
- The mixed CDs, novels, and artistic gifts

- Losing the sexy "bad boy" and how hot that part of him made you feel
- Having a BFF/girlfriend and a boyfriend in one
- The intense, philosophical conversations
- How insightful and compassionate he could be
- Feeling protected and cherished by him

**Praise the universe that you never have to deal with...**
- Paying off his debts
- Handling all the boring reality
- Feeling like his mother
- Worrying if he's going to kill himself with his crazy risks
- Wondering if he's keeping secrets from you
- His addictive behaviors and habits
- Feeling like the "guy" in the relationship

# Love Matcher:

## Can you find a common language?

| You are a(n)... | He thinks you're... | You think he's... | Common Language |
|---|---|---|---|
| Aries | Aggressive. | Passive-aggressive. | Being hypersensitive and overdramatic, love of shopping |
| Taurus | His perfect companion, with the same taste in music, art, and culture. | Completely oversensitive, but has great taste in the arts. | Music, art, culture, food, wine, socializing, snobbish tastes |
| Gemini | Clinically insane, but in a really sexy way. | Clinically depressed, but in a really fascinating way. | Kinky sex, language, books, secret lives, the sexy challenge of trying to figure each other out, seeing what you can get away with |
| Cancer | His future wife and the mother of his kids. | Romantic, but upsets your sense of security and keeps too many secrets. | Marriage, children, family, security, nurturing, emotional eating, binge drinking |
| Leo | An intimidating powerhouse—the Alpha-female heartbreaker of his dreams. | A sensitive romantic who will worship you and allow you to rule the roost. Perfection. | Romance, fantasy, playing master and servant, spoiling yourselves and each other |

| You are a(n)... | He thinks you're... | You think he's... | Common Language |
|---|---|---|---|
| Virgo | Controlled and together in a way he admires (and envies). | Charming and suave, but way too flaky for your neurotic nature to take seriously. | Love of luxury shoes and accessories, books, wine, healing the planet, being martyrs, intimate dinners |
| Libra | An ethereal beauty who's as dreamy as he is, but could lack depth. | The most romantic person you've ever met, but a little depressive at times. | Being hopeless romantics, daydreaming, living in a fantasy world, poetry, music, chocolate, blowing all your money on an extravagant affair |
| Scorpio | His favorite dominatrix. | Your sexy slave. | Sex, secretiveness, mystery, candlelit dinners, marriage, children, values, love of water, a need for privacy and intimacy, spirituality |
| Sagittarius | Funny to joke around with, but way too heavy-handed and all over the place. | A wishy-washy wuss who needs to pick a side already. | Gossip, analyzing people, trading books and article links, love of freedom, fear of commitment, indulging beyond your limits (whatever those are) |

| You are a(n)... | He thinks you're... | You think he's... | Common Language |
|---|---|---|---|
| Capricorn | Cool and collected, but a bit too earthbound and literal. | Full of s**t—a smooth talker who can't keep his word consistently or commit to anything. | Wine, upscale tastes, label whoring |
| Aquarius | A cool, unreachable babe who's impervious to your seductive charms—he'll pine for you in semi-secret for years. | Your cute best buddy whose sensitive side makes you queasy. | Humanitarian principles, compassion, New Age pursuits, partying in seedy nightclubs, attracting tortured souls |
| Pisces | His mother. | Your son. | Romance, nurturing, sensitivity, films, movies, codependent enabling |

# About the Authors

Tali and Ophira Edut (The AstroTwins) began their astrological journey in 1992, when a computerized printout of their charts jolted them into a metaphysical awakening. Wanting to know how the heck someone's time, date, and place of birth could reveal so much about their character, they delved into an inquiry, using friends, family members, historical figures, and pop stars as case studies. Their fascination grew into an obsession—and then, a career.

Today, The AstroTwins reach over 40 million readers a month with their horoscopes in print, online, and broadcast. Their columns and predictions have appeared in *Teen People*, *Us Weekly*, *OK!*, Brides.com, Lifetime TV's website, and numerous other places. The AstroTwins have been featured on MTV, E!, The Style Network, and in the *New York Times*. They have read charts for celebrities including Beyoncé, Stevie Wonder, and Sting at red-carpet events, and appear regularly on Sirius Radio to give live astrological advice.

Tali and Ophira are Detroit natives who live in New York City with their posse of miniature dachshunds. Ophira also lives with her husband and stepdaughter. Visit them online at www.astrostyle.com.